Knowledge in Flux

Knowledge in Flux
Modeling the Dynamics of Epistemic States

Peter Gärdenfors

A Bradford Book
The MIT Press
Cambridge, Massachusetts
London, England

This book was set in Times Roman by Asco Trade Typesetting Ltd., Hong Kong, and printed and bound by Halliday Lithograph in the United States of America.

Library of Congress Cataloging-in-Publication Data

Gärdenfors, Peter.
  Knowledge in flux: modeling the dynamics of epistemic states/Peter Gärdenfors.

  p. cm.
  "A Bradford book."
  Bibliography: p.
  Includes index.
  ISBN 0-262-07109-6
  1. Epistemics. 2. Knowledge, Theory of. I. Title.
  B820.3.G37 1988   121'.6—dc19   87-31505

Contents

Preface   ix

Introduction   1

I   **Models**   5

1   **The Elements of Epistemological Theories**   7

1.1   Program   7

1.2   Epistemic States   9

1.3   Epistemic Attitudes   12

1.4   Epistemic Inputs   13

1.5   Changes of Belief   15

1.6   Belief Systems, Language, and the External World   18

2   **Models of Epistemic States**   21

2.1   Program   21

2.2   Belief Sets   21

2.3   Ellis's Belief Systems   26

2.4   Models Based on Possible Worlds   28

2.5   Spohn's Generalized Possible Worlds Models   30

2.6   An Example from Artificial Intelligence:
Doyle's Truth Maintenance System   32

2.7   Bayesian Models   36

2.8   Generalized Probabilistic Models   40

2.9   Johnson-Laird's Mental Models   43

3   **Expansions, Revisions, and Contractions**   47

3.1   The Three Basic Types of Changes of Belief   47

3.2   Expansions   48

3.3   Revisions   52

3.4   Contractions   60

3.5   On the Notion of Minimal Change   66

3.6   From Contractions to Revisions and Vice Versa   68

3.7   Spohn's Generalization of Revisions and
Contractions   72

**4   Epistemic Entrenchment and Construction of
      Contraction Functions**   75

4.1   The Problem of How to Construct a Contraction
      Function   75
4.2   Maxichoice Contraction Functions   76
4.3   Full Meet Contraction Functions   78
4.4   Partial Meet Contraction Functions   80
4.5   Grove's Systems of Spheres   83
4.6   Epistemic Entrenchment   86
4.7   The Origins of Epistemic Entrenchment   91
4.8   Constructing Contraction and Revision Functions from
      the Ordering of Epistemic Entrenchment   94
4.9   Safe Contractions   97
4.10 Two Further Application Areas: Logical Databases and
      Legal Codes   99

5   The Dynamics of Probabilistic Models   105

5.1   Bayesian Models and Their Dynamics   105
5.2   Why Conditionalize? Some Representation Results   106
5.3   Imaging   108
5.4   A Representation Theorem for Imaging   112
5.5   Imaging versus Conditionalization   114
5.6   Preservative Imaging   117
5.7   Contractions of Probability Functions   118
5.8   Revisions of Probability Functions   121
5.9   From Contractions to Revisions and Vice Versa   124
5.10 Construction of Probabilistic Revision Functions   125

II   Applications   129

6   The Dynamics of Belief As a Basis for Logic   131

6.1   Propositions Defined from Possible Worlds   131
6.2   Propositions Defined by Changes of Belief   132
6.3   Basic Postulates for Propositions   134

6.4   Negation and Disjunction   137
6.5   Completeness Results   138
6.6   Propositions Corresponding to Contractions and
      Revisions   142
6.7   Concluding Remarks   144

7   Conditionals   147

7.1   The Ramsey Test for Conditionals   147
7.2   The Logic of Counterfactuals   148
7.3   Other Kinds of Conditionals   152
7.4   The Incompatibility of (RT) and (K*4)   156
7.5   Weaker Versions of the Ramsey Test   160
7.6   Discussion of the Inconsistency Result   162
7.7   Conditional Beliefs and Beliefs in Conditionals   165

8   Explanations   167

8.1   Program   167
8.2   Background   168
8.3   Second-Order Probabilistic Models of Epistemic States   170
8.4   An Analysis of Explanations   176
8.5   Applications of the Analysis   180
8.6   Some Consequences of the Analysis   185
8.7   Conclusion   188

9   Causal Beliefs   191

9.1   Background   191
9.2   The Information Problem   192
9.3   An Epistemic Analysis of Causal Beliefs   194
9.4   Analysis of Some Examples   197
9.5   A Comparison with Granger Causality   202
9.6   Causation and Explanation   203
9.7   Some Further Aspects of the Causal Analysis   206
9.8   Limitations of the Analysis   208

Appendix A   Proofs of Main Lemmas and Theorems of
              Chapter 3   211
Appendix B   Proofs of Main Lemmas and Theorems of
              Chapter 4   217
Appendix C   Proofs of Main Lemmas and Theorems of
              Chapter 5   227
Appendix D   Proofs of Main Lemmas and Theorems of
              Chapter 6   237
Appendix E   Proofs of Main Lemmas and Theorems of
              Chapter 7   239
Notes   243
References   249
Index   257

Preface

This is a book about how to change your mind. More precisely, I present a theory of rational changes of belief. The epistemic changes that are at focus are *revisions* that occur when the agent receives new information that is inconsistent with the present epistemic state. In part I I formulate rationality postulates for revisions and other types of epistemic changes. I also present some explicit constructions of ideally rational changes. The postulates and the constructions are connected by a number of representation theorems. The book is thus part of a general investigation of rationality.

Although I do not develop computer implementations of the constructions, I believe that my theory is of interest to AI (artificial intelligence) researchers. After all, the problem of finding an appropriate knowledge representation is a key problem for AI. But a solution to this problem is of little help unless one also understands how to *update* the epistemic states in the light of new information.

In part II I apply the theory of the dynamics of epistemic states to some philosophical problem areas within cognitive science: Chapter 6 is devoted to showing that the dynamics of belief and knowledge may be seen as more fundamental than logic. Chapter 7 presents an epistemic semantics for conditional sentences. Chapter 8 gives a pragmatic analysis of explanations, and Chapter 9 provides a closely related analysis of causal beliefs.

In developing the theory and its applications, I commit heresy in relation to a number of philosophical doctrines. I do not believe in possible worlds, and I do not think they should be used as primitive entities. However, I sometimes find the possible worlds approach a useful heuristic. My theory is not a realist theory but rather a conceptualistic or cognitive one: The "external world" plays only a marginal role in determining the rationality of belief changes. Consequently the notion of truth is not used at all in specifying the rationality postulates for the dynamics of belief. Instead of truth conditions I use acceptability criteria. Finally, even though most of the belief models discussed here presume an object language governed by a logic, I do not regard logical concepts, let alone linguistic concepts, as sacrosanct primitive notions. As I show in chapter 6, it is possible to develop an epistemological theory that takes epistemic states and their dynamics as primitive and use it to *generate* a logic.

During my work I have received helpful comments and useful criticism from several friends and colleagues. First, I would like to thank David Makinson, who has painstakingly worked through my material in various stages, corrected my proofs, added new results, and provided me with all sorts of constructive criticism. Together with Carlos Alchourrón we jointly developed much of the theoretical material in chapters 3 and 4. Bengt Hansson and Nils-Eric Sahlin mangled the first draft of the manuscript, sheet by sheet, at a number of informal seminars. Their frank but friendly opinions helped in smoothing the text. Isaac Levi's comments have, as usual, been exponential: Whenever I send him an n-page letter, he sends me a 2^n-page response, all of which is useful, even if I do not always agree. My wife, Annette, has been a guinea pig for the intelligibility of my ideas, and I am grateful for her support.

A visiting fellowship at the Australian National University from October 1986 to January 1987 gave me the opportunity of presenting my manuscript to a qualified audience. I would like to thank John Broome, Peter Forrest, André Fuhrmann, Frank Jackson, Peter Lavers, Philip Pettit, Peter Roeper, Jack Smart, and Neil Tennant for helpful discussions. Conall O'Connell did a great job in adjusting my depraved English to suit.

The list of other people who have commented on my manuscript is long. I hope I do not offend anyone by mentioning only Wolfgang Balzer, John Collins, Max Cresswell, Zoltan Domotor, Jon Doyle, Brian Ellis, Norman Foo, Adam Grove, Sören Halldén, Paul Hemeren, Richard Jeffrey, Peter Menzies, David Pearce, Wlodek Rabinowicz, Anand Rao, Hans Rott, Gerhard Schurz, Krister Segerberg, Wolfgang Spohn, Johan van Benthem, and Bas van Fraassen. I owe them all a lot. Thanks also to Harry Stanton and the staff of the MIT Press for advice and careful editing.

The book has basically been written backward. I began working in this area by thinking about the pragmatics of explanations. The result was "A Pragmatic Approach to Conditionals" (*Philosophy of Science*, 1980, 47:404–423), a first version of which was written during 1976. This paper now forms the core of chapter 8. At that time I thought that explanations were based on various forms of conditional sentences. This led me to develop an epistemic semantics for conditionals presented in chapter 7. This chapter draws on "Conditionals and Changes of Belief" (in *The Logic and Epistemology of Scientific Change*, I. Niiniluoto and R. Tuomela, eds., North-Holland, Amsterdam, 1978, 381–404), "Even if" (in *Proceedings from the Fifth Scandinavian Logic Symposium*, F. V. Jensen, B. H. Mayoh, and K. K. Møller, eds., Aalborg University Press, Aalborg, 1979, 189–203), "An Epistemic Approach to Conditionals" (*American Philosophical Quarterly*, 1981, 18:203–211), "Belief Revision and the Ramsey Test for Conditionals"

(*Philosophical Review*, 1986, 95:81–93), and "Variations on the Ramsey Test: More Triviality Results" (*Studia Logica*, 1987, 46(4):319–325).

Only after this did I turn to the more general problems of characterizing contractions and revisions. The results are presented in chapters 3 and 4, which use material from "Rules for Rational Changes of Belief" (in ⟨*320311*⟩: *Philosophical Essays Dedicated to Lennart Åqvist on his Fiftieth Birthday*, T. Pauli, ed., Philosophical Studies 34, Philosophical Society and Department of Philosophy, Uppsala University, Uppsala, 1982), "Epistemic Importance and Minimal Changes of Belief" (*Australasian Journal of Philosophy*, 1984, 62:136–157), "On the Logic of Theory Change: Partial Meet Functions for Contraction and Revision" (*Journal of Symbolic Logic*, 1985, 50:510–530; written jointly with Carlos Alchourrón and David Makinson), and "Epistemic Importance and the Logic of Theory Change" (in *Foundations of Logic and Linguistics*, G. Dorn and P. Weingartner, eds., Plenum Press, New York, 1985, 345–367). This theory was then extended to probabilistic models, which now forms chapter 5, containing material from "Imaging and Conditionalization" (*Journal of Philosophy*, 1982, 79:747–760) and "The Dynamics of Belief: Contractions and Revisions of Probability Functions" (*Topoi*, 1986, 5:29–37; © 1986 by D. Reidel Publishing Company).

In the meantime I had discovered that it is possible to start from the dynamics of epistemic states as primitive and use this to generate logic. This is now chapter 6, which draws on "The Dynamics of Belief as a Basis for Logic" (*British Journal for the Philosophy of Science*, 1984, 35:1–10) and "Propositional Logic Based on the Dynamics of Belief" (*Journal of Symbolic Logic*, 1985, 50:390–394). Chapter 9 is a rather late addition concerning the epistemology of causal beliefs. This chapter uses some material from "Causation and the Dynamics of Belief" (in *Causation in Decision, Belief Change, and Statistics*, W. L. Harper and B. Skyrms, eds., Reidel, Dordrecht, vol. 2, 85–104). I wish to acknowledge permission from the publishers and editors to use all the material mentioned.

My work has been supported in part by a grant from the Anders Karitz Foundation, which I gratefully acknowledge.

Knowledge in Flux

Introduction

To attain knowledge, add things every day.
To attain wisdom, remove things every day.
(Lao Tzu, *Tao-te Ching*, ch. 48)

Oscar used to believe that he had given Victoria a gold ring at their wedding. He had bought their two wedding rings at a jeweler's shop in Casablanca. He thought it was a bargain. The merchant had claimed that the rings were made of 24 carat gold. They certainly looked liked gold, but to be on the safe side Oscar had taken the rings to the jeweler next door who had testified to their gold content.

However, some time after the wedding, Oscar was repairing his boat and he noticed that the sulfuric acid he was using stained his ring. He remembered from his school chemistry that the only acid that affected gold was aqua regia. Somewhat surprised, he verified that Victoria's ring was also stained by the acid.

So Oscar had to revise his beliefs because they entailed an inconsistency. He could not deny that the rings were stained. He toyed with the idea that, by accident, he had bought aqua regia rather than sulfuric acid, but he soon gave up this idea. So, because he had greater confidence in what he was taught in chemistry than in his own smartness, Oscar somewhat downheartedly accepted that the rings were not made of gold after all. Consequently he was convinced that both the jewelers had been lying. He also came to believe that they were in collusion with each other, although he was not completely certain of this.

This story is an everyday example of a *belief revision* caused by some piece of information (the stained ring) that *contradicts* the beliefs that are accepted by a person. Before the discovery Oscar was fully convinced that the rings were made of gold (otherwise he would not have given Victoria one of them as a wedding ring), and thus he accepted this as knowledge and not just as a probable fact. We see not only that the revision affects his epistemic attitude concerning the material of the rings but also that this change has consequences for many other beliefs as well.

We find Oscar's revision of his beliefs rational. However, if he had avoided the inconsistency by denying that the rings were stained or by claiming that the chemical theory of gold is wrong, we would at least wish to hear some further arguments for such an expedient before accepting its rationality.

The kind of belief revision that occurs here is different from the kind of change that happens when Oscar observes or learns something that is *consistent* with his present beliefs, for example, when he notices that his bank account is empty. This latter kind of change is called an *expansion*, because one simply adds the new belief together with its consequences to the old state of beliefs without bothering to eliminate any conflicting beliefs.

Shifting to the philosophical mood, several questions now present themselves: What makes a belief revision or expansion *rational*? What logical and nonlogical *rules* govern rational belief revisions? How can we describe the epistemic states of an agent? Can a computer program appropriately model epistemic states and changes in such states? Questions like these are the motivation for this book.

To continue the story: Oscar's marriage to Victoria turned out to be a disaster. Oscar often found himself pondering what would have happened if he had not married her. The interesting problem for Oscar is to decide which among his present beliefs are consequences of the fact that he married Victoria and which he would have held in any case. Oscar is certain that he would not be living in his suburban house and that he would have to make his morning coffee by himself. He believes that he would have continued his life as a sea captain. He might have married another woman, and he might not have. He thinks that he would still have been balding but perhaps would not have gained quite so much weight. Probably he would have developed his slight alcohol problem anyway...

Here Oscar is making a different type of epistemic change: a *contraction*. He retracts the information that he has married Victoria and tries to find out which other beliefs he would have to give up as a consequence of this retraction and which beliefs he would retain. Again, the resulting epistemic state should be coherent. If Oscar, for example, gave up his belief that he is left-handed as a consequence of retracting his belief that he has married, it would be difficult to consider this a rational belief change.

This book is about expansions, revisions, contractions, and other types of changes of belief. One of the main goals is to present *rationality criteria* for such changes. The book is divided into two parts: The first part presents a *theoretical framework* for modeling the dynamics of belief; the second part contains a number of *applications* of this theory.

The focus of the first theoretical part is the rationality principles that govern epistemic changes of different kinds. These principles are formulated within a general epistemological framework containing, among other things, *models of epistemic states* and a *typology of epistemic changes*. The epistemic states are modeled in a logically idealized way, which entails that they are amenable to computer implementations. Both propositional and probabilistic models are investigated.

Epistemic changes, and in particular expansions, revisions, and contractions, are studied in two ways here: On the one hand, these changes are characterized by a number of *rationality postulates*, and, on the other hand, they are presented as explicit *constructions*. A number of representation theorems are proved; they show that the rationality postulates determine precisely the epistemic changes covered by the suggested constructions. Again, these constructions are suitable for computer programs, although the implementation details are not pursued here. In particular, the constructions are useful for the problem of representing changing knowledge within AI (the frame problem) and the problem of updating logical databases.

As a first application in the second part of the book, I show how *propositional logic* can be generated from a theory of epistemic dynamics. This result suggests that a theory of epistemic dynamics may be philosophically more fundamental than logic and semantics.

The second application is an outline of an epistemic semantics for *conditional sentences*. The semantics is based on the idea that a conditional sentence signals the outcome of a potential epistemic change. I show that there is a close correspondence between different forms of conditional sentences and the typology of epistemic changes presented in the theoretical part of the book. However, I also show that the epistemic semantics faces some serious problems.

The two final applications concern *explanation* and *causation*, which obviously are central topics within philosophy of science. Both these problem areas are attacked with tools from the dynamics of belief. I argue that, when evaluating explanations and causal beliefs, one relies crucially on the outcome of certain *contractions* of the agent's present epistemic state.

I MODELS

1 The Elements of Epistemological Theories

1.1 Program

The concepts at focus in this book are *epistemic states* and *changes* of epistemic states. A number of models of epistemic states and their dynamics are studied. The theoretical framework in which these models are embedded is here called an *epistemological theory*. The main task for an epistemological theory is to provide a conceptual apparatus for investigating problems about changes of knowledge and belief. Among other things, such a theory should provide a representation of the *epistemic elements* and the *criteria of rationality* that are relevant for an understanding of epistemic dynamics.

Let me begin by giving a brief introduction to the epistemic factors that form the core of the epistemological theories. Each of these factors is presented in greater detail later. The first and most fundamental factor in an epistemological theory is a class of models of *epistemic states* or *states of belief*. The intended interpretation is that such a model is a representation of a person's knowledge and belief at a certain point in time, as, for example, Oscar's state of belief at the moment he discovered that his ring was stained. However, the epistemic states here are not seen as psychological entities; they are presented as *rational idealizations* of psychological states. This means that a state in a computer program may also be seen as a model of an epistemic state.

A second factor in an epistemological theory is a classification of the *epistemic attitudes* that describe the status of various elements of belief that are contained in an epistemic state. For example, a person may accept or not accept a particular fact as true or he may judge it to be certain, probable, or possible. These are different attitudes toward the same fact. The epistemic attitudes can often be detected linguistically by what a person is willing to assert in a given state of belief. It should be noted that I use the word "epistemic" as a covering term for different attitudes (and other factors) in an epistemological theory, so that, for example, 'belief', which sometimes is called a "doxastic" attitude, also falls under this term.

A third element is an account of the *epistemic inputs* that may lead to changes of epistemic states. These inputs can be thought of as the deliverances of experience or as linguistic (or other symbolic) information provided by other individuals (or machines). For example, when Oscar noticed that his ring was stained, this observation served as an epistemic input that lead to a revision of his state of belief. However, for my purposes

I need not give a general account of the different forms of epistemic inputs, but they will be more abstractly defined with the aid of the effects they have on epistemic states.

A fourth component, which is of central concern here, consists of a classification of *epistemic changes* or *changes of belief*. Different kinds of epistemic input result in different types of change of in the epistemic states. The most important epistemic changes are expansions, revisions, and contractions as exemplified in the introduction. Epistemic changes are generated from epistemic inputs by an *epistemic commitment*, which is defined as a rule determining how an epistemic state would change as a result of various inputs. For example, Oscar's epistemic commitment determined that he should give up believing that the rings were of gold rather than giving up his knowledge about chemistry.

On the metalevel an epistemological theory also contains *criteria of rationality*, which are used for *evaluating* the other factors of the theory. For example, if sets of sentences are used as models of epistemic states, then *consistency* is a basic rationality requirement on such a set. Or, when evaluating changes of belief, we require that the change be the *minimal* one needed to accommodate the epistemic input that generates the change.

The general way of structuring an epistemological theory outlined here is to a large extent parallel to (and to some extent inspired by) Bas van Fraassen's account (1980b) and also Isaac Levi's writings [in particular, Levi (1980)]. However, these authors are mainly concerned with probabilistic models of epistemic states, whereas I aim at developing a more general perspective that should be applicable to various types of models.

The epistemological theories considered here are *nonlinguistic* in the sense that, in general, the description of the components of a theory are not dependent on any particular object language in which the beliefs of an individual are expressed. On the contrary, I argue in chapter 6 that an elaborated epistemological theory is fundamental for an understanding of the logical aspects of language. This means that I view an epistemological theory as a necessary presupposition for an analysis of the logic and semantics of a language. Thus I view language basically as a tool for communicating the contents of epistemic states between individuals and not as something these states are built up from.

It is true, however, that many of the *models* of epistemic states in this book are *propositional*; that is, the basic elements of the states are propositions expressed in some object language. Propositional models have been used frequently in the philosophical literature, and they allow us to use logical techniques. However, I want to emphasize that, even if propositional models provide the main examples in this work, my basic position is that epistemological theories are more fundamental than linguistic and semantic ones.

Furthermore, the epistemological theories are *conceptualistic* in the sense that they do not presume any account of an "external world" outside of the individuals' epistemic states. It is true that the epistemic inputs in general have their origin in such a "reality," but I argue that epistemic states and changes of such states as well as the rationality criteria governing epistemic dynamics can be, and should be, formulated independently of the factual connections between the epistemic inputs and the outer world. A consequence of this position is that the concept of truth is irrelevant, or at least secondary, for the type of epistemological theory considered here. After presenting the components of an epistemological theory in greater detail, I return in section 1.6 to the relations between the contents of such a theory and language on the one hand and the external world and truth on the other.

1.2   Epistemic States

Epistemic states are the central entities in the epistemological theories studied in this book. Epistemic states are used for representing an actual or a possible cognitive state of some individual at a given point of time. However, the concept of a state of belief is *not* meant to be a psychological concept that expresses something about how beliefs are represented and handled in our brains. Rather, it is an *epistemological* concept that is an *idealization* of the psychological concept—an idealization that is judged in relation to the rationality criteria of the epistemological theory. For example, in the epistemological theories that will be discussed later, states of belief are assumed to be consistent and closed under logical consequences. Clearly these conditions are often violated in practice.

One can think of the idealized epistemic states as being *equilibrium states*.[1] To give but two examples of what this means: If a set of beliefs is not consistent or if a probability assignment to a field of beliefs is not coherent, then the individual should, if she is to fulfill the rationality criteria, adjust her state of belief until it reaches an equilibrium that satisfies the criteria. A rational state of belief is one that is in equilibrium under all forces of internal criticism. The internal forces pushing an epistemic state toward an equilibrium should be distinguished from the epistemic inputs that serve as *external* forces taking a state from one equilibrium to another.[2]

In this way the rationality criteria serve as regulative ideals. Actual psychological states of belief normally fail to be ideally rational in this sense. This is due to several factors, the most important of which are that the states are continually disturbed by new inputs (perceptual or others) and that the internal criticism, which functions as the adjusting mechanism, is not sufficiently effective. The equilibrium idealization of states of belief is analogous to idealizations in physics: mass points without extension, perfectly black bodies, ideal gases, etc. And the rationally ideal epistemic states function in the same way as idealized physical entities—they appear in the formulation of the fundamental laws, and they provide a framework for understanding the systems that approximate them.[3]

As I see it, *inductive reasoning* belongs to the process of adjusting a state of belief to an equilibrium. The active "force" here is the desire to have a representation of the current information that is as parsimonious as possible, and for this purpose inductive generalizations may play an important role. However, the theme of induction is not pursued here. Thus this "internal" form of the dynamics of belief is also not treated.[4]

Rational epistemic states are normally seen as idealizations of *human* cognitive states. However, in some contexts it is interesting to try to extend the application area of the ideal systems. One may, for example, ask whether the state of a computer program can fruitfully be described as a rational state of belief or something approximating such a state. This interpretation is discussed in sections 2.6 and 4.10. Or one may wish to extend the application area to animals or to human organizations. It should be noted that in these applications it is important that an epistemological theory not presume any particular linguistic notions.

At this point it is interesting to introduce Robert Stalnaker's idea that the cognitive state of a person is best described by *several* systems of belief rather than by only one:

A person may be disposed, in one kind of context, or with respect to one kind of action, to behave in ways that are correctly explained by one belief state, and at the same time be disposed in another kind of context or with respect to another kind of action to behave in ways that would be explained by a different belief state. This need not be a matter of shifting from one state to another or vacillating between states; the agent might, at the same time, be in two stable belief states, be in two different dispositional states which are displayed in different kinds of situations. (Stalnaker 1984, p. 83)[5]

Stalnaker sees this kind of phenomenon as a sign of the lack of perfection of the human cognitive abilities. The beliefs of an ideally rational agent *ought to* fit together in a single coherent system. However, it may be a nontrivial problem to put separate belief states together. Stalnaker argues that this process is a plausible way of explaining the use of *deduction* in human reasoning:

Inquiry in general is a matter of adjusting one's beliefs in response to new information, but in the case of deductive inquiry, the information that initiates the change is new, not to the agent, but only to one of his belief states. By dividing the agent into separate centers of rationality, we make it possible to see the processing of the information an agent already has as a phenomenon with the same structure as the reception of new information." (Stalnaker 1984, p. 87)

In the next chapter I present different models of epistemic states that are used in epistemological theories. In order not to leave the rest of this chapter hanging in the air, I here give a brief outline of the models that are most common in the philosophical literature.

The best-known models of epistemic states are the Bayesian models used in decision theory. Here a state of belief is represented by a *probability measure* defined over some object language or over some space of events. It is assumed within the Bayesian tradition that all information that is relevant for decision making is conveyed by such a probability measure. An important rationality criterion governing this type of model is that of *coherence*.

A second kind of model, which is simpler than the Bayesian but also less informative, consists in representing an epistemic state as a *set of propositions*, expressed by sentences from some given object language. The intended interpretation of such a model is that the set consists of those propositions that the person *accepts* in the modeled state. The central rationality criterion here is *consistency*, but *logical omniscience* is also often assumed in the sense that the set of propositions representing an epistemic state is supposed to be closed under logical consequences.

A third way of modeling epistemic states is to represent a state by a set of possible worlds. The interpretation of such a set is that the person associated with the modeled state knows that the "actual world" is a member of the set of worlds, but it is also compatible with his beliefs that any world in the set could be the actual one.

These three types of models are related to each other, and their connections are also investigated in chapter 2. Although models of states of belief are most important, some other applications are also considered; in particular, logical databases and legal codes, which are the topic of section 4.10.

1.3   Epistemic Attitudes

In the models of epistemic states different "kinds" of belief are expressible. For example, in a model based on a set of propositions, one can distinguish three different kinds: (1) a proposition A may be *accepted*, which simply means that A belongs to the set representing the epistemic state; (2) A may be *rejected*, which is to say that the negation of A is accepted in the state; and (3) A may be *kept in suspense* or *indetermined*, which means that neither A nor its negation is an element of the relevant set of propositions. Or, in a model of an epistemic state based on a probability measure P, a richer typology of beliefs is possible: One may say that a proposition A *is more probable than B*, meaning that $P(A) > P(B)$; that A is *likely*, meaning that $P(A) > 0.5$, and so on.[6] In this type of model we can also say that A is accepted if $P(A) = 1$ and similarly that A is rejected if $P(A) = 0$ and indetermined if $0 < P(A) < 1$.

All these examples show beliefs with different *epistemic attitudes*. Depending on which type of model is used to represent a state of belief, different epistemic attitudes are expressible. In general, the epistemic attitudes can be described in terms of a *valuation* of the items in a model of an epistemic state. For example, in models based on sets of propositions, the valuation is given by the membership relation; and in probabilistic models the valuation is given by the probability measure.

The epistemic attitudes are reflected by the linguistic idioms we use to express the attitudes. Such expressions are called *epistemic judgments*. Some of the most common examples are that someone "believes that A," "is convinced that A," "finds it extremely likely that A," "does not know whether A," "finds it possible that A," and "finds A more likely than B."

Expressions of these kinds can be interpreted with the aid of a model of an epistemic state and the epistemic attitudes expressible in the model. Given a type of model of epistemic states, for example, a probabilistic model, it is possible to define a Tarskian kind of *satisfaction relation* for most of the expressions. Thus we can say that an epistemic judgment is *valid* or *accepted* relative to a given representation of an epistemic state if the epistemic attitude expressed by the judgment is satisfied by the relevant valuation function. Note that, even if an epistemic judgment is accepted in a given state, it does not follow that it is assertable, because this is in general ruled by Gricean types of conditions. However, I take acceptability to be a necessary condition for sincere assertability.

On this account the valuation function of an epistemic state determines the epistemic attitudes, which then determine the epistemic judgments that are accepted in the state. For some types of models of epistemic states the state is uniquely determined by the class of judgments accepted in the state. This is trivially true of models based on sets of propositions in relation to epistemic judgments expressed in terms of acceptability. For other models the case is more complicated. It is possible that the models of epistemic states contain some "hidden variables" that do not have any correspondence in the class of epistemic judgments. Such a model, involving second-order probabilities, is presented in chapter 8. In this case there are things that may be a part of our epistemic state but that we cannot express in the available language. (This sounds more like the early Wittgenstein than I intend it to do.)

1.4   Epistemic Inputs

On the idealized interpretation of epistemic states that is assumed here, the states are supposed to be in reflective equilibrium. On this approach all changes of a state of belief must be accounted for by some "external forces." These external forces can be described as the "deliverance of experience" by linguistic or nonlinguistic means, and they are called *epistemic inputs* here. A simple figure illustrates the process (figure 1.1). Because the *content*

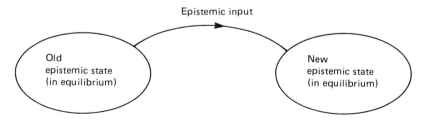

Figure 1.1
A framework for the dynamics of epistemic states.

of the epistemic states is at focus, the "form" of the epistemic inputs (for example, whether it is linguistic or nonlinguistic) is not important. What matters is the *effect* the input has on a given epistemic state.

Depending on what type of model of epistemic states is assumed, different typologies of epistemic inputs will be of interest. In order to illustrate such a typology, I here assume that a state of belief is modeled by a deductively closed set of sentences, with the interpretation that the sentences in the set express exactly the beliefs that are accepted in the modeled state. As discussed in section 1.3, this type of model allows for three different epistemic attitudes: A sentence may be accepted, rejected, or indetermined.

A change of an epistemic state involves a change in some of the epistemic attitudes. In the assumed model there are two kinds of changes, corresponding to two different kinds of epistemic inputs. First, a sentence A, which was not earlier accepted, may be *added* to the set of sentences, either as a result of new evidence or as a hypothetical assumption in an argument (the latter situation is exemplified in chapter 7). Second, a sentence A that was accepted may be *given up*. This kind of input can be the result of conflicting evidence or a desire to open up for investigation a sentence that contradicts what was previously accepted (the latter situation is exemplified in connection with a theory of explanations in chapter 8 and an analysis of causal claims in chapter 9). This kind of epistemic input may be called the *derogation* of A. Addition and derogation are the only relevant kinds so long as the inputs are confined to single sentences.

If we turn to probabilistic models of epistemic states, we may obtain a more complicated typology of epistemic inputs. The most important kind of input is the addition of a sentence A as certain evidence, for example, as a piece of data in statistical calculations where the new probability of A is 1. This is the only kind of input considered in the traditional Bayesian approach, where it is also assumed that the prior probability of A is greater than 0. However, there are other kinds of epistemic inputs that are clearly relevant to the Bayesian way of modeling states of belief. For example:

(1.1)   The new probability of A is x (where $0 \leqslant x \leqslant 1$).

(1.2)   The new probability of A lies between x and y (where $0 \leqslant x \leqslant y \leqslant 1$).

(1.3)   The new quotient of the probabilities of A and B is x (where $0 \leqslant x$).

These and some other examples of inputs to the probabilistic kind of models are discussed by van Fraassen (1980b). As has been argued by several authors, there are a number of situations in which the evidence obtained by an individual cannot be described by simply adding a sentence *A*, that is, changing its probability to 1. But some of the other forms may be appropriate.[7] It is certainly a limitation of the traditional Bayesian theory that it only accounts for the simplest form of epistemic input.

A general way of describing epistemic inputs, which seems to be applicable to most kinds of models of epistemic states, is to formulate the inputs as *constraints* on the resulting state of belief. On this approach the addition of a sentence *A* as new evidence corresponds to the constraint that *A* be accepted in the new epistemic state, and the derogation of *A* corresponds to the constraint that *A* be indetermined in the new state of belief. Similarly inputs of the forms (1.1)–(1.3) can easily be formulated as constraints on the resulting probability measure representing the new state of belief. As van Fraassen (1980b) notes, the constraints can also be expressed as commands to the believer. For example, the addition of *A* corresponds to the command, "Have full belief that *A*!"

An even more abstract way of representing epistemic inputs is to describe them as *functions* taking states of belief into new states of belief. Representing epistemic inputs in this way amounts to identifying them with the *effects* they have on different epistemic states. This avenue is discussed in the next section and elaborated in chapter 6.

1.5 Changes of Belief

On the view that rational epistemic states are equilibria, a *change* of a rational epistemic state is caused only by an epistemic input. This means that a typology of changes of belief is determined by the typology of epistemic inputs.

The general connection between epistemic inputs and changes of belief that emerges here is that there is some *functional rule* that, for a given state of belief and a given epistemic input, determines a new state of belief. This kind of rule is called an *epistemic commitment function*.

To give a simple example of a typology of changes of belief, I return to the two kinds of epistemic input for sets of sentences as models of epistemic states, to wit, additions and derogations. In the case where a sentence *A* is added to an epistemic state *K*, represented by a set of sentences, we can distinguish two subcases: (1) *A* is *consistent* with the beliefs in *K*, and (2) *A* *contradicts* the beliefs in *K*.

If the addition of *A* does not conflict with the sentences in *K*, then the simplest way to model the change induced by A is to add A set theoretically to K and then form the deductive closure of the expanded set. This kind of change is called the *expansion* of K by A. If, on the other hand, A contradicts the sentences in K, there is no simple way of modeling the change induced by the addition of A. The epistemic commitment function picks out a unique new state of belief, which in this case is called the *revision* of K by A. An important question is then, What can be said about the relation between the original epistemic state K and the revision of K by A? This question is the focus of chapters 3 and 4. The central rationality criterion on revisions is that the revision of K by A should be the *minimal* change of K that is consistent and includes A.

The change of a state of belief K induced by the derogation of a sentence A is called the *contraction* of K with respect to A. In some contexts such changes have been called "question openings." [8] When giving up a sentence A in K, it may become necessary to give up other sentences as well in order to keep the set of accepted sentences deductively closed. The rationality criterion that governs contractions is that the loss of information be as small as possible so that no belief is given up unnecessarily. Contractions and their relations to expansions and revisions are analyzed in detail in chapter 3.

Linguistically we inform others about our commitment functions by using various forms of *conditional sentences*. The connections between belief changes and conditional sentences are the topic of chapter 7. The key idea is the so-called *Ramsey test*, which says that a sentence of the form 'If A, then B' is accepted in an epistemic state K if and only if B is accepted in the revision of K with respect to A.

If we next turn our attention to the Bayesian way of modeling states of belief with the aid of probability measures, it is easy to find a process that corresponds to the expansion of a set of sentences. The traditional way of describing the change induced by the addition of a sentence A in probabilistic terms is to *conditionalize* the given probability measure on A. This process can be defined in the following way: If the probability function P represents the present state of belief, then the new state of belief that results from the addition of A is represented by the probability measure P', which is defined by $P'(B) = P(B/A)$ for all sentences B [as usual, $P(B/A)$ is here defined as $P(B \& A)/P(A)$]. For this measure we have $P'(A) = 1$; so A is accepted in the new state of belief, as desired.

The conditionalization process provides a partial definition of a commitment function for the Bayesian models of belief. It should be noted that the conditionalization is defined only if $P(A) \neq 0$. The traditional Bayesian theory gives no solution to the problem of how the changes of belief should be defined for other types of epistemic inputs. Methods of extending the conditionalization process to revisions, that is, the case when $P(A) = 0$, have been discussed by several authors.[9] Inputs of the type (1.1) were first discussed by Jeffrey (1965) and have later been investigated by several researchers.[10] I return to an analysis of some of these nonstandard forms of epistemic inputs for probabilistic models in chapter 5.

The representation of changes of belief outlined here is based on the assumption that the connection between epistemic inputs and changes of belief is given by the epistemic commitment function. As mentioned in section 1.4, there is, however, another way of presenting the relation between epistemic inputs and changes of belief: One may start from states of belief as the only fundamental entities and then *define* an epistemic input as a *function* from epistemic states to epistemic states. This means that the epistemic input is determined by the changes of epistemic states it induces. When a function representing a certain epistemic input is applied to a given state of belief K, the value of the function is the state that would be the result of accommodating the input to K. If two inputs always produce the same new epistemic state for the same input, that is, if the inputs are identical as functions, then there is no epistemological reason to distinguish them.

This alternative method of describing epistemic inputs and changes of epistemic states is ontologically simpler than the earlier method because the epistemic inputs need not be postulated as separate entities. Instead of an epistemic commitment function, one now needs an account of the class of inputs, that is, the class of functions from epistemic states to epistemic states, which then can form a basis for a typology of the changes of belief. This approach to epistemic inputs and epistemic dynamics is taken in chapter 6 as a starting point for a reconstruction of propositional logic from changes of belief.

One question that has not been considered so far is how the epistemic commitment function can be determined. As I argue in chapter 4, the mechanism generating the commitment function is based on the assumption that different beliefs have different degrees of *epistemic entrenchment*. This degree is not determined by how probable a belief is judged to be but rather by how important the belief is in inquiry and deliberation. The commitment function can then be determined from these degrees of epistemic entrenchment by means of a rule that roughly says that, when an epistemic state is revised, the most important beliefs should be retained so long as the rationality criteria are not violated. This construction is made precise in chapter 4, where the epistemological origins of the degree of epistemic entrenchment are also discussed.

1.6   Belief Systems, Language, and the External World

I have now introduced the main components of an epistemological theory. A natural unit for the analysis in the following chapters is a system formed from (1) a class of models of epistemic states, (2) a valuation function determining the epistemic attitudes in the state for each epistemic state, (3) a class of epistemic inputs, and (4) a commitment function that is defined for all epistemic states and all epistemic inputs. Let us call a system containing these four components a *belief system*. A belief system is a *cognitive* or *conceptual* structure, the material basis of which is irrelevant in the present context. The purpose of this section is to discuss the connections between belief systems and language on the one hand and belief systems and the "external world" on the other.

A belief system does not presuppose any object language in which beliefs, epistemic attitudes, or epistemic inputs are described. This view of belief systems entails that we can ascribe a belief system to an animal and discuss whether the animal's beliefs and changes of belief, as inferred from its behavior, are rational according to some given standards of rationality.

On the other hand, a belief system is a necessary prerequisite when giving meaning to linguistic expressions. Contrary to what is claimed in many classical semantical theories, I suggest that a sentence does *not* get its meaning from some correspondence with the "world" but that the meaning can be determined only *in relation to a belief system*. The primary reason why an individual utters a sentence is because he has a particular *belief* concerning the utterance (and a goal in uttering it). Thus it is the relation between a sentence and the individual's beliefs (and desires) that is most important when determining the meaning of the sentence. A *semantical theory* consists of a *mapping* from a linguistic structure to a belief system. Thus the meaning of an expression "resides" in a belief system (a cognitive entity) and not in the (material) external world. As I see it, belief systems function as *mediators* between language and the external world (figure 1.2).

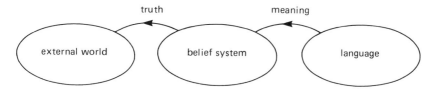

Figure 1.2
The relations between language, belief systems, and the external world.

A consequence of this view of the relations among language, belief systems, and the external world is that *epistemic attitudes* such as "acceptability" are more primitive notions for a semantical theory than "truth" [see Ellis (1979, p. viii)], at least when truth is seen as some form of correspondence between language and the external world. Thus, when understanding the meaning of an expression, *acceptability criteria* are primary to truth conditions. In this book I do not aim at any full-fledged semantical theory, but I do apply the epistemic approach outlined here to two types of linguistic entity: *logical constants* in chapter 6 and *conditional sentences* in chapter 7. Furthermore, I analyze *explanations* (chapter 8) and *causal claims* (chapter 9) using similar techniques. These analyses accordingly are based on acceptability criteria—truth conditions play a peripheral role.

I next turn to the relation between belief systems and the external world. On the theory presented here a belief system can almost be regarded as a closed system; the only external factor it presumes is the class of epistemic inputs. And, as was argued in section 1.5, we need not even know what the inputs really are; what matters are the effects they have on a belief system. This means that it does not matter much for the internal *theory* of belief systems what the factual connections with the external world are. However, my theory is not totally relativistic in the sense that the *contents* of a belief system are not related to the facts of the external world. On the contrary, beliefs are to a large extent produced by sensorily mediated contacts between the belief system and the world. What I claim is only that the logical *structure* of the belief system is not directly dependent on these contacts.

Even if the analysis of belief systems presented in this book does not depend on any account of the relation between such systems and reality, I still believe that rational belief systems to a large extent mirror an external world. Or, more precisely, a belief system contains *representations* of factual objects, properties, and relations. Thus I find my view congenial with Stalnaker's causal-pragmatic analysis (1984, chs. 1 and 2). And I think it is a central task for epistemology to give an account of the relations between these representations and what they represent. However, I do not aim at such an account here; the epistemological theories I present are restricted to the "cognitive" components of belief systems, which do not ontologically presuppose an "objective reality."

A consequence of this separation of subjective and objective epistemological factors is that the concepts of truth and falsity are *irrelevant* for the analysis of belief systems. These concepts deal with the relation between belief systems and the external world, which I claim is not essential for an analysis of epistemic dynamics. This entails that from within a belief system there is *no* difference between *knowledge* and *full belief*. From the subject's point of view there is no way to tell whether she *accepts* something as knowledge, that is, has full belief in it, or whether her accepted knowledge is also *true*.[11] When I speak of particular pieces of knowledge, I use the word "knowledge" in the sense of full belief, and I do not assume that this concept entails anything about the truth of the beliefs.

My negligence of truth may strike traditional epistemologists as heretical. However, one of my aims is to show that many epistemological problems can be attacked without using the notions of truth and falsity.

2 Models of Epistemic States

2.1 Program

A cornerstone concept in an epistemological theory is that of an epistemic state or state of belief. In this chapter I present a number of *models* of epistemic states that have been used within different areas of philosophy, computer science, psychology, and linguistics. I do not aim at presenting a complete list of models; I confine myself to the models that allow me to say something relevant about their *dynamics*, that is, how the states change as a result of epistemic inputs. This chapter, however, is restricted to a presentation of the *static* features of some models of epistemic states as well as the rationality criteria that are used to motivate them. The dynamics of different kinds of models are treated in chapters 3–6.

2.2 Belief Sets

A simple way of modeling the epistemic state of an individual is to represent it by a *set* of sentences. The intended interpretation of such a set is that it consists of exactly those sentences that the individual *accepts* in the modeled state of belief. Instead of saying that the individual accepts the sentence, we can also say that the individual *believes it to be true* or *regards it as certain*.

This kind of model is *linguistic* in the sense that it presupposes an object language **L** from which the sentences in the set are to be selected. For the most part I leave the details of **L** open, assuming only that **L** contains expressions for the standard sentential connectives. These connectives are symbolized as follows:

negation: $-$
conjunction: &
disjunction: $\vee$
material implication: $\rightarrow$

As sentential variables I use $A, B, C, \ldots$. It is also convenient to introduce symbols for two sentential constants:

truth: $\top$
falsity: $\perp$

Note that these sentences are used only as "ideal points"; they imply nothing about the correspondence between a state of belief and the external world, and they do not represent truth values.

In later chapters the same formulas will be used to denote *propositions*, that is, the "content" of sentences. However, it will be clear from the context what the symbols denote. And, because it is assumed that logically equivalent sentences cannot be distinguished within an epistemic state, there is little risk of equivocation.

Modeling epistemic states by sets of sentences is connected with a typology of epistemic attitudes that for any sentence *A* allows only the following three possibilities:

A is *accepted*,
A is *rejected*,
A is *indetermined*, that is, *A* is neither accepted nor rejected.

This typology can be reduced to two items by requiring *A* to be rejected iff $-A$ is accepted (compare this with section 2.3).

Not every set of sentences can be used to represent *rational* epistemic states. Sets of sentences that may be rationally held by an individual are called *belief sets*. In order to determine which sets of sentences constitute belief sets, I focus on two rationality criteria:

(2.1)   The set of accepted sentences should be *consistent*.

(2.2)   *Logical consequences* of what is accepted should also be accepted.

Both these criteria presuppose a *logic* for the language **L** in order to determine what is meant by "consistent" and "logical consequence." Both criteria are supported by the view of states of belief as idealized equilibria. But the criteria can also be motivated by more pragmatic considerations— inconsistent sets of belief are of no help when seeking guidance for how to act, and, in order to use one's knowledge effectively, one must be able to draw the consequences of the information one has on a topic.[1] It is clear, however, that the two criteria are not realistic as descriptions of individuals' actual sets of belief. In particular, this is the case for the requirement of including logical consequences—because of the limitations of our mental powers, we often do not see all the consequences of what we accept. I still believe, however, that the criterion is useful, at least as an ideal of rationality.

Because the concept of acceptance is central in the account of epistemic states and epistemic changes developed here, I want to make some remarks on my use of the concept. First, acceptance is a broader concept than belief; it also includes such attitudes as assuming, presupposing, and positing. To accept a proposition is to *treat* it as true in one way or another.[2] For example, in debates one often hypothetically assumes that one does not believe the proposition under discussion in order not to beg the question. In connection with an analysis of conditional sentences in chapter 7, assumed acceptance plays a central role. This position entails that acceptance is relative to context: A person may accept something in one context but reject it or leave it indetermined in another.

Second, one must distinguish the acceptance of a sentence from the *awareness* of this acceptance.[3] Because of limited calculation ability and memory failure, humans are not aware of all the consequences of their beliefs. Harman (1986, pp. 12–14) makes a distinction between *explicit* belief, which means that one's belief involves an explicit mental representation whose content is the content of the belief, and *implicit* belief, which is a belief that is derivable from the explicit beliefs. Because epistemic states are conceived of as rational equilibrium states, the beliefs that are accepted in these states include all implicit beliefs.[4]

Finally, accepting a proposition A in an epistemic state K entails *full belief* in the sense that in K there is no doubt that A is false (Levi expresses this by saying that the negation of A is not a serious possibility in K). This means that I take all accepted propositions to have maximal probability, that is, probability 1. The consequences of this position are elaborated in section 2.7 and in chapter 5. In contrast to this, some authors (for example, de Finetti and Carnap) allow that a proposition with maximal probability need not be accepted as true or, equivalently, that some propositions with zero probability are not inconsistent with the accepted beliefs.[5] However, even if on my account acceptance entails full belief, acceptance does not entail *infallibility* in the sense that an accepted belief will never be doubted. Because an agent is always influenced by different epistemic inputs, sometimes these inputs will contradict or in other ways undermine the accepted beliefs. Then, as Peirce puts it: "The scientific spirit requires a man to be at all times ready to dump his whole cartload of beliefs, the moment experience is against them" (Peirce 1932, pp. 46–47).[6]

After this digression on the notion of acceptance, I now return to the description of belief sets. The rationality criteria (2.1) and (2.2) can be seen as minimal requirements on representations of epistemic states. Belief sets are here defined for weakly specified languages. If more is known or assumed about the structure of the object language, it may be possible to formulate other, more specific rationality criteria.

I assume that the language **L** is governed by a logic that is identified with its consequence relation $\vdash$; that is, a sentence A is logically valid iff it is a consequence of the empty set. The relation $\vdash$ is assumed to satisfy the following conditions:

($\vdash$1)   If A is a truth-functional tautology, then $\vdash A$.

($\vdash$2)   Modus ponens. That is, if $\vdash A \to B$ and $\vdash A$, then $\vdash B$.

($\vdash$3)   Not $\vdash \bot$. That is, $\vdash$ is consistent.

It follows that $\vdash$ contains classical propositional logic. Furthermore it is assumed that $\vdash$ satisfies the deduction theorem that is, that $\vdash A \to B$ iff $A \vdash B$), and that it is compact; in other words, if A is a logical consequence of some set X, then A is a consequence of some finite subset of X). I note explicitly further assumptions about the logic as they are used. We can then formulate the two rationality criteria (2.1) and (2.2) more precisely in the following definition:

(Def BS)   A set K of sentences is a (nonabsurd) *belief set* iff (i) $\bot$ is not a logical consequence of the sentences in K and (ii) if $K \vdash B$, then $B \in K$.

This means that technically a belief set is what logicians normally call a *theory*. However, the interpretation here in terms of subjective beliefs is somewhat different from the standard interpretation of a theory.

It is easy to show that (Def BS) is equivalent to Stalnaker's (1984, pp. 81–82) definition of an acceptance state. He uses the following three conditions:

(2.3)   If A is a member of a set of accepted sentences and A entails B, then B is a member of that set.

(2.4)   If A and B are each members of a set of accepted sentences, then $A \,\&\, B$ is a member of that set.

(2.5)   If A is a member of a set of accepted sentences, then $-A$ is not a member of that set.

Stalnaker then argues that each of these conditions applied to belief is motivated by his pragmatic picture.

The set of all logical consequences of a set K, that is, $\{A: K \vdash A\}$, is denoted $Cn(K)$ and is called the *consequence set* of K. A basic and useful fact about this set is that $B \in Cn(K \cup \{A\})$ iff $(A \to B) \in Cn(K)$. From (Def BS) it follows that all belief sets satisfy the following condition, which is one way of expressing the idea that epistemic states are in equilibrium:

(Cn) $K = Cn(K)$.

It turns out to be convenient for technical reasons to regard the set **L** of all sentences as a belief set. This set is called the *absurd* belief set and is denoted $K_\perp$. Note that it follows from condition (ii) in (Def BS) that the set of logically valid sentences is included in every belief set. This set, which may also be denoted $Cn(\varnothing)$, is thus the smallest belief set.

An important feature of belief sets is that they need not be *maximal* in the sense that for every sentence A either A belongs to the belief set or $-A$ belongs to it. The epistemic interpretation of this is that an individual is normally not *omniscient*. However, in some of the technical contexts to follow, maximal belief sets are of interest. Such belief sets correspond to omniscience with respect to what is expressible in **L**. In some contexts maximal belief sets have been called "state descriptions" and even "possible worlds."

In some of the applications in part II a richer language than what has been assumed so far is needed. In standard propositional languages only finite disjunctions and conjunctions are defined, but sometimes infinite disjunctions and conjunctions are useful. Let us say that the language **L** is *complete* iff, for every sequence $(A_i)_{i \in I}$, where I is an index set, there exist sentences $\bigcup_{i \in I}(A_i)$ and $\bigcap_{i \in I}(A_i)$ in **L** representing the disjunction and conjunction, respectively, of the sentences in $(A_i)_{i \in I}$. (In what follows the index set I is suppressed from the notation.) Furthermore, let us say that the relation $\vdash$ of logical consequence is complete iff it satisfies the following conditions:

($\vdash$4)   For all A_i, $A_i \vdash \bigcup(A_i)$.

($\vdash$4')   For all A_i, $\bigcap(A_i) \vdash A_i$.

($\vdash$5)   If $A_i \vdash B$ for all A_i, then $\bigcup(A_i) \vdash B$.

($\vdash$5')   If $C \vdash A_i$ for all A_i, then $C \vdash \bigcap(A_i)$.

In fact, it follows from de Morgan's laws that ($\vdash$4) is equivalent to ($\vdash$4') and that ($\vdash$5) is equivalent to ($\vdash$5'). The notion of a complete logic is closely related to complete Boolean algebras.[7]

Finally, let us say that a belief set is complete iff it is closed under a complete logic. An important feature of a complete belief set K is that the conjunction of all the sentences in K is a sentence, which also is in K. Let us denote this conjunction $\bigcap K$ and call it the *determiner* for K. The name is motivated by the fact that $\bigcap K$ determines K in the sense that, for any sentence A, $A \in K$ iff $\bigcap K \vdash A$; that is, everything that is believed in K is a consequence of the single sentence $\bigcap K$.

2.3   Ellis's Belief Systems

Ellis (1976, 1979) has put forward a type of model of epistemic states that is closely related to belief sets. According to Ellis, a *belief system* is in the simplest case a set of assignments of the values T, F, and X to the sentences of a language **L**. $T(A)$ denotes the conviction (or "firm belief") that A is true, $F(A)$ the conviction that A is false, and $X(A)$ the absence of any firm belief concerning A.[8] This type of model is thus a direct way of representing a set of epistemic attitudes toward the sentence in a language **L**.

Ellis writes down a number of rationality criteria for belief systems, which he calls *acceptability* criteria (in contrast to truth conditions). The criteria are dependent on the structure of the language that is considered. In the simplest case, when **L** has the syntactic structure of the propositional calculus, the conditions are of the form '$T(A \& B)$ occurs in a belief system only if neither $F(A)$ nor $F(B)$ occur' and '$T(A \to B)$ occurs in a belief system only if $T(A)$ and $F(B)$ do not both occur'. As regards the status of these rationality criteria, Ellis says that they are "as much linguistic competence requirements as rationality laws, since they serve to define the connectives and operators [of the language **L**]" (Ellis 1979, p. 8). The ideal of rationality is satisfied mainly because of Ellis's requirement that belief systems be *completable* through every extension of **L**. This means that, for every language that syntactically includes **L**, there is some way of replacing the X evaluations that occur in a given belief system by T or F evaluations without violating any of the remaining acceptability criteria. Completability as an ideal of rationality is a consequence of "the requirement that a rational belief system be defensible against all internal criticism" (Ellis 1979, p. 9), that is, reductio ad absurdum arguments. This requirement is, of course, the same as the requirement of consistency [condition (i) in (Def BS)] in section 2.2.

Ellis states without proof that the acceptability criteria for the propositional language entail that a sentence A is a theorem of the classical propositional calculus iff $F(A)$ does not occur in any rational belief system [for a proof, see van Fraassen (1980a)].

In order to compare Ellis's belief systems with the belief sets of section 2.2, it should be noted that it is not required that $T(A \lor -A)$ occur in a belief system or that, if both $T(A)$ and $T(A \to B)$ occur, that $T(B)$ also occur. Ellis calls a belief system *strictly rational* if it satisfies these two additional requirements. In such a system one accepts as true all logical consequences of already accepted sentences. The two additional requirements thus correspond to the requirement of deductive closure [condition (ii) of (Def BS)]. Ellis seems to think that these requirements are too strong; he says that "strictly rational belief systems are really only for the gods, and they have no need for logic anyway. Therefore, I prefer the weaker concept of rationality" (Ellis 1979, p. 32). Against this it can be said that strict rationality in Ellis's sense is an idealization for certain, but so are the acceptability criteria governing rational belief systems. As mentioned earlier, Ellis also works with the equilibrium model of epistemic states. Because these criteria can be simplified if we confine ourselves to strict rationality [they can essentially be replaced by (Def BS)], there is much to be gained by such an idealization.

I now show that a strictly rational belief system in Ellis's sense is essentially identical with a belief set. Let us first assume that a nonabsurd belief set K satisfying (Def BS) is given and that the assumed logic is classical propositional logic. Define a set B_K of T, F, and X assignments in the following way: For any sentence A, A is assigned T iff $A \in K$, A is assigned F iff $-A \in K$, and A is assigned X otherwise. Then it is easy to show that B_K is a strictly rational belief system in Ellis's sense.

Conversely, suppose that a strictly rational belief system B is given. Define a set K_B of sentences as follows: $A \in K_B$ iff $T(A) \in B$. Then it is easy to show that K_B is a nonabsurd belief set governed by standard propositional logic.

These simple results show that belief sets and Ellis's strictly rational belief systems are equivalent ways of modeling epistemic states. When applying sets of sentences as models of epistemic states in what follows, I restrict myself to deductively closed sets. I prefer the belief set representation because it is more perspicuous.

I have given here only an outline of how Ellis develops, in terms of acceptability criteria, an alternative to the standard truth-condition semantics for the simplest propositional language. Ellis extends this approach to other classical and modal logics and logics of conditionals. He states completeness results for about ten different systems of logic. As regards conditional sentences, a semantical theory based on acceptability criteria that is closely related to Ellis's approach is developed in chapter 7.

2.4   Models Based on Possible Worlds

An obvious objection to using sets of sentences as models of epistemic states is that the *objects* of belief are normally not sentences but rather the *content* of sentences, that is, propositions. The characterization of propositions that has been most popular among philosophers during recent years is to identify them with *sets of possible worlds.* (An alternative construction of propositions is presented in chapter 6.) The basic semantic idea connecting sentences with propositions is then that a sentence expresses a given proposition iff it is true in exactly those possible worlds that constitute the set of worlds representing the proposition.

This set-theoretical approach to propositions makes it possible to describe some standard operations on propositions in a straightforward manner: Let $[A]$ and $[B]$ denote propositions, that is, sets of possible worlds. The conjunction of two propositions $[A]$ and $[B]$ interpreted as sets of possible worlds is represented by $[A] \cap [B]$, disjunction by $[A] \cup [B]$, and the negation of a proposition $[A]$ is $[\top] - [A] = W - [A]$. Here W is the set of all possible worlds, which also may be taken as the proposition "truth" $[\top]$ (corresponding to the sentence $\top$). We can also use the representation to introduce a relation of logical consequence between propositions: $[A]$ is a logical consequence of a set of propositions S iff the intersection of S is a subset of $[A]$. As is easily seen, the logic generated by this definition of sentential connectives includes classical propositional logic. The logic of propositions is discussed further in chapter 6.

By taking beliefs to be beliefs in propositions, we can then model an epistemic state by a set $[K]$ of possible worlds. This kind of model is called a *possible worlds model.* The epistemic interpretation of $[K]$ is that it is the *narrowest* set of possible worlds in which the individual is certain to find the actual world or, in other words, the largest set of possible worlds that is compatible with the individual's convictions.[9] Harper (1976) calls the set $[K]$ the individual's "acceptance context."

The interpretation of the set $[K]$ entails that what you accept as known in a given epistemic state is exactly what is true in all worlds in $[K]$. In a sense the use of possible worlds is a way of describing what you do *not* know. The more you learn, the fewer possible worlds are compatible with what you know. For example, I do not know whether the person who just called me on the telephone has blue or brown eyes; I do not know whether there are bats in the tower of the cathedral; and I do not know whether the train I am waiting for will be on time. Each of these possibilities demarcates a set of worlds that are compatible with what I accept as knowledge.

The central acceptability criterion is that a proposition $[A]$ is accepted in $[K]$ iff $[K]$ is a *subset* of the set of worlds representing $[A]$. Similarly $[A]$ is rejected iff $[K]$ and the set representing $[A]$ are *disjoint*. From these criteria it follows immediately that the set of accepted propositions is closed under logical consequences. The criterion that an epistemic state be consistent corresponds to the requirement that the set $[K]$ be nonempty.

Following the seminal work of Hintikka (1962), *epistemic logic* has developed as a special branch of intensional logic.[10] In this kind of logic the object languages are augmented by epistemic *operators*, so that, for example, "a knows that B" is expressed in these languages by the formula $K_a B$. A formal semantics for these operators is then developed in terms of possible worlds (the corresponding notion in Hintikka's writings is a model set). In contrast to this, my strategy is to "epistemize" the whole semantics, in the sense that I locate the epistemological machinery in the belief systems rather than in the object language. This does not mean that I have any aversion to epistemic logic—on the contrary. However, because I believe that the study of epistemic operators in a formal or natural language is not of primary concern for understanding the dynamics of knowledge and belief, I have chosen to keep the object language as simple as possible.

There is a close correspondence between belief sets and possible worlds models of epistemic states. An *interpretation function I* is a mapping from sentences of the language **L** to sets of possible worlds from W that satisfies the following conditions:

(I1) $I(-A) = W - I(A).$

(I2) $I(A \& B) = I(A) \cap I(B).$

(I3) $I(A \vee B) = I(A) \cup I(B).$

(I4) $I(A \rightarrow B) = (W - I(A)) \cup I(B).$

(I5) $I(\top) = W.$

(I6) $I(\bot) = \varnothing.$

Let the language **L** and an interpretation function I for **L** into W be given. It is easy to show that, if K is a nonabsurd belief set and if I assigns some sentence in K a nonempty set $I(A) = [A]$, then the intersection $[K]$ of all the sets $I(A)$ for $A \in K$ is nonempty. This intersection can then be taken as a possible worlds model. In this model all sentences in K (or rather their propositional interpretations) are accepted, and no other *sentences* from **L** are accepted. However, there may be *propositions*, that is, subsets of W, that are accepted in $[K]$, but these are not the interpretations of any sentences in K. This is possible simply because not all subsets of W need be interpretations of any sentences from **L**.

Conversely, given any nonempty possible worlds model $[K]$ together with an interpretation function I, we can define a set K of sentences as follows: $A \in K$ iff $[K] \subseteq I(A)$. It is easy to show that K is a nonabsurd belief set. Here it can be noted that, if we assume that all propositions have a name in **L**, that is, for every subset W' of W there is some sentence A in **L** such that $I(A) = W'$, then the belief set generated in this way is complete, that is, closed under infinite disjunctions and conjunctions. In particular, there is then a determiner $\bigcap K$ for the belief set such that $I(\bigcap K) = [K]$. And in this case there will be a one-to-one mapping from sentences in **L** to propositions in the power set of W.

2.5 Spohn's Generalized Possible Worlds Models

A possible worlds model (as well as a belief set) gives a crude representation of a subject's beliefs because we can express only the most elementary epistemic attitudes. This is a consequence of the fact that the set $[K]$, representing the epistemic state, divides the possible worlds into only two classes. For these models there is no possibility of expressing any degree of plausibility of different possible worlds or propositions. The best-known way of modeling *degrees* of belief is to introduce probabilities defined over a language or a class of propositions. This is the topic of the next section. In this section I present Spohn's (1987) ordinal conditional functions, which are a different way of introducing degrees of belief. Isaac Levi has pointed out that Shackle's (1961) measure of "potential surprise" is closely related to Spohn's construction.

An *ordinal conditional function*, according to Spohn, is a function k from a given set W of possible worlds into the class of ordinals such that some possible worlds are assigned the smallest ordinal 0. Intuitively k represents a *plausibility grading* of the possible worlds. The worlds that are assigned the smallest ordinals are the most plausible, according to the beliefs of the individual.

The plausibility ordering of possible worlds can be extended to an ordering of propositions, (sets of possible worlds), by requiring that the ordinal assigned to a proposition A be the *smallest* ordinal assigned to the worlds included in A; that is, $k(A) = \min\{k(w): w \in A\}$. This definition entails that the plausibility ordering of propositions have the following two properties:

(2.6) For all propositions A, either $k(A) = 0$ or $k(-A) = 0$.

(2.7) For all nonempty propositions A and B, $k(A \cup B) = \min\{k(A), k(B)\}$.

We can now identify the set $[K]$ of the previous section by the set of the most plausible possible worlds, that is, the set of worlds w such that $k(w) = 0$. Following this, we can introduce the basic acceptability criterion: A proposition A is *accepted* in the epistemic state represented by the ordinal conditional function k iff $k(-A) > 0$. That this definition is the natural one follows from the fact that $k(A) = 0$ means that A and $[K]$ have some world in common; that is, A is not believed false in $[K]$. So if $k(-A) > 0$, this means that all worlds in $[K]$ must belong to A.

An important feature of ordinal conditional functions is that it makes sense to talk of greater or lesser plausibility or firmness of belief, relative to some function k. We can distinguish several cases: If both A and B are accepted [that is, if $k(-A) > 0$ and $k(-B) > 0$], we can say that A is *believed more firmly than B* iff $k(-A) > k(-B)$, that is, if the most plausible worlds outside A are less plausible than the most plausible worlds outside B. There are other cases where A is more plausible than B. First, the case where A is accepted and B is not, that is, where $k(-A) > k(-B) = 0$. Second, there is the case where A is not believed false but B is; that is, $k(A) = 0 < k(B)$. Finally, we have the case where both A and B are believed false but A less firmly so, that is, $0 < k(A) < k(B)$. This leads us to the following definition: A is *more plausible than B* relative to k iff $k(-A) > k(-B)$ or $k(A) < k(B)$.

We thus see that representing epistemic states by ordinal conditional functions makes it possible to introduce more interesting epistemic attitudes, to wit, "believed more firmly than" and "more plausible than," beside the standard "accepted," "rejected," and "kept in suspense." However, the full forces of the ordinal conditional functions appears only in the next chapter, when I turn to changes of epistemic states.

2.6   An Example from Artificial Intelligence: Doyle's Truth Maintenance System

So far the models of epistemic states that have been presented have been taken from the philosophical literature. There are, however, other areas of research where models of epistemic states are important. In general terms it can be said that such models are important for cognitive science. In this section I briefly comment on the use of semantic networks as models of epistemic states and then present a particularly interesting example from artificial intelligence (AI), to wit, Doyle's (1979) truth maintenance system.

Probably the most common models of epistemic states used in cognitive science are those called *semantic networks*. A semantic network typically consists of a set of *nodes* representing some objects of belief and, connecting the nodes, a set of *links* representing relations between the nodes. The networks are then complemented by some implicit or explicit interpretation rules that make it possible to extract beliefs and epistemic attitudes. Changing a semantic network consists in adding or deleting nodes or links.

Different semantic networks have different types of objects as nodes and different kinds of relations as links. In fact, the diversity is so large that it is difficult to see what the various networks have in common. It seems that any kind of object can serve as a node in the networks and that any type of relation or connection between nodes can be used as a link between nodes. This diversity seems to undermine the claims that semantic networks represent epistemic states, and it raises the question of what they have to do with semantics. In his excellent methodological article, Woods (1975) admits that "we must begin with the realization that there is currently no 'theory' of semantic networks" (p. 36). As a preliminary to such a theory, Woods formulates requirements for an adequate notation for semantic networks and explicit interpretation rules for such a notation. My aim here is not a presentation of his ideas but a brief outline of semantic networks as models of epistemic states.

Turning now to artificial intelligence, the philosophically most important problem seems to be the frame problem. In general terms, this problem can be defined as the problem of finding a (basically epistemic) model that permits changing and complex information about the world to be represented in an adequate and efficient way.[11] A solution to the frame problem would be a way of describing the *form* of the world (or a substantial part of it) that would enable us to translate efficiently our knowledge and beliefs about the world into a computer program. It should be noted that the frame problem is not a question of content but one of form: The simple belief sets presented in section 2.2 are perfectly capable of representing the blocks worlds studied in AI, but these models are badly suited for describing *actions* that may be performed in such worlds and the *changes* of the world the actions bring about.

Doyle's (1979) truth maintenance system (TMS) is an attempt to model changes of belief within an AI setting and, as such, is of direct relevance for the frame problem. As Doyle remarks (p. 232), the name "truth maintenance system" not only sounds like Orwellian Newspeak, but is also a misnomer, because what is maintained is the consistency of beliefs and reasons for belief. Doyle (1983) later changed the name to "reason maintenance system." In a broad sense TMS can be said to be a semantic network model, but its belief structure and its techniques for handling changes of belief are more sophisticated than in other semantic network models.

There are two basic types of entities in TMS: *nodes* representing propositional beliefs and *justifications* representing reasons for beliefs. These justifications may be other beliefs from which the current belief is derived. A node may be *in* or *out*, which corresponds to the epistemic attitudes of accepting and not accepting the belief represented by the node. As should be expected, if a certain belief is out in the system, this does not entail that its negation is in. On the other hand, as a rationality requirement, if both a belief and its negation are in, then the system will start a *revision* of the set of nodes and their justifications in order to reestablish consistency.

A justification consists of a pair of lists: an inlist and an outlist. A node is in if and only if it has some justification (there may be several for the same node), the inlist of which contains only nodes that are in and the outlist of which contains only nodes that are out. A particular type of justification, called "nonmonotonic justification," is used to make tentative guesses within the system. For example, a belief in A can be justified simply by the fact that the belief in $-A$ is out. Beliefs that are justified in this way are called *assumptions*. This technique gives us a way of representing commonsense "default" expectations. It also leads to *nonmonotonic* reasoning in the following sense: If belief in A is justified only by the absence of any justification for $-A$, then a later *addition* of a justification for $-A$ will lead to a *retraction* of the belief in A. The general problem of non-monotonic reasoning and retraction of beliefs is analyzed in chapter 3.

The basic concepts of TMS are best illustrated by an example:

Node	Justification		Status
	Inlist	Outlist	
(N1) Oscar is not guilty of defamation.	(N2)	(N3)	in
(N2) The accused should have the benefit of the doubt.	–	–	in
(N3) Oscar called the queen a harlot.	(N4), (N5)	–	out
(N4) It may be assumed that the witness's report is correct.	–	–	in
(N5) The witness says he heard Oscar call the queen a harlot	–	–	out

In this situation (N1) is in because (N2) is in and (N3) is out. Node (N3) is out because not both of (N4) and (N5) are in. If (N5) changes status to in (this may be assumed to be beyond the control of the system), (N3) will become in and consequently assumption (N1) is out.

Apart from the representations of nodes and justifications as presented here, TMS contains techniques for handling various problems that arise when the system of beliefs is adjusted to accommodate the addition of a new node or justification. In particular, when a contradiction is found, the system uses a form of backtracking to find the fundamental assumptions that directly or indirectly give support to the contradiction. One of these assumptions is chosen as the culprit and is given the status out. This process sometimes needs to be iterated, but it is beyond the scope of this chapter to give a full description of the mechanics of TMS.

However, the TMS representation of beliefs is not without epistemological problems. The example can be used to illustrate some of the drawbacks of TMS. In the handling of beliefs and justifications, TMS takes no notice of what the nodes happen to stand for. The sentences that I have added to the node names are not interpreted in any way by the system. This means that much of the *logic* of propositions is lost in the TMS representation of beliefs. All forms of logical inferences that are to be used by the system have to be reintroduced as special systems of justifications.

Doyle discusses conditional proofs, but the process for handling such inferences seems extremely complex.

Furthermore, as regards the frame problem, TMS is not an ideal solution because it leaves much of the work to the programmer. The programmer produces the nodes and their justifications; she has to organize the information in levels, and she also has to decide on how contradictions are to be engineered. In short, the programmer may end up in a task that is no easier than describing the relevant beliefs and their connections in a belief set.

I find TMS to be an interesting way of modeling epistemic states. In particular, the idea of including justifications for the beliefs held seems fruitful. This aspect of belief systems seems to be neglected in other models of epistemic states. An exception, however, is Spohn (1983a), who tries to define the notion of one belief being a *reason* for another within his model of states of belief.

Harman (1986, ch. 4) introduces a distinction between two competing theories of belief revision that is helpful here: the *foundations theory*, which holds that one needs to keep track of one's original justifications for belief, and the *coherence theory*, which holds that one need not.

The foundations theory holds that some of one's beliefs "depend on" others for their current justification; these other beliefs may depend on still others, until one gets to foundational beliefs that do not depend on any further beliefs for their justification. In this view reasoning or belief revision should consist, first, in subtracting any of one's beliefs that do not have a satisfactory justification and, second, in adding new beliefs that either need no justification or are justified on the basis of other justified beliefs one has.

On the other hand, according to the coherence theory, it is not true that one's ongoing beliefs have or ought to have the sort of justificational structure required by the foundations theory. In this view ongoing beliefs do not usually require any justification. Justification is taken to be required only if one has a special reason to doubt a particular belief. Such a reason may consist in a conflicting belief or in the observation that one's beliefs could be made more "coherent," that is, more organized or simpler or less ad hoc, if the given belief were abandoned (and perhaps if certain other changes were made). According to the coherence theory, belief revision should involve minimal changes in one's beliefs in a way that sufficiently increases overall coherence. (Harman 1986, pp. 29–30)

Levi (1980) defends the coherence theory. He claims (p. 1) that knowledge is not "a matter of pedigree." It is clear that, with the exception of Doyle's TMS, all models of epistemic states presented in this chapter adhere to the coherence theory. This is true also of the probabilistic models to be presented in the following sections. Harman (1986, ch. 4) discusses the pros and cons of the foundations theory versus the coherence theory. Among other things he reviews some psychological experiments [see Ross and Anderson (1982)] that tend to support the coherence theory. It seems to be a matter of fact that people do not keep track of the justifications for their beliefs. The main reason for this is that it would soon lead to a combinatorial explosion, and it is a matter of the *economy of thought* to avoid cluttering one's mind. Harman sees this as the decisive reason in favor of the coherence theory. However, it should be admitted that, in the view of epistemic states as equilibrium points adopted here, combinatorial considerations are of less importance than other rationality criteria.

2.7   Bayesian Models

The best-known models of epistemic states and of how epistemic inputs affect an epistemic state are models that are based on *subjective* or *personalistic probabilities*. A central part of the Bayesian doctrine is that the epistemic state of an individual can be represented by a *probability function* defined over a language or a set of possible worlds. The intended interpretation is that such a probability function provides a measure of the individual's *degrees of belief* in the sentences or propositions. These degrees of belief then provide us with a richer repertoire of epistemic attitudes than is possible with belief sets or traditional possible worlds models.

The criterion of rationality that is used to motivate the assumption that degrees of belief should be represented by a probability function is that degrees of belief should be *coherent*. The meaning of coherence is best explained by a brief description of the so-called Dutch book theorem. In the form of Bayesianism advocated by Ramsey (1931b) and de Finetti (1937), it is assumed that the probability an individual assigns to a sentence can be determined with the aid of his inclination to accept *bets* concerning the truth of the sentence. If he, for example, accepts a bet that A is true at the odds of $1:4$, then this is taken to imply that he estimates the probability of A to be at least $1/(1 + 4) = 0.2$. The Dutch book theorem says that if it is not possible to construct a bet where the individual will lose money no matter what happens (a Dutch book), then there is a unique probability measure that describes the individual's degrees of belief in the different sentences of the language.[12] It should be noted that a necessary assumption for this theorem is that, if an individual is not willing to bet on A at odds of $a:b$, then he should be willing to bet on $-A$ at odds of $b:a$. In the betting context the requirement that the individual's beliefs be coherent is simply that no Dutch book can be made against him. The Dutch book theorem then shows that coherence entails that the individual's degrees of belief can be represented by a probability function.

The Bayesian models of epistemic states have been used extensively within many areas of decision theory and game theory. In combination with a utility measure the subjective probabilities have been used in various forms of decision rules, the most familiar being the principle of maximizing expected utility. In decision-theoretic contexts it is often assumed that all information about the world that is relevant for the decision maker is conveyed by his subjective probability function, that is, the Bayesian model of an epistemic state.

I have not yet raised the question of how the probability function on **L** (or W) is to be defined. We want to consider a numerical function defined on **L** that obeys the laws of probability. The standard formulation of these laws is as follows:

(2.8) $0 \leqslant P(A) \leqslant 1$ for all sentences A in **L**.

(2.9) $P(\top) = 1$.

(2.10)   For all sentences A and B, if A and B are logically disjoint [that is, if $\vdash -(A \,\&\, B)$], then $P(A \vee B) = P(A) + P(B)$.

However, this formulation of the axioms presumes that we know the *logic* of **L**, because otherwise we cannot determine when two sentences are logically disjoint. In order to prepare the ground for chapter 6, I use instead an axiomatization of the laws of probability that shows that we need not presuppose a logic. On the contrary, the axiomatization can be used to *define* a logic for **L**. Historically the first axiomatization of this kind is Popper's (1959, app. *iv) axioms for conditional probability. For my purposes an axiomatization of unconditional probability is sufficient, and I can use the following definition, which is adopted from Stalnaker (1970):

(Def Prob)   A (language-based) *probability function* is a function P from sentences in **L** into real numbers that meets the following six conditions for all sentences A, B, and C:

(i) $0 \leqslant P(A) \leqslant 1$.

(ii) $P(A) = P(A \& A)$.

(iii) $P(A \& B) = P(B \& A)$.

(iv) $P(A \& (B \& C)) = P((A \& B) \& C)$.

(v) $P(A) + P(-A) = 1$.

(vi) $P(A) = P(A \& B) + P(A \& -B)$.

In this definition we assume that $-$ and $\&$ are the only primitive connectives and that the remaining connectives are defined in the standard way. It is worth noting that Stalnaker introduces these probability functions "as an autonomous semantics for propositional calculus, based on the concept of knowledge rather than truth" (Stalnaker 1970, p. 65). This semantic program has since been developed by Leblanc (1983) and Field (1977) among others.

It is easy to show that, on the standard axiomatization of probability functions, the six conditions in (Def Prob) are satisfied. In order to show that we can use (Def Prob) to derive the standard axiomatization of probability functions, we must first show how it can be used to generate a *logic* for **L**. Let us say that a sentence A is *logically valid* iff $P(A) = 1$ for all probability functions that satisfy conditions (i)–(vi). On the basis of this we can then say that two sentences A and B are *logically disjoint* iff $-(A \& B)$ is logically valid. From these definitions the following lemmas can be established:[13]

LEMMA 2.1   A sentence is logically valid iff it is a truth-functional tautology.

LEMMA 2.2   If A and B are logically disjoint, then, for any probability function P, $P(A \vee B) = P(A) + P(B)$.

Lemma 2.2 expresses the key axiom in the standard axiomatization of probability functions. Because the other axioms are trivial, we conclude that the standard axiomatization and the one presented here are essentially equivalent.

I next turn to the connections between belief sets and the probability models presented here. Probabilities represent degrees of belief, and belief sets represent beliefs that are accepted as certain. In a probabilistic model it is natural to define the second notion by saying that a sentence A is *accepted as certain relative to P* iff $P(A) = 1$. We can then introduce a relation between probability functions and sets of sentences:

(Def Gen)   A probability function P defined over **L** *generates* the set K of sentences iff, for all sentences A in **L**, $P(A) = 1$ iff $A \in K$.

In other words, the set generated by P is the set of sentences that are accepted as certain relative to P. The relation is many to one—different probability functions may generate the same set of sentences. The following result is trivial but useful [for a proof, see Gärdenfors (1978a), p. 398]:

LEMMA 2.3 K is a nonabsurd belief set iff there exists some probability function P that generates K.

This result shows that, in applications where we are interested only in the sentences that are accepted as certain, we need not use the full complexity of probability functions but can confine ourselves to belief sets.

(Def Gen) identifies the accepted sentences with the sentences that have *full belief*, that is, probability 1. Some authors, for example, de Finetti, Carnap, and Levi, drive a wedge between acceptability and maximal probability and thus allow that some sentences that have probability 1 are not accepted [see Levi (1980, ch. 5)]. For example, in a problem of estimating the value of a real-valued parameter x that ranges between 0 and 1, the hypothesis that x has an irrational value normally has probability 1, but, according to these authors, it should not be accepted. Even if a distinction between acceptability and full belief is motivated in some cases, it does not play any role in this book; so, in order to avoid unnecessary complications, I assume (Def Gen) in chapter 5 and to some extent in the applications in part II.

   Corresponding to his belief systems, Ellis (1979) also discusses a class of models of epistemic states that use probability values. These models are based on a set of "P-evaluations," which are assignments of subjective probabilities to sentences in **L**. In addition to evaluations of the form $P(A) = x$, Ellis also allows evaluations of the form $Y(A)$, which occur in the model of an individual's epistemic state when she has no determinate degree of belief in A. Thus these systems of P-evaluations are related to standard Bayesian probability models just like Ellis's belief systems are related to belief sets. Forrest (1986) develops Ellis's probabilistic models into a *dynamic* setting. An important difference between the dynamics of probabilistic models to be presented in chapter 5 and Forrest's system is that he does not make the idealizing assumption that belief systems be closed under logical implications. Besides this, his typology of epistemic changes is different from the one presented there. Some further models of "indeterminate" degrees of belief are discussed in the next section.

It is, of course, also possible to have a probabilistic version of the possible worlds models. Such a model consists of a probability function defined over sets of possible worlds taken from some given set W. This kind of model is studied by several authors, and an extended version of it is introduced in chapter 8.[14]

A central feature of probabilistic possible worlds models is that, because propositions are defined as sets of possible worlds, we can immediately assign probabilities to propositions as soon as we have a probability function defined over W. And if we have an interpretation function I available that takes sentences into propositions, we can assign probabilities to sentences by saying that the probability of the sentence is the same as the probability of the set of possible worlds that is its interpretation. It should come as no surprise that such a probability assignment to the sentences in L satisfies (Def Prob). Thus it is clear that, in light of the results of section 2.6, a probability model defined over a set W of possible worlds is but a slight generalization of a probability model defined over a language L.

2.8   Generalized Probabilistic Models

The main rationale for the Bayesian way of modeling epistemic states is the Dutch book theorem or closely related results. As was mentioned earlier, a presupposition for the theorem is that an individual be willing to take either side of a bet so that, if he is not willing to bet on a sentence A at odds of $a:b$, he should be willing to bet on $-A$ at odds of $b:a$. A general criticism of the Bayesian models is that this requirement demands too much of people's willingness to accept bets, and, perhaps more important, it is far from certain that the requirement is rationally motivated. People are often not willing to accept either of the two bets, and they may have good reasons for not doing so. This criticism of the standard Bayesian models of epistemic states is directed against the assumptions needed for the Dutch book theorem, but similar points can be made against other arguments for representing beliefs by a single probability measure.

A probability function is one way of representing beliefs that are partial in the sense that they are neither accepted nor rejected. The probability function provides detailed information about how strongly the beliefs are held, but, as we have seen, such a function may be unrealistically detailed.

In this section I present some other ways of representing partial beliefs that have been suggested within theories of decision making. These models are based on less demanding assumptions about an individual's behavior than in the standard Bayesian model.

The first alternative way of describing partial beliefs is to associate with each sentence in a language (or each proposition in a possible worlds context) a *probability interval*.[15] The intended interpretation of such an interval is that the information available to the individual entails that the "true" probability of the sentence is a point in the interval and that no narrower interval is justified by this information. On this interpretation the width of the probability interval associated with a sentence A can be taken as a measure of the individual's degree of ignorance of the probability of A. The interval associated with a sentence A can be denoted $(P_*(A), P^*(A))$, where $0 \leqslant P_*(A) \leqslant P^*(A) \leqslant 1$. $P_*(A)$ and $P^*(A)$ are called the *lower* and *upper* probabilities of A, respectively.

The rationality criteria governing the assignment of probability intervals take the form of certain restrictions that guarantee that the assignment is *coherent*. If we consider only a single sentence A, then it must be the case that $P_*(A) = 1 - P^*(-A)$ and $P^*(A) = 1 - P_*(-A)$ in order to maintain the interpretation that every value within the interval assigned to A is a "possible" probability of A. Generally the coherence restriction is that, for every value x within the interval $(P_*(A), P^*(A))$, there must be values within the intervals associated with the other sentences in the language such that x together with these values form a standard probability function over the language [see Gärdenfors (1979b), p. 169]. If this criterion is not fulfilled for some assignment of intervals, it is possible to construct a Dutch book against an individual using these intervals as a basis for his betting behavior.

The second generalization of the traditional Bayesian models that I consider is based on utilizing a *class* **P** of probability functions, instead of a single probability function, to represent the beliefs of an individual. The interpretation of the set **P** is that the information available to the individual is not sufficient to single out a unique probability function, but it determines a class of *epistemologically possible* [or, as Levi (1974) calls them, "permissible"] probability functions. A probability function is said to be epistemologically possible if it does not contradict the individual's knowledge in the given epistemic state. Several authors have suggested that a state of belief be represented by such a class of probability functions.[16]

Levi (1974) also assumes that the set **P** is *convex*, which means that, if P and P' are two functions in **P**, then for all a, $0 \leqslant a \leqslant 1$, the "mixture" function $a \cdot P + (1 - a) \cdot P'$ is also in **P**. (The mixture function is defined by $[a \cdot P + (1 - a) \cdot P'](A) = a \cdot P(A) + (1 - a) \cdot P'(A)$ for all A. Mixture functions and their properties are analyzed in section 5.2.) The interpretation of this assumption is that, if P and P' are both epistemologically possible probability functions according to the beliefs of an individual, then any mixture of these functions is also possible.

Note that, if **P** is assumed to be convex, then for any sentence A the set of probabilities assigned to A by the functions in **P** form an interval (possibly open). In this sense we can say that the set **P** generates an interval assignment to the sentences of **L**. Representing beliefs by a convex set of probability functions is, however, a more general method than representing them by probability intervals, because from a convex set of probability functions a unique set of associated intervals can be computed; but if we start from a given assignment of coherent probability intervals, there is in general a large number of convex sets of probability functions that generate the intervals. And when it comes to decision making, this may make a difference. Levi (1974, pp. 416–417) presents an example that shows that there may be two decision situations with the same alternative states and outcomes but with different sets of "permissible" probability functions, which give different decisions when his theory is used, although the probability intervals that are generated are identical.

It is argued in Gärdenfors and Sahlin (1982) that not all aspects of an individual's beliefs that are relevant for decision making can be captured by a set of probability functions. As a second element in the models of states of belief, in addition to the set **P** a measure r of the *epistemic reliability* of the probability functions in **P** is introduced. The motivation for including r is that, even if several probability functions are epistemologically possible, some distributions are more reliable to the individual—they are backed up by more evidence or information than other distributions. The measure of epistemic reliability is intended to represent these degrees of information. In a sense the measure r can be seen as a probabilistic generalization of Spohn's notion of believing more firmly, as presented in section 2.5.

The concept of epistemic reliability is also closely related to the "weight of evidence" that was introduced by Keynes (1921, p. 71). In fact, this way of extending the Bayesian representation of beliefs was forestalled by Peirce:

To express the proper state of belief, not *one* number but *two* are requisite, the first depending on the inferred probability, the second on the amount of knowledge on which that probability is based. (Peirce 1932, p. 421)

For a discussion of the weight of evidence, see Gärdenfors (1979b, pp. 176–178).

I have now presented some of the main extensions of the standard Bayesian models of belief. There are several variants of each of the types that have been presented here, but my aim has not been to give a complete list. A general approach to both belief set representations and probabilistic models can be found in Domotor (1983). Yet another extension of the Bayesian model is presented in chapter 8 as a tool for analyzing explanations.

2.9   Johnson-Laird's Mental Models

Most of the models of epistemic states presented so far have presumed sentences or propositions as the building blocks of the models. Furthermore, the models have been governed by a propositional logic. In this concluding section I give an outline of Johnson-Laird's (1983) "mental models," which deal with reasoning in first-order logic and which have "things" as building blocks.

One of the main applications of Johnson-Laird's models is *syllogistic reasoning*. He considers syllogisms that involve two premises of the forms 'All X are Y', 'Some X are Y', and 'No X are Y'. The key step in the modeling of premises in a syllogism is to set up a *table* of "actors" taking different "roles" (Johnson-Laird 1983, ch. 5). For example, the premise 'All artists are beekeepers' may be represented as follows:

artist = beekeeper
artist = beekeeper
artist = beekeeper
      (beekeeper)
      (beekeeper)

Here three actors are playing the joints roles of artists and beekeepers, and two (optional) actors are taking the role of the beekeepers who are not artists. If a second premise, 'All the beekeepers are chemists', is now added, the table is *expanded* to accommodate this premise in the following way:

```
artist = beekeeper = chemist
artist = beekeeper = chemist
artist = beekeeper = chemist
          (beekeeper) = (chemist)
          (beekeeper) = (chemist)
                        (chemist)
```

By inspecting this table, we can readily determine that the conclusion 'All the artists are chemists' follows.

Similarly the premise 'None of the authors are burglars' can be modeled by "fencing off" the actors:

```
author
author
author
_____
          burglar
          burglar
          burglar
```

Suppose now that we want to add the premise 'Some of the chefs are burglars'. The most straightforward way of doing this is as follows:

```
(i)   author
      author
      author
      _____
                burglar = chef
                burglar = chef
                (burglar)
                          (chef)
```

If this table is used, it is tempting to conclude that 'None of the authors are chefs', which some experimental subjects do. However, here are two other ways of modeling the premises:

```
(ii)  author
      author
      author    =          chef
      _____
                burglar = chef
                burglar = chef
                (burglar)
```

(iii) author   =   chef
       author   =   chef
       author   =   chef
       _____
                 burglar = chef
                 burglar = chef
                 (burglar)

Because all these tables are consistent with the premises, it follows that the conclusion 'None of the authors are chefs' is invalid (and so is 'Some of the authors are not chefs'). Given these three tables, it may be tempting to claim that there is no valid conclusion connecting the authors with the chefs (as many subjects do). However, in all three 'Some of the chefs are not authors' is valid.

I have here only presented Johnson-Laird's method of modeling syllogistic reasoning by way of examples. The reader is referred to Johnson-Laird (1983) for the theoretical basis of these models. He there uses the tables and the various places where the constructions can go *wrong* in the subjects' minds (for example, not seeing all possible types of tables for a particular pair of premises) to explain several experimental findings concerning people's performance in syllogistic reasoning.

Another application in Johnson-Laird's book is a computer program that constructs models of *spatial descriptions*. For example, if given the input

X is to the right of Y
Z is in front of Y
W is to the left of Z,

the program constructs the following spatial representation:

      Y   X
W   Z

The interesting cases occur when the program is given indeterminate descriptions, such as

X is to the right of Y
Z is to the left of X.

Even if this information does not fully specify the model, the program nevertheless constructs a model, for example:

Z   Y   X

However, if the program is subsequently informed that

Z is to the right of Y,

then this information *contradicts* the constructed model. This forces the program to check whether there is any *revision* of the model that is consistent with all the information available. This is accomplished by (recursively) rearranging the indetermined positions of the items in the model and checking whether the rearrangement satisfies the premises. In the example given here, the program returns the model

Y   Z   X,

as expected.

Also for this application I have chosen to present Johnson-Laird's theory by means of examples. My main reason for presenting these applications is that the models do *not* use sentences or propositions as building blocks. As we have seen, however, it is still possible to make *inferences* from the models. Furthermore, I want to emphasize that *expansions* and *revisions* can be represented in a systematic manner for these models.

3 Expansions, Revisions, and Contractions

3.1 The Three Basic Types of Changes of Belief

In chapter 2 I treated the *statics* of belief, that is, the representation of epistemic states. I now turn to the first steps of the *dynamics* of belief. For the main part of this chapter I presume that epistemic states are modeled by belief sets. My main aim is to formulate and discuss some criteria for different kinds of changes of belief and then analyze the relations between the criteria. In the final section I extend the approach to Spohn's generalized models (as presented in section 2.5). The dynamics of probabilistic models are investigated in chapter 5.

A belief set is admittedly a crude way of representing a state of belief. However, as will be seen in this and the next chapter, several important epistemological problems have already appeared at this low level of sophistication. In order not to obscure these problems, I think it is preferable to use a representation of beliefs that is as simple as possible.

If K is a consistent belief set, then for any sentence A only three different epistemic attitudes concerning A can be expressed:

(i) $A \in K$: A is accepted.
(ii) $-A \in K$: A is rejected.
(iii) $A \notin K$ and $-A \notin K$: A is indetermined.

So a change of belief concerning A consists in changing one of these epistemic attitudes into one of the others. In all, six such changes are possible, but for reasons of symmetry they are naturally grouped into three types.

The first type is when the epistemic attitude 'A is indetermined' is changed into either 'A is accepted' or '$-A$ is accepted' (that is, 'A is rejected'). I call this kind of change an *expansion*, because it consists in adding a new belief (and its consequences) to the belief set without retracting any of the old beliefs. Such changes of belief are commonly the results of observations or of accepting linguistically transmitted information.

The second kind of change occurs when one of the attitudes 'A is accepted' or 'A is rejected' is changed into 'A is indetermined'. This kind of change is called a *contraction*, because it consists in giving up the belief in A (or the belief in $-A$). This kind of change can be made by an agent in order to open up for investigation some proposition that contradicts what the agent previously believed. In a debate a belief in A may be (hypothetically) retracted in order to give the negation of A a hearing without begging the question. And, as argued in chapters 8 and 9, contractions play an essential role in explanations and in causal reasoning.

A common property of expansions and contractions is that they are *consistent* changes of a state of belief; there is no belief that is accepted in an expansion or a contraction that contradicts any belief in the earlier state of belief.

The third type of change is when either '*A* is accepted' is changed to '*A* is rejected' (that is, '$-A$ is accepted') or '*A* is rejected' is changed to '*A* is accepted'. This type of change is called a *revision*, because a belief whose negation was accepted earlier is accepted. Thus this kind of change is not a consistent change. A typical example of a revision is when you are about to pay your bill at a restaurant and, to your great surprise, there is no money in your wallet, even though you are certain that it contained enough money to pay the bill. A revision may also be made when you, for the sake of argument, hypothetically accept a proposition, although you presently believe in its negation. In chapter 7 the relation between revisions of belief and the use of counterfactual sentences is investigated.

So long as we restrict ourselves to the belief set representation of epistemic states and the three kinds of epistemic attitudes that are expressible for such models, these three kinds of change of belief are the only relevant ones. Thus, in order to determine the *epistemic commitment* for a belief system based on belief sets, one needs to specify rules for how expansions, contractions, and revisions are made. The main task in this and the following chapter is to provide *formal representations* of the three types of belief change. There are two basic strategies that can be used to this aim. The first, which is pursued in this chapter, is to formulate various *rationality postulates* that should be satisfied by the appropriate belief changes. The second strategy, which is the topic of chapter 4, is to present *constructive models* of epistemic dynamics.

3.2   Expansions

Expansion is a simple way of modeling the epistemic change that follows *learning* something—the epistemic attitude toward some sentence *A* is changed from indetermined to accepted. The most common causes of such changes are observations and the information provided by other people (through various information channels). Where *K* is the initial belief set, the expansion of *K* by *A* is denoted K_A^+. Formally it is assumed that $+$ is a function from pairs of belief sets and sentences, that is, from $\mathbf{K} \times \mathbf{L}$, to belief sets, that is, $\mathbf{K}$. We can express this by the following postulate:

(K^+1) K_A^+ is a belief set.

Because belief sets are used as representations of states of belief, we need not worry about the details of the epistemic inputs. The appropriate input can be identified with the change it causes; that is, it can be described as the requirement that A be accepted in the expanded state of belief. This requirement can be put more formally:

(K^+2) $A \in K_A^+$.

The next postulate for expansions can be justified by the "economic" side of rationality. The key idea is that, when we change our beliefs, we want to retain as much as possible of our old beliefs—information is in general not gratuitous, and unnecessary losses of information are therefore to be avoided [compare Hilpinen (1981)]. This heuristic criterion is called the criterion of *informational economy*. This criterion plays an important role in several places in this book.

If A is indetermined in K (or if A is accepted), then $-A$ is not accepted; so A does not contradict any of the beliefs in K. It is therefore possible to retain all the old beliefs in the expansion of K by A; so the criterion of informational economy justifies the following:

(3.1)   If $-A \notin K$, then $K \subseteq K_A^+$.

However, in the abnormal case when $-A \in K$, adding A produces an inconsistency. So in this case it is natural conventionally to let K_A^+ be the absurd belief set, that is, $K_\perp$. Because $K_\perp$ is a superset of all belief sets, (3.1) can be generalized to the postulate

(K^+3) $K \subseteq K_A^+$.

This axiom also motivates the name "expansion."

A degenerate case of expansion occurs when A is already accepted in K. In this case an epistemic input in the form of a requirement to accept A should have no effect on the state of belief because the epistemic attitude toward A is already as required. This justifies the following axiom:

(K^+4) If $A \in K$, then $K_A^+ = K$.

For the next postulate suppose that more is known in the state of belief H than in the state of belief K. In the terminology of belief sets this amounts to the supposition that $K \subseteq H$. If K and H are expanded by A, then it is natural that K_A^+ should not contain any beliefs that are not also included in H_A^+ (see the discussion in section 2.6). Formally we have the following *monotonicity* postulate:

(K^+5) If $K \subseteq H$, then $K_A^+ \subseteq H_A^+$.

From these five postulates it is now possible to derive some useful consequences.

(3.2)   If $B \in K_A^+$, then $K_B^+ \subseteq K_A^+$.

When interpreting this result, the interesting case is when $B \notin K$ but $B \in K_A^+$. This means that the belief in B in K_A^+ is a consequence of the addition of A to K. It then follows from (3.2) that, if K is expanded by B instead, nothing is accepted in K_B^+ that is not accepted in K_A^+.

An immediate consequence of (3.2) is

(3.3) $K_A^+ = K_B^+$ if and only if $B \in K_A^+$ and $A \in K_B^+$.

The postulates for expansions that have been presented so far do not presume any form of logical structure on the belief sets. If we take into account that belief sets are closed under logical consequences, that is, that they satisfy the condition (Cn), we can derive some further consequences. First, we have a trivial corollary to (3.3):

(3.4)   If $\vdash A \leftrightarrow B$, then $K_A^+ = K_B^+$.

In other words, the content of K_A^+ is determined by the logical strength of A, not by its linguistic formulation.

Second, there is a composition principle:

(3.5) $(K_A^+)_B^+ = K_{A\,\&\,B}^+$.

The epistemic interpretation of this identity is that first learning A and then learning B is the same as learning $A \& B$ in a single step. Because $K_{A\,\&\,B}^+$ is the same as $K_{B\,\&\,A}^+$, this shows one of the idealizations of the expansion process, to wit, that the order of the new pieces of information is irrelevant; that is, expansion is commutative:

(3.6) $(K_A^+)_B^+ = (K_B^+)_A^+$.

Another immediate consequence of (3.5) is

(3.7)   If $-A \in K$, then $K_A^+ = K_\perp$.

In the idealized form of learning represented by expansions, $K_\perp$ is the inconsistent endpoint that should be shunned at all costs. It is impossible to get out of $K_\perp$ by expansion because $(K_\perp)_A^+ = K_\perp$ for all A. Figuratively $K_\perp$ is epistemic hell. It follows from (3.6) that, if $-A$ is accepted in K and one wishes to change K by accepting A, then, on pain of inconsistency, the expansion process cannot be used.

The postulates (K^+1)–(K^+5) do not, except in the limiting case when $A \in K$, exclude the possibility that K_A^+ contains a lot of beliefs, not included in K, that have no connection whatsoever with A. Because we want to avoid endorsing beliefs that are not justified, we should require that K_A^+ not contain any beliefs that are not required by other postulates. Technically this idea can be formulated as follows:

(K^+6) For all belief sets K and all sentences A, K_A^+ is the smallest belief set that satisfies (K^+1)–(K^+5).

In the light of this axiom, it is now interesting to consider the set $Cn(K \cup \{A\})$, that is, the set of all logical consequences of the old beliefs together with the new belief A. In fact, it is not difficult to show that, in the presence of the other axioms, (K^+6) is equivalent to the requirement that $K_A^+ \subseteq Cn(K \cup \{A\})$. Even without (K^+6) it is easy to show that

(3.8) $Cn(K \cup \{A\}) \subseteq K_A^+$.

So with the aid of (K^+6) this inclusion can be strengthened to an identity; that is, $Cn(K \cup \{A\})$ is indeed the smallest set of beliefs that satisfies (K^+1)–(K^+5).

THEOREM 3.1   The expansion function $+$ satisfies (K^+1)–(K^+6) iff $K_A^+ = Cn(K \cup \{A\})$.

This simple result can be seen as a *representation theorem* for expansion because it provides us with an explicit definition of this process.

Once the identity in theorem 3.1 has been established, we can derive further properties of the expansion process. The following two will be useful:

(3.9) $(K \cap H)_A^+ = K_A^+ \cap H_A^+$.

(3.10) $K_{A \vee B}^+ \subseteq K_A^+$.

To sum up this section, a set of postulates for expansions of belief sets has been presented. These postulates uniquely determine the expansion of K by A as the set of all logical consequences of K together with A. Thus the axioms lead to an explicit definition of the expansion process. As will be seen in the next two sections, it is not possible to give definitions in the same way for revisions and contractions.

3.3   Revisions

The next type of belief change is when the sentence A, which represents the epistemic input to K, *contradicts* the beliefs that are already in K. In this case it becomes necessary to revise K in order to maintain consistency. This means that this kind of belief change is *nonmonotonic*—a new belief is added, but not all of the old ones are retained.

Even if traditional theories of belief changes have concentrated on modeling expansions and other consistent changes, I believe that we frequently are forced to revise our beliefs. One of the main reasons for this is that many of the things we accept as certain are not well founded—we believe things because of prejudice, because of faulty inferences, or because we trust too many authorities. In fact, modeling revisions of belief seems much more important for understanding human reasoning than modeling expansions.

The problem of analyzing rational revisions of epistemic states is more difficult than the case of expansions. The main reason is that some of the old beliefs must be given up, and logically there is always a multitude of ways to select these beliefs. Stalnaker (1984, pp. 96–97) has the following comment on the problem:

A belief change in response to conflicting information will always force one to choose between alternative revisions, none of which can be seen, on logical grounds alone, to be preferable to the others. The choice will depend on assumptions about epistemic and causal dependence and independence [see chapter 9 of this book], on the reasons one has for one's beliefs as well as on the beliefs themselves. Whether we represent belief states by lists of sentences or by sets of possible worlds, we will need to impose additional structure on our notion of a belief state before we can say very much about the way beliefs change or ought to change in response to new information.

My main purpose in this and the next chapter is to spell out this "additional structure."

Another difference between expansions and revisions is that expansions are monotonic in the sense of $(K^+ 5)$, whereas revisions, because they are nonincreasing, are often *nonmonotonic* in the sense that, even if the beliefs of one state K are included in the beliefs of another state H, the revision of K with respect to sentence A need not be included in the revision of H with respect to A. The importance of such nonmonotonic changes has been recognized for many applications within AI.[1] Thus the project of modeling revisions also seems central for developing the *theory of nonmonotonic reasoning*.

When revising K to accommodate the conflicting epistemic input A, some of the earlier beliefs must be retracted in order to avoid inconsistencies. The criterion of informational economy demands that as few beliefs as possible be given up so that the change is in some sense a *minimal* change of K to accommodate for A. The notion of minimality is discussed in section 3.5. It should be noted here, however, that there are in general several ways of fulfilling the minimality requirement.

For example, I may now believe that all philosophers are scatterbrained, that Wittgenstein was a philosopher, and consequently that Wittgenstein was scatterbrained. If I then, somehow, receive compelling evidence that Wittgenstein was *not* scatterbrained, I will be forced to revise my earlier beliefs, on pain of inconsistency. The revision can be made by giving up either my belief that all philosophers are scatterbrained or my belief that Wittgenstein is a philosopher. So long as only *logic* is considered, both of these ways will do. A third possibility is that I give up both beliefs but retain their disjunction. However, it follows from the criterion of informational economy that this disjunction, at least, should not be retracted because the loss of information should be kept as small as possible.

An important problem concerning revisions is thus how one determines which beliefs are to be retained and which are to be removed from the given set of beliefs. The postulates presented in this section are based on logical considerations. They do not give a unique solution to this problem; instead they circumscribe the set of rational solutions.

As mentioned, the main thrust of the criterion of informational economy is that the revision of a belief set not be greater than what is necessary in order to accept the epistemic input. My main goal in this section is to delimit the meaning of "minimal change" by formulating some rationality postulates that apply to revisions of belief sets. It is assumed that, for any belief set K and any sentence A, there is a *unique* revision representing a selected minimal change. In more mathematical terms this amounts to the assumption that there is a *revision function* ∗ from **K** × **L** to **K** that takes a belief set K and a sentence A into a new belief set, which is denoted K_A^*. This is admittedly a strong assumption, in particular because K_A^* is not uniquely determined from K and A by the postulates presented. However, I believe that these postulates together with certain *nonlogical* factors determine the exact content of K_A^*. Because such nonlogical factors cannot be expressed in the terminology of belief sets only, they are not dealt with until chapter 4.

The first postulate simply requires that the outputs of the revision process indeed be states of belief:

(K∗1)   For any sentence A and any belief set K, K_A^* is a belief set.

The second postulate is a postulate of "success" in line with (K^+2). It guarantees that the epistemic input A is accepted in K_A^*:

(K∗2) $A \in K_A^*$.

The normal application area of a revision process is when the input A contradicts what is already in K, that is, $-A \in K$. However, in order to have the revision function defined for all arguments, we can easily extend it to cover the case when $-A \notin K$. In this case, the revision is, of course, identified with an expansion. For technical reasons to appear later, the condition is divided into two parts:

(K∗3) $K_A^* \subseteq K_A^+$.

(K∗4)   If $-A \notin K$, then $K_A^+ \subseteq K_A^*$.

In (K∗4) the clause $-A \notin K$ expresses that A is consistent with the beliefs in K. This proviso is not needed in (K∗3) because, if $-A \in K$, then $K_A^+ = K_\perp$ and (K∗3) is trivially fulfilled. These postulates entail that, except for the limiting case when $K_A^+ = K_\perp$, expansion is a special case of revision.

As mentioned earlier, we want to avoid inconsistent beliefs, which would amount to being in the absurd state of belief $K_\perp$, as much as possible. It is assumed that K_A^* is a *consistent* belief set unless $-A$ is logically necessary, in which case postulate (Cn) forces an inconsistency:

(K∗5) $K_A^* = K_\perp$ if and only if $\vdash -A$.

From the postulates introduced so far and the postulates for expansions, it follows that

(3.11)   If $A \in K$, then $K_A^* = K$.

This is of course as it should be: If A is already included in K, then the minimal change needed to include A is no change at all.

With the aid of (K*3), (3.11), and (3.9), it is then easy to show that

(3.12) $K_A^* = (K \cap K_A^*)_A^+$.

This simple result will be useful in section 3.6.

Because it is propositions rather than sentences that form the elements of belief sets as well as the epistemic inputs that generate belief changes, it is the *content* of the epistemic input that determines the change rather than its particular linguistic formulation. This means that logically equivalent sentences should lead to identical changes. The sixth postulate is a generalization of (3.4):

(K*6)   If $\vdash A \leftrightarrow B$, then $K_A^* = K_B^*$.

On the other hand, even if $K_A^* = K_B^*$, we can, of course, not conclude that A is logically equivalent to B. It follows, however, that in this case the material equivalence $A \leftrightarrow B$ is included in K_A^* (and even in K).

The postulates (K*1) through (K*6) are elementary requirements on the revision function * that connects K, A, and K_A^*. For reasons that will be clear in chapter 4, this set is called the *basic set* of postulates for revisions.

I next turn to a less elementary condition on revisions. My aim is to formulate a generalization of (K*3) and (K*4) that applies to *iterated* changes of belief. The idea is that, if K_A^* is a revision of K and K_A^* is to be changed by adding further sentences, such a change should be made by using expansions of K_A^* whenever possible. More generally, the minimal change of K to include both A and B (that is, $K_{A \& B}^*$) ought to be the same as the expansion of K_A^* by B, so long as B does not contradict the beliefs in K_A^*.

To give an informal example of the condition, suppose that I revised my present belief state K by accepting the belief that J. S. Bach did not compose the famous Toccata and Fugue in D minor for organ. In the revised state K_A^*, I would have to give up some of my beliefs concerning Bach's originality among eighteenth-century composers. If I then added to the new state K_A^* the belief B that the composer of the Toccata and Fugue also wrote a duet for flute and lute (which Bach never did), then B would be consistent with K_A^* and accommodated by a simple expansion. The net result of these two changes [that is, $(K_A^*)_B^+$] should then be the same as revising K by the composite belief $A \& B$ that someone, not identical with J. S. Bach, wrote the Toccata and Fugue in D minor and also wrote a duet for flute and lute, that is, $K_{A \& B}^*$.

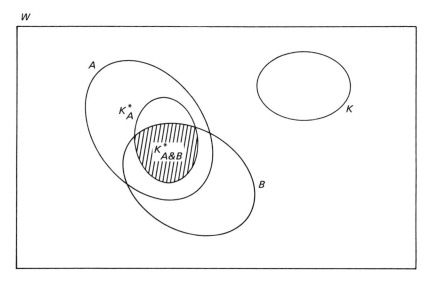

Figure 3.1
A possible worlds representation of the relation between K_A^* and $K_{A \& B}^*$.

For mainly technical reasons the precise formulation of the postulate is split into two axioms:

(K*7) $K_{A \& B}^* \subseteq (K_A^*)_B^+$.

(K*8)   If $-B \notin K_A^*$, then $(K_A^*)_B^+ \subseteq K_{A \& B}^*$.

When $-B \in K_A^*$, $(K_A^*)_B^+$ is $K_\perp$, which is why the proviso is needed in (K*8) but not in (K*7).

The content of the postulates can also be given a pictorial description in terms of possible worlds. To do this, assume that W is the set of all possible worlds and that K is represented by the set of possible worlds in which all the sentences in the belief set are true (this is the correspondence between belief sets and possible worlds models that was discussed in section 2.4). Suppose that A is a proposition that is inconsistent with K, which in terms of possible worlds means that the set of worlds corresponding to A is disjoint from the set of worlds representing K. Let K_A^* be the set of worlds corresponding to the revision of K by A. A consequence of (K*2) is that this set is a subset of the set representing A. Let B be a proposition that is consistent with K_A^*, that is, $-B \notin K_A^*$. We then have figure 3.1. The postulates (K*7) and (K*8), taken together, say that the set representing

$K^*_{A \& B}$ is identical with the intersection of the set representing B and the set representing K^*_A.

Let us return to the belief set representation of epistemic states. To see how powerful postulates (K*7) and (K*8) are, we note that they entail, in combination with the postulates for expansions, the following identity criterion:

(3.13) $K^*_A = K^*_B$ if and only if $B \in K^*_A$ and $A \in K^*_B$.

This criterion can also be given an independent motivation in terms of the interpretation of K^*_A as the minimal change of K needed to accept A: If B is accepted in K^*_A, which is the minimal mutilation of K to include A, then the change of K necessary to include B is at least not greater than the change of K necessary to include A. Similarly, if A is included in K^*_B, then the change of K necessary to include A is at least not greater than the change necessary to include B. Because it has been assumed that for each sentence A there is a *unique* minimal change of K that includes A, K^*_A and K^*_B must be identical.

Another consequence of (K*7) that is of interest is the following:

(3.14) $K^*_A \cap K^*_B \subseteq K^*_{A \vee B}$.

It turns out that, in the presence of the basic set of postulates, (3.14) is indeed equivalent to (K*7). It is somewhat difficult to formulate an independent motivation for (3.14) in terms of minimal changes of belief, but it is given an interpretation in terms of conditional sentences in section 7.2. In order to see that the inclusion in (3.14) cannot be replaced by an identity, one can choose an A that is already in K. Then by (3.11) $K^*_A = K^*_{A \vee B} = K$, but K is not included in K^*_B if K^*_B is a genuine revision of K.

Also, for (K*8) it is possible to give an equivalent reformulation that involves disjunction instead of conjunction:[2]

(3.15)   If $-B \notin K^*_{A \vee B}$, then $K^*_{A \vee B} \subseteq K^*_B$.

Another principle that is useful is the following "factoring" condition [see (3.27) in the next section]:

(3.16) $K^*_{A \vee B} = K^*_A$ or $K^*_{A \vee B} = K^*_B$ or $K^*_{A \vee B} = K^*_A \cap K^*_B$.

It can be shown that, given the basic postulates (K*1) through (K*6), the criterion (3.16) is in fact equivalent to the conjunction of (K*7) and (K*8).[3]

It is easy to see that, if (K*7) and (K*8) are added to the basic set

(K*1)–(K*6), some of these postulates become superfluous: If we assume that $K_\top^* = K$, then postulates (K*3) and (K*4) are special cases of (K*7) and (K*8) (when A in these axioms is taken to be a tautology); and (K*6) follows directly from (3.13). However, because (K*1)–(K*6) are referred to separately in this book, the redundancy is retained.

The postulates that have been introduced are motivated by the interpretation of K_A^* as the minimal change of K needed to accept A. The consequences of the postulates that have been established also support this interpretation. One may now ask whether there are further postulates for revisions that are justified by this interpretation. In chapter 4 (and to some extent also in chapters 5 and 7) I argue that the postulates (K*1)–(K*8) in a certain sense cover the *logical* properties of the revision process, so that no further axioms are necessary.

The postulates (K*1)–(K*8) do not uniquely characterize the revision K_A^* in terms of only K and A in contrast to the expansion K_A^+, which was characterized as $Cn(K \cup \{A\})$ by the axioms (K$^+$1)–(K$^+$6). However, this is as it should be. I believe that it would be a mistake to expect that only logical properties are sufficient to characterize the revision process. This would be like requiring that the standard (Kolmogorov) axioms for probability functions should pick out one unique rational probability function. It is argued in chapter 4 that there are other epistemic factors that are important when determining the exact content of a belief revision.

I close this section by discussing three principles that have a certain prima facie plausibility but that must be rejected as general postulates for revision functions. The first principle is connected with the criterion of informational economy. One way of applying this criterion to revisions is to require that K_A^* contain a *maximal* subset of K that does not contradict A. This idea can be expressed more formally as

(3.17)   If $B \in K$, then $B \notin K_A^*$ or $-B \in K_A^*$.

Or, in words, the only reason for excluding a belief B, which is in K, from K_A^* is that it would contradict beliefs in K_A^*. This principle seems attractive, but it has unpalatable consequences. To see this, let me introduce the following notion: A belief set K is said to be *maximal* iff for any sentence A in **L** either $A \in K$ or $-A \in K$. The epistemic interpretation of a maximal belief set is that it represents a state of belief where the agent has a firm opinion on every matter, thus the belief state of a *besserwisser*. This would be the kind of knowledge possessed by Laplace's demon.

It was shown in Gärdenfors (1978a) that (3.17) entails

(3.18)   If K is maximal, then, for any A, K_A^* is also maximal.

However, Alchourrón and Makinson (1982, observation 3.2) strengthen this result considerably. They show that for any belief set K (3.17) is equivalent to

(3.19) K_A^* is maximal for any sentence A such that $-A \in K$.

In other words, (3.17) not only entails that maximality be preserved in revisions but that maximality be *created*. When K is a nonmaximal belief set, which is the normal case, K_A^* is a maximal belief set that obviously is too large to represent any intuitive process of rational belief revision—just because you revise your beliefs with respect to A, you should not be led to have a definite opinion on every matter. Thus (3.17) cannot be accepted as a postulate for belief revisions. It should be mentioned, however, that Makinson (1985a) has argued that revision is an operation that is most naturally applied not to a belief set K as a whole but to some nonredundant *base* $K_0 \subseteq K$ (compare this with the discussion in section 4.10). For such a context the derivation of (3.19) from (3.17) is no longer possible, and (3.17) itself retains its plausibility. In this book, however, I always apply belief change operations directly to belief sets themselves, not to their bases.

The second principle to be discussed is a generalization of axiom (K^+5), which also covers the genuine revision case. Because this principle will play an important role in chapter 7, it is given a name. Here is the principle of *monotonicity*:

(K*M)   If $K \subseteq H$, then $K_A^* \subseteq H_A^*$.

To see the general problems confronting (K*M), consider a belief set K such that $-A \notin K$ and $B \in K$, and let H be $K_{(B \to -A)}^+$, that is, K expanded by $B \to -A$. It follows that $-A \in H$. Let us also assume that $B \in K_A^*$. Now, in H_A^* we cannot keep both B and $B \to -A$ because this would contradict (K*5); one of these sentences must be retracted from the belief set. In many situations there may be strong reasons for giving up B rather than $B \to -A$. The implication may, for example, be supported by a well-established scientific law. However, in such a case, $B \in K_A^*$ but $B \notin H_A^*$, which contradicts (K*M). In section 7.6 (K*M) is discussed again, and there a more concrete counterexample, illustrating this general argument, is given.

A formal but conclusive counterexample to (K*M) is the following:[4] Let

B and C be sentences such that not $B \vdash C$, not $C \vdash B$, and consequently not $\vdash B \& C$. Put $K = Cn(B)$, $K' = Cn(C)$, and $H = Cn(B \& C)$. Then $K \subseteq H$ and $K' \subseteq H$. Now put $A = -(B \& C)$. Then $K'_A = Cn(B \& -C)$ and $K'^*_A = Cn(-B \& C)$. Thus, if (K*M) holds, we have B, $-B$, C, and $-C$ all in H^*_A, and thus $H^*_A = K_\perp$, which is impossible by (K*5) because not $\vdash -A$.

The final, prima facie promising principle to be discussed is the following strengthening of (K*6):

(3.20)   If $\vdash A \to B$, then $K^*_B \subseteq K^*_A$.

There are familiar counterexamples to this principle: Let A be the sentence 'This match is wet and it is struck', and let B be 'This match is struck'. Let K be a state of belief in which it is known that the match is not struck, that is, $-B \in K$. Most reasonably K^*_B includes the belief that the match will light, but K^*_A does not. Hence K^*_B is not a subset of K^*_A. This example indicates a connection between our use of counterfactual sentences and belief revisions. This connection is developed in detail in chapter 7.

A formal counterexample can also be given here:[5] Choose B and C such that not $B \vdash C$ and not $\vdash -(B \& C)$. Put $K = Cn(B \& -C)$ and $A = B \& C$. Then $A \vdash B$. But $K^*_B = K$, so $-C \in K^*_B$, whereas K^*_A contains $B \& C$ and is consistent [by (K*5)] and so $-C \notin K^*_A$.

The fact that the three suggested principles (3.17), (K*M), and (3.20) all must be rejected lends some indirect support for the claim that (K*1)–(K*8) make up the appropriate set of postulates for belief revisions. However, this claim is directly supported by some representation theorems, which are established in chapter 4.

3.4   Contractions

A contraction of a belief set occurs when some beliefs are retracted but no new belief is added. Recall Oscar's speculations about what would have happened if he had not married Victoria. This kind of change may, for example, also occur in a debate. One of the disputants may include A in her belief state K while the other includes $-A$ in his state K'. In order to avoid begging the question, both disputants should, at least temporarily, give up their beliefs in A and $-A$, respectively (and all beliefs that imply these beliefs). From the remainder of their beliefs it may then be possible to carry on a debate, where the task of the debaters is to find arguments that support A and $-A$, respectively. It is argued in chapters 7 and 8 that a similar argumentative strategy is followed when someone gives an explanation or when someone makes a claim about causal relations. Indeed, in these chapters contractions play a crucial role in the analyses.

The main problem concerning contractions of belief sets is that, when retracting a belief A from a belief set K, there may be other beliefs in K that entail A (or other beliefs that jointly entail A without separately doing so). So, if we want to comply with the criterion (Cn), that is, keep the contracted state of belief closed under logical consequences, it is necessary to give up other beliefs as well. For example, if A is accepted in K just because it is a logical consequence of B and C, which are also in K, then either B or C (or perhaps both) must be rejected. The problem is then to determine which beliefs should be given up and which should be retained. We want the criterion of informational economy to apply also to contractions, so that no beliefs should be given up unnecessarily.

The contraction of a belief set K with respect to a sentence A, that is, the sentence to be rejected, is denoted K_A^-. It is assumed that, for any belief set K and any sentence A, there is a *unique* contraction so that the expression K_A^- is well defined. As with revisions, this can be made mathematically precise by the assumption that there is a *contraction function* − from $\mathbf{K} \times \mathbf{L}$ to $\mathbf{K}$, that takes a belief set K and a sentence A into a new belief set K_A^-.

My main objective now is to formulate a set of rationality postulates for contraction functions. To a large extent these postulates are motivated by the criterion of informational economy. As for revisions, the rationality postulates are not sufficient to determine uniquely a contraction function; other epistemic factors play a role as well. These factors are discussed in chapter 4.

The first postulate is of a familiar kind:

(K⁻1)   For any sentence A and any belief set K, K_A^- is a belief set.

Because K_A^- is formed from K by giving up some beliefs, it should be required that no new beliefs occur in K_A^-:

(K⁻2) $K_A^- \subseteq K$.

When $A \notin K$, the criterion of informational economy requires that nothing be retracted from K:

(K⁻3)   If $A \notin K$, then $K_A^- = K$.

We also postulate that the contraction be successful, that is, that the sentence to be contracted not be a logical consequence of the beliefs retained in K_A^- (unless A is logically valid):

$(K^- 4)$ If not $\vdash A$, then $A \notin K_A^-$.

When A is logically valid, (Cn) would be violated if A was retracted.

The contraction of a belief set K with respect to a logically valid sentence A may, for simplicity, be defined as K itself. [This definition is in fact a consequence of postulate $(K^- 6)$, to be introduced later.]

The following consequence of $(K^- 1)$–$(K^- 4)$ together with the postulates for expansions serves as a guide to the next postulate for contractions:

(3.21)   If $A \in K$, then $(K_A^-)_A^+ \subseteq K$.

This result guarantees that, if we first contract K with respect to A and then expand the resulting belief set by A again, the final set of beliefs will not include anything that was not already in K. The criterion of informational economy requires that K_A^- be a "large" subset of K. In analogy with $(K^+ 6)$, we postulate that *all* beliefs in K are *recovered* after first contracting and then expanding with respect to the same belief. Formally this can be expressed as

$(K^- 5)$ If $A \in K$, then $K \subseteq (K_A^-)_A^+$.

In probabilistic contexts the validity of $(K^- 5)$ can be questioned. For example, let K be my present state of belief, and let A describe the event that at breakfast today I dropped my toast and B the event that it landed with the buttered side down (I take it that this is a random process and that it is about equally likely that the toast lands with the buttered side up). Because B is a consequence of A (causal consequence, not logical), it follows that in K_A^- I no longer accept B. But if I start from K_A^- and imagine that I drop my toast, that is, expand by A, B does not follow because $-B$ is equally likely. For probabilistic models of epistemic states a weaker form of $(K^- 5)$ can be formulated [see postulate $(P^- 5w)$ in section 9.3]. However, in nonprobabilistic contexts $(K^- 5)$ seems to be a valid principle.

One may wonder what happens if K is first expanded by A and then contracted with respect to A. Do we always get K back? This cannot be true in general, even in nonprobabilistic contexts, because if $-A \in K$, then $K_A^+ = K_\perp$, and if H is another belief set such that $-A \in H$, then also

$H_A^+ = K_\perp$ and hence $(K_A^+)_A^- = (H_A^+)_A^-$. It follows that $(K_A^+)_A^-$ cannot always be identical with K.[6]

A consequence of (K^-1)–(K^-5) and the axioms for expansion is

(3.22) $K_A^- = K \cap (K_A^-)_{-A}^+$.

The importance of this result will be seen in section 3.6. As an additional connection, note that (3.22) together with (K^-1)–(K^-4) entails (K^-5). This shows that (K^-5) and (3.22) are equivalent, given the background of (K^-1)–(K^-4).

In parallel with (K^*6) I introduce the following postulate:

(K^-6) If $\vdash A \leftrightarrow B$, then $K_A^- = K_B^-$.

This postulate can be motivated in the same way as (K^*6).

Postulates (K^-1)–(K^-6) are called the *basic set* of postulates for contractions. As will be seen in section 3.6, this set is closely connected with the basic set (K^*1)–(K^*6) for revisions.

The basic set of postulates is assumed to be given as a background for all the results mentioned. In addition to these postulates, two further postulates that deal with the relation between K_A^- and $K_{A \& B}^-$ are introduced. As a motivation for the first of these postulates, one can note that, when a belief of the form $A \& B$ is to be rejected, there is normally a choice between rejecting A and rejecting B. So it seems that, in general, one would have to give up less when contracting a belief set K with respect to $A \& B$ than when contracting K with respect to A. More formally this amounts to requiring that $K_A^- \subseteq K_{A \& B}^-$ or, more generally,

(3.23)   If $\vdash B \to A$, then $K_A^- \subseteq K_B^-$.

Although this principle looks reasonable at first sight, it cannot be a generally valid rule for contractions. For example, let A be the belief that the morning train will be on time, let B be the belief that my car will start this morning so I can go to the station, and let C be the belief that I will be able to catch the train. Suppose that my present state of belief includes all the beliefs A, B, and C (and hence also $A \& B$). If I now contract K with respect to A, I would still believe in C. If I, on the other hand, contract K with respect to $A \& B$, then I would have to give up either A or B. Knowing that the train is reliable and my car is not, I would reject B but not A. But then I would also give up C, because if my car does not start and the train is on time, I will miss the train. Hence C is in K_A^- but not in $K_{A\&B}^-$; thus (3.23) cannot be generally valid for contractions.

The case against (3.23) can be strengthened by noting that, given the basic postulates, it is equivalent to the clearly unintuitive principle[7]

(3.24) $K_{A\&B}^- = K_A^- \cap K_B^-$.

Instead, the following weaker postulate is introduced:

(K^-7) $K_A^- \cap K_B^- \subseteq K_{A\&B}^-$.

Or, in words, the beliefs that are in both K_A^- and K_B^- are also in $K_{A\&B}^-$. In relation to the car and train example, it can be noted that, although C was in K_A^-, it is not in K_B^- (for the same reason as it was not in $K_{A\&B}^-$), so this example gives some support for (K^-7). Another way of supporting the postulate comes from comparing it with the following alternative weakening of (3.23):

(3.25) $K_A^- \cap Cn(\{A\}) \subseteq K_{A\&B}^-$.

This condition does not require that all beliefs in K_A^- also be in $K_{A\&B}^-$; only the beliefs in K_A^- that are logical consequences of A are required. This may seem to be a weak condition, but it can be shown that, given the background of the basic postulates for contractions, (3.25) is in fact *equivalent* to (K^-7).[8]

I now come to the final postulate for contractions. When contracting K with respect to $A\&B$, either A or B (or both) must be rejected. If A is rejected, this is because A is less epistemologically entrenched than B (this idea is expanded in chapter 4). In this case the minimal change of K necessary to give up $A\&B$ is closely related to the minimal change necessary to reject A itself. This motivates the following postulate:

(K^-8) If $A \notin K_{A\&B}^-$, then $K_{A\&B}^- \subseteq K_A^-$.

It will soon be seen why the inclusion cannot, in general, be replaced by an identity. An immediate consequence of (K^-8) and (K^-4) is the following useful principle, which says that $K_{A\&B}^-$ is "covered" either by K_A^- or by K_B^-:

(3.26)   Either $K_{A\&B}^- \subseteq K_A^-$ or $K_{A\&B}^- \subseteq K_B^-$.

In most cases, when $A \notin K_{A\&B}^-$, $K_{A\&B}^-$ is identical with K_A^-. However, this is not always the case: If A and B are equally epistemologically entrenched (but not logically equivalent), *both* A and B are rejected in $K^-_{A \& B}$, whereas only A is rejected in K^-_A. However, it can be shown (Alchourrón et al. 1985, observation 6.5) that (K^-7) and (K^-8) together with the basic postulates for contractions entail the following "factoring" condition:

(3.27)   Either $K^-_{A \& B} = K^-_A$ or $K^-_{A \& B} = K^-_B$ or $K^-_{A \& B} = K^-_A \cap K^-_B$.

In fact the converse is also true: In the presence of the basic axioms, (3.27) entails *both* (K^-7) and (K^-8).[9]

In analogy with the identity criterion for revisions, we have the following criterion for contractions:[10]

(3.28)   If $B \to A \in K^-_A$ and $A \to B \in K^-_B$, then $K^-_A = K^-_B$.

As will be seen in section 3.6, postulates (K^-7) and (K^-8) are closely related to postulates $(K*7)$ and $(K*8)$ for revision functions. Before turning to a presentation of the relations between contractions and revisions, I would like to mention some principles that have not been added as postulates. The first is a monotonicity condition and thus an analogue to $(K*M)$:

(K^-M) If $K \subseteq H$, then $K^-_A \subseteq H^-_A$.

The arguments against this principle can be taken over, mutatis mutandis, from the arguments against $(K*M)$. And after revisions and contractions have been connected in section 3.6, it can be shown that $(K*M)$ and (K^-M) are essentially two ways of formulating the same condition.

The second principle is, in a similar way, closely connected with (3.17). When contracting K with respect to A, the loss of information should be as small as possible. The recovery postulate (K^-5) is one way of guaranteeing this. Another idea is to require that K^-_A be a maximal subset of K such that $A \notin K$. More precisely we have the following *fullness condition*, which will play a certain role in section 4.2:

(K^-F) If $B \in K$ and $B \notin K^-_A$, then $B \to A \in K^-_A$.

It can be shown that (K^-F) entails (K^-5). To see the drawbacks of (K^-F), we note that it is equivalent to the following principle:[11]

(3.29)   If $B, C \in K$ and $B \vee C \in K^-_A$, then either $B \in K^-_A$ or $C \in K^-_A$.

This principle makes K_A^- "too large" because there are many cases in which we accept a disjunction as true but do not accept any of the disjuncts as true. To see the problem, consider the following example [adapted from Quine (1952)]. Assume that the belief set K representing my state of belief contains, among other beliefs, the following:

(A)   Bizet was French.
(B)   Verdi was Italian.

These two beliefs imply

(C)   Bizet and Verdi were not compatriots.

which is thus also accepted in K. Now assume that I for some reason or other want to contract my state of belief K with respect to C. Which beliefs do I retain in the contraction K_C^-? Well, at least one of the beliefs A and B must be retracted. But which one? In my opinion these beliefs are of equal epistemic entrenchment, and I see no reason whatsoever for retracting one and retaining the other. However, at least one of A and B is contained in any maximal subset of K that does not imply C. So if K_C^- is a maximal subset of K, either A or B is in K_C^-, which seems to be counterintuitive. This example shows that $(K^- F)$ cannot be accepted as a general postulate for contraction functions.

An even stronger principle is the following:

(3.30)   Either $K_{A \& B}^- = K_A^-$ or $K_{A \& B}^- = K_B^-$.

This condition obviously entails (3.27) and hence $(K^- 7)$ and $(K^- 8)$. However, it is shown in Alchourrón et al. (1985, observation 6.3) that (3.30) also entails $(K^- F)$ and thus is subject to the same criticism as that principle. Again, these observations lend some support to the claim that $(K^- 1)$–$(K^- 8)$ is an appropriate set of postulates for contraction. This claim is further supported by the representation theorems in chapter 4.

3.5   On the Notion of Minimal Change

Several of the postulates that have been formulated for contractions and revisions have been motivated by an appeal to the requirement that epistemic changes ought to be *minimal* changes necessary to accommodate the input. However, the notion of minimality needs some further clarification.

Because belief sets, which have a meager internal structure, have been used as models of epistemic states, the only way to estimate the "magnitude" of a change is to compare the *sizes* of the involved sets of sentences. Postulates (K^+3), (K^+5), $(K*4)$, and (K^-2) are examples of such comparisons. These postulates can be motivated by the following *conservativity principle* [see Harman (1986, p. 46)]:

(Cons)   When changing beliefs in response to new evidence, you should continue to believe as many of the old beliefs as possible.

However, belief sets cannot be used to express that some beliefs may be *reasons* for other beliefs. (This deficiency was one of the motivations behind Doyle's TMS presented in section 2.6.) And intuitively, when we compare degrees of similarity between different epistemic states, we want the structure of reasons or justifications to count as well. And in such a case we may end up contradicting (Cons). The following example, adopted from Tichy (1976), illustrates this point:[12] Suppose that I accept as known in my present state K that there is a man who always wears his hat when it rains, but when it does not rain, he wears his hat completely at random (about 50% of the days). I also know that it rained today and that he wore his hat. Let A be the proposition 'It rained today' and B 'The man wears his hat'. Thus both A and B are accepted in K. What can we say about the state K^*_{-A}? According to (Cons), B should still be accepted in K^*_{-A} because the addition of $-A$ does not conflict with B. However, I no longer have any *reason* for believing B, so intuitively neither B nor $-B$ should be accepted in K^*_{-A}.[13]

This example shows that the structure of belief sets is not rich enough to describe our intuitions concerning the minimality of revisions of epistemic states. I admit that the postulates for contractions and revisions that have been introduced here are quite simpleminded, but they seem to capture what can be formulated for the meager structure of belief sets. In richer models of epistemic states, admitting, for example, reasons to be formulated, the corresponding conservativity postulates must be formulated much more cautiously.

A similar point can be made, but less forcefully, against the postulate (K^+3) for expansions: Suppose that I believe in K that there is a $10 prize for drawing a black ball from an urn and that I must pay $1 for the chance to draw a ball. As a result I also believe that at most 10% of the balls are black (call this belief B). Nothing I believe *contradicts* A, where A is the belief 'This is an experiment in psychology and the budget is lavish'. Yet in the expansion K_A^+, I would no longer have reason to believe B.[14] However, here it can be objected that B is not fully accepted in K but only has a high probability, so that (K^+3) is not applicable in this case.

The dynamics of probabilistic models of belief are developed in chapter 5, but it seems appropriate to say a few words about the relevant notion of minimal change already here. For probabilistic models it is possible to introduce evaluations of "similarity" and "degree of change" based on information-theoretic *measures* (the principle of maximal entropy is central here). This means that the loss of information involved in contractions and revisions can be given a precise meaning. Consequently more sophisticated evaluations of minimality can be made for these models than are possible for belief sets where only the size of the sets is relevant. However, neither of the probabilistic models of epistemic states to be considered in chapter 5 represents that one belief is a reason for another. So, again, these models are open to the same criticism as the belief sets, for example, by exploiting some variant of Tichy's example.

These considerations show that the relevant notion of minimality is dependent on which models of epistemic states are used. And because our intuitions are based on a richer structure on beliefs than what can be represented in the models investigated in this book, these intuitions, as we have seen, sometimes conflict with the consequences of the postulates that can be formulated for the models.

3.6   From Contractions to Revisions and Vice Versa

In sections 3.3 and 3.4 revisions and contractions were characterized by two sets of postulates. The postulates are independent in the sense that the postulates for revisions do not refer to contractions (whereas they do refer to expansions) and the postulates for contractions do not refer to revisions.

A natural question is now whether either contraction or revision can be defined in terms of the other. If this is possible, the set of primitive concepts will be reducible and the epistemological theories studied here will be simpler and more coherent. In this section I present two arguments that support the contention that either contraction or revision can be defined in terms of the other (assuming expansions as given).

Isaac Levi (1977) argues that the only two legitimate forms of changes of belief are expansions and contractions. Levi advances the thesis that revisions can be analyzed as a sequence of contractions and expansions. In the terminology of belief sets this idea can be interpreted as follows: In order to construct the revision K_A^* for a belief set K and a sentence A, one first contracts K with respect to $-A$ and then expands K_{-A}^- by A. Figuratively the ground is prepared for adding the conflicting A to K by first eliminating $-A$ and all other beliefs that entail $-A$. Formally Levi's thesis can be expressed by the following definition:

(Def *) $K_A^* = (K_{-A}^-)_A^+$.

This identity gives us a definition of revisions in terms of contractions and expansions. This identity is called the *Levi identity* here.

If K_A^* is defined in this way, it can be argued that it is the minimal change of K necessary to include A, as should be expected of an appropriate definition, for any revision of K to include A, where A is inconsistent with K, must involve a rejection of $-A$. And K_{-A}^- is defined to be the minimal change of K necessary to remove $-A$. Then A must be added in some way, and the expansion of K_{-A}^- is the minimal change needed to accomplish this. Because both these steps are necessary, the only alternative to (Def *) is to perform the steps in reverse order. However, as was argued in section 3.5, it is not clear that the reverse process can be defined—first expanding by A and then contracting with respect to $-A$ may not give the desired result in the principal case when A contradicts K.

It follows from (K^-1) and the definition of expansions that K_A^* defined by the Levi identity is a belief set. The obvious question is now whether the remaining postulates for revisions are satisfied. The following two theorems give a comforting answer.

THEOREM 3.2   If the contraction function $-$ satisfies (K^-1)–(K^-4) and (K^-6) and the expansions satisfy (K^+1)–(K^+6) (that is, expansions can be defined as in theorem 3.1), then the revision function * obtained from (Def *) satisfies $(K*1)$–$(K*6)$.

Note that postulate (K^-5) is not used in this derivation.

THEOREM 3.3   Suppose that the assumptions of theorem 3.2 are fulfilled. Then (a) if (K^-7) is satisfied, $(K*7)$ is satisfied for the defined revision function, and (b) if (K^-8) is satisfied, $(K*8)$ is satisfied for the defined revision function.

These results strongly support the appropriateness of (Def *) as a definition of a revision function.

I now turn to the converse problem of defining contractions in terms of revisions. The idea here, first presented in Harper (1977), is that a sentence B is accepted in the contraction K_A^- if and only if B is accepted in both K and K_{-A}^*. The rationale for this analysis is that, because K_{-A}^* is the minimal change of K needed to accept $-A$, it contains as much as possible from K that does not entail A. Of course, K_{-A}^* also contains $-A$ and its consequences and K (normally) contains A and its consequences, but the beliefs that K and K_{-A}^* have in common are as much as possible of K that does not entail A. Formally this analysis amounts to the following definition:

(Def $-$) $K_A^- = K \cap K_{-A}^*$.

This identity provides us with a definition of contractions in terms of revisions. The identity is called the *Harper identity* here.

Because the intersection of two belief sets is a belief set, it follows that K_A^- defined as in (Def $-$) is a belief set. Thus this definition satisfies (K$^-$1). In fact, it is easy to prove the following theorem.

THEOREM 3.4   If the revision function $*$ satisfies (K$*$1)–(K$*$6), then the contraction function $-$ generated by (Def $-$) satisfies (K$^-$1)–(K$^-$6).

Furthermore, we also have the converse of theorem 3.3.

THEOREM 3.5   Suppose that the revision function $*$ satisfies (K$*$1)–(K$*$6) so that theorem 3.4 is applicable. Then (a) if (K$*$7) is satisfied, (K$^-$7) is satisfied for the defined contraction function, and (b) if (K$*$8) is satisfied, (K$^-$8) is satisfied for the defined contraction function.

In the same way as for the Levi identity, these results strongly support the appropriateness of the Harper identity. Theorems 3.2 through 3.5 show that the defined revisions and contractions have the right properties. But we also want the two definitions to be *interchangeable* in the sense that, if we start with one definition to construct a new contraction (or revision) function and after that use the other definition to obtain a revision (or contraction) function again, then we ought to get the original function back. If this can be proved, we will have shown that contractions and revisions are interdefinable in a strong sense.

To show this, we first apply definition (Def $-$) to K_{-A}^- in definition (Def $*$). Because $K_{--A}^* = K_A^*$, by (K$*$6), the result is

(3.31) $K_A^* = (K \cap K_A^*)_A^+.$

However, this is the same identity as (3.12), which was shown to be a consequence of the basic postulates for revisions; so in this direction the definitions are interchangeable.

To check the other direction, we apply (Def *) to $K_{\underline{-}A}^*$ in (Def $-$). Because $K_{\underline{-}-A}^- = K_A^-$, by (K$^-$6) the result is

(3.32) $K_A^- = K \cap (K_A^-)_{-A}^+.$

Again, this identity is the same as (3.22), which was shown to be a consequence of the basic postulates for contractions. These two results show that, assuming only the basic postulates for revisions and contractions, these two processes are indeed interdefinable with the aid of the Levi identity and the Harper identity.

It was mentioned in section 3.4 that the recovery postulate (K$^-$5) may not be valid in all contexts. It is therefore interesting to ask what happens if this postulate is dropped. Makinson (1987) has shown that we lose something; that is, (K$^-$5) is not derivable from the postulates (K$^-$1)–(K$^-$4) and (K$^-$6), but we do not lose much.

To make this more precise, let us, following Makinson, call an operation $-$ that satisfies (K$^-$1)–(K$^-$4) and (K$^-$6) a *withdrawal function*. Because (K$^-$5) was not used in theorem 3.2, we know that each withdrawal function, by means of the Levi identity, generates a revision function that satisfies (K*1)–(K*6). If $-$ and $\dot{-}$ are two withdrawal functions that generate the same revision function, we say that $-$ and $\dot{-}$ are *revision equivalent*. We write $[-]$ for the class of all withdrawal functions that are revision equivalent to $-$. Let us say that the withdrawal function $\dot{-}$ is *greater than* $-$ on K if $K_A^- \subseteq K_A^{\dot{-}}$ for all A. Makinson proves the following.

LEMMA 3.6   Let K be any belief set. Then for each withdrawal operation $-$ on K, there is a *unique* contraction function $\dot{-}$ on K that is revision equivalent to $-$, and this $\dot{-}$ is the greatest element of $[-]$.

The upshot is that, if one's main interest is in revision, then, although a given revision operation on a belief set K may be generated by several withdrawal functions, there is a unique function also satisfying the recovery postulate (K$^-$5). This function is also the unique withdrawal operation that eliminates from K as *little* as possible. This makes clearer the specific role of recovery and also lends some support to its intuitive acceptability for the idealized belief sets treated in this chapter.

3.7   Spohn's Generalization of Revisions and Contractions

In section 2.5 I presented Spohn's (1987) generalized belief models, which
admitted degrees of acceptance or plausibility (different from probabilities).
In this final section I present an outline of how Spohn models revisions
and contractions and show how these processes relate to contractions and
revisions of beliefs sets.

Recall that Spohn models a consistent state of belief by an ordinal
conditional function k from a set W of possible worlds to the class of
ordinals such that at least some world is assigned 0. This function provides
a plausibility grading of all worlds in which the worlds assigned the smallest
ordinals are the most plausible. This grading is extended to the class
of propositions (that is, sets of possible worlds) by the rule that $k(A) =$
$\min\{k(w)\colon w \in A\}$ for all propositions A. A proposition A is accepted relative to k iff $k(-A) > 0$ [and consequently $k(A) = 0$].

We now turn to Spohn's model of the dynamics of belief. A key feature
is that the epistemic inputs are not only propositions but *propositions
together with a degree of plausibility*. The typical form of an input is thus
a pair (A, a) of a proposition A and an ordinal a. The interpretation of this
input is that A is the information that the agent wants to accept in the new
state of belief and a is the degree of *firmness* with which this information
is incorporated into the new state. [Recall that the degree of firmness of an
accepted proposition is measured by the value of $k(-A)$—the higher the
value, the more firmly A is believed.]

Suppose that the present state of belief is described by the ordinal
conditional function k and that the state changes as a result of an epistemic
input (A, a). How is the new state of belief, call it $k^*(A, a)$, to be described?
Interestingly enough, Spohn presents an explicit construction, not only
postulates. Spohn calls $k^*(A, a)$, the (A, a)-*conditionalization of* k.

As an auxiliary concept, Spohn introduces the notion of the *A-part of* k,
which I denote $k(\cdot/A)$. This function, which is defined only for the worlds
in A, is determined by the following rule:

(3.33)   For all $w \in A$, $k(w/A) = -k(A) + k(w)$.

For technical reasons Spohn here makes use of the notion of left-sided
subtraction of ordinals, which is defined as follows: If a and b are two
ordinals with $a \leqslant b$, then $-a + b$ is the uniquely determined ordinal c such
that $a + c = b$. In the case when all ordinals are finite, this notion coincides

with standard subtraction, and rule (3.33) can be written more perspicuously as $k(w/A) = k(w) - k(A)$. Thus one might say that the A-part of k is the restriction of k to A shifted to 0, that is, in such a way that $k(A/A) = 0$.

With the aid of this concept, we can now define the ordinal conditional function $k^*(A, a)$ representing the new state of belief:

(3.34)   Let A be a proposition such that $A \neq \varnothing$. If $w \in A$, then $k^*(A, a)(w) = k(w/A)$, and, if $w \in -A$, then $k^*(A, a) = a + k(w/-A)$.

Thus the (A, a)-conditionalization of k is the union of the A-part of k and the $-A$-part of k shifted up by a degrees of plausibility. It follows from the definition that $k^*(A, a)(A) = 0$ and $k^*(A, a)(-A) = a$. This means that A is accepted in $k^*(A, a)$ with firmness a. Furthermore, definition (3.34) is constructed so that getting informed about A does not change the epistemic state restricted to A or to $-A$. In other words, the (A, a)-conditionalization of k leaves the A-part as well as the $-A$-part of k unchanged; they are only shifted against each other.[15]

If $a > 0$ and $-A$ is accepted in k [that is, $k(-A) = 0$ but $k(A) > 0$], then the process of forming the (A, a)-conditionalization is a generalization of *revisions* of belief sets as presented earlier in this chapter. To make this more precise, let us define the belief set K *associated with* the ordinal conditional function k as the set of all propositions that are accepted in k. If we let K_A^* denote the belief set associated with $k^*(A, a)$, where $a > 0$, then it can be shown that the revision function defined in this way satisfies postulates (K*1)–(K*8).

However, it is interesting to note that Spohn's notion covers other cases as well. In particular, the $(-A, k(A))$-conditionalization of k corresponds to a *contraction* with respect to A! In the principal case when A is accepted relative to k, that is, when $k(-A) > 0$ and $k(A) = 0$, this is identical with the $(A, 0)$-conditionalization. For this kind of change we have both $k^*(A, 0)(A) = 0$ and $k^*(A, 0)(-A) = 0$; that is, A is not accepted in relation to $k^*(A, 0)$, and thus we have a proper contraction. Again, if we let K_A^- denote the belief set associated with $k^*(-A, k(A))$, it can be shown that the contraction function defined in this way satisfies (K⁻1)–(K⁻8).

Another special case is when A is not accepted in relation to k, that is, when $k(-A) = 0$. In this case the (A, a)-conditionalization of k corresponds to an *expansion*. Also in this case it can be shown that the associated belief set has exactly the properties of an expansion, as described in section 3.2.

Finally, there is a case that has no correspondence in terms of belief sets. Suppose that $k(A) = 0$ and $k(-A) = b$; that is, A is already accepted in relation to k with degree b of firmness. Now if $a > b$, then A is still believed in $k*(A, a)$, but with a higher degree of firmness. This corresponds to a case when one obtains additional reasons for A. And if $a < b$ but $a > 0$, then A is still accepted in $k*(A, a)$, although with a lesser degree of firmness. This represents a case when one has obtained some reason against A whereby the belief in A is weakened but not retracted. It is an advantage of Spohn's model of the dynamics of belief that it can handle this case. This kind of change cannot be modeled in terms of belief sets only. However, the so-called Jeffrey conditionalization is a probabilistic version of the same kind of belief change.

4 Epistemic Entrenchment and Construction of Contraction Functions

4.1 The Problem of How to Construct a Contraction Function

In chapter 3 contraction and revision functions were investigated indirectly by means of a number of postulates imposed on the functions. It was also shown in section 3.6 that, if it is possible to give an explicit construction of a contraction function, then this also yields a revision function by means of the Levi identity (or vice versa through the Harper identity). Because contractions and revisions (which include expansions as a special case) are the only relevant types of epistemic change for belief sets, the commitment function for a belief system based on belief sets is thus completely determined by a contraction function (or a revision function). The goal of this chapter is to present a series of constructions of contraction functions leading up to two basically equivalent proposals.

When forming the contraction K_A^- of a theory K with respect to a proposition A, the principle of informational economy requires that K_A^- contain as much as possible from K without entailing A. Therefore the *maximal subsets* of K that do not contain A are of particular interest when looking for a constructive definition of a contraction function. Some suggestions for constructions based on such maximal subsets of K are studied in detail in sections 4.2 through 4.4. A model based on *possible worlds* is presented in section 4.5. These investigations lead to some *representation theorems* for contraction functions.

Another guiding idea for a construction of a contraction function is that the propositions accepted by an agent in a state of belief have different *epistemic entrenchments* for the agent—some propositions are more useful than others in inquiry and decision making.[1] If the relative epistemic entrenchment of the propositions in K can be determined, then this degree of entrenchment should be used when forming the contraction so that the propositions that are retracted are those with the lowest epistemic entrenchment. In sections 4.6 and 4.7 I present the concept of epistemic entrenchment in greater detail. It is partially characterized by a set of qualitative postulates, which, among other things, require that propositions be *ordered* according to their degree of epistemic entrenchment. I discuss the cognitive and epistemological origins of such an ordering. This ordering of epistemic entrenchment is then used to give a formal definition of a contraction function.

In section 4.8 the construction based on maximal subsets and the construction based on an ordering of epistemic entrenchment are linked to each other. I show that these two methods lead to basically the same result and that the resulting contraction functions satisfy postulates (K^-1)–(K^-8). I also show that these postulates guarantee the existence of an ordering of epistemic entrenchment in the following sense: For any contraction function satisfying the postulates, there exists an underlying ordering of the propositions that generates the contraction function by means of the definition mentioned.

In section 4.9 I present a third approach, due to Alchourrón and Makinson, to the problem of constructing a contraction function. The final section is devoted to two other areas where the constructions may be applied, namely, updating logical databases and derogating and amending legal codes.

4.2 Maxichoice Contraction Functions

The problem in focus is how to define the contraction K_A with respect to a belief set K and a proposition A. A general ideal is to start from K and then give some recipe for choosing which propositions to delete from K so that K_A^- does not contain A as a logical consequence. If we turn our attention to the criterion of informational economy, it seems natural to require that K_A^- should be as large a subset of K as possible—K_A^- should contain as much as possible of the information in K. For this reason I first focus on the belief sets that are subsets of K and that do not contain A and then search among these for the "largest," that is, those containing as much information as possible. This is a first, tentative solution to the problem of defining a contraction function.

The following notion will be useful: A belief set K' is a *maximal subset of K that fails to imply A* if and only if (i) K' is a subset of K, (ii) $A \notin K'$, and (iii) for any proposition B that is in K but not in K', $B \rightarrow A$ is in K'. The last clause means that, if K' were to be expanded by B, it would entail A.

Because it has been assumed that K is a belief set, it is easy to verify, using the assumption that $\vdash$ is compact, that there always exist subsets of K that are maximal subsets of K that fail to imply A, unless A is logically valid. However, there are in general several such subsets. The set of all belief sets K' that are maximal subsets of K that fail to imply A is denoted $K \perp A$. This set forms the basis for all the constructions in this and the next two sections.

The construction idea can now be formulated more precisely: The contraction K_A^- of K with respect to A is determined by a *selection function* S that picks out an element $S(K \perp A)$ of $K \perp A$ for any K and any A whenever $K \perp A$ is nonempty. We then define K_A^- by the following rule:

$$\text{(Def Max)} \quad K_A^- = \begin{cases} S(K \perp A) & \text{when not } \vdash A, \\ K & \text{otherwise.} \end{cases}$$

Thus K_A^- is some maximal subset of K that fails to imply A, if such subsets exist; otherwise it is K itself. Contraction functions determined by some such selection function are called *maxichoice contraction functions.*

A first test for this construction of a contraction function is whether it has the desirable properties. A partial answer to this question is easily obtained:

LEMMA 4.1   Any maxichoice contraction function satisfies $(K^- 1)$–$(K^- 6)$.[2]

From the definition of maxichoice functions it is clear that they also satisfy the fullness condition $(K^- F)$, which we recall here:

$(K^- F)$ If $B \in K$ and $B \notin K_A^-$, $B \to A \in K_A^-$ for any belief set K.

In a sense, condition $(K^- F)$ identifies the maxichoice functions because one can show the following *representation theorem.*[3] Let us say that a contraction function $-$ can be *generated* by a maxichoice contraction function iff there is some selection function S such that $-$ is identical with the function obtained from S by means of (Def Max).

THEOREM 4.2   Any contraction function that satisfies $(K^- 1)$–$(K^- 6)$ and $(K^- F)$ can be generated by a maxichoice contraction function.

Alchourron and Makinson (1982) also note that $(K^- 7)$ and $(K^- 8)$ do not hold in general for maxichoice contraction functions. To obtain these postulates, the maxichoice functions must be further constrained. They investigate the following constraint: A maxichoice function is *orderly* iff there is some partial ordering (that is, a reflexive, transitive, and anti-symmetric relation) $\leqslant$ of the power set of K such that $K' \leqslant K_A^-$ for all propositions A and all $K' \in K \perp A$. In other words, the maxichoice function is orderly if K_A^- is one of the "best" elements of $K \perp A$ according to $\leqslant$. They can then prove the following.

LEMMA 4.3   Any orderly maxichoice contraction function satisfies $(K^- 1)$–$(K^- 8)$ and the decomposition condition (3.30).[4]

It was shown in chapter 3 that (3.30) is a strong condition—among other things it implies $(K^- 7)$ and $(K^- 8)$. Indeed it is possible to show the following representation theorem for orderly maxichoice contraction functions.[5]

THEOREM 4.4   Any contraction function that satisfies $(K^- 1)$–$(K^- 6)$ and (3.30) can be generated by an orderly maxichoice contraction function.

We can now apply the criticism of (3.30) in section 3.4 to show that maxichoice contractions are in general *too large*. This point can be made even more strongly using a technical result from Alchourrón and Makinson (1982). Let us recall that a maximal belief set K is a belief set such that, for every proposition B of its language, either $B \in K$ or $-B \in K$. We then have the following discomforting result.

LEMMA 4.5   If $A \in K$ and K_A^- is defined by means of a maxichoice contraction function, then for any proposition B either $A \lor B \in K_A^-$ or $A \lor -B \in K_A^-$.

COROLLARY 4.6   If a revision function $*$ is defined from a maxichoice contraction function $-$ by means of the Levi identity, then, for any A such that $-A \in K$, K_A^* will be maximal.

This corollary shows that, in a sense, maxichoice functions *create* maximal belief sets. Thus the set K_A^* is much too large to correspond to any intuitive process of revision. I believe that these results compel us to look at other possible ways of constructing contraction functions.

4.3   Full Meet Contraction Functions

We have seen that a maximal subset of K that fails to imply A in general contains too much to be used as the contraction K_A^-. But the elements of $K \perp A$ can be used in other ways. A second tentative idea is to assume that K_A^- contains only the propositions that are *common to all* of the maximal subsets in $K \perp A$. More technically this means that, for any K and any A, K_A^- is defined as follows:

$$(\text{Def Meet}) \quad K_A^- = \begin{cases} \bigcap(K \perp A) & \text{whenever } K \perp A \text{ is nonempty,} \\ K & \text{otherwise.} \end{cases}$$

Thus a proposition B is in K_A^- iff it is contained in *all* maximal subsets of

K that fail to imply A. We call such a contraction function a *full meet contraction function.*

Once again the question arises whether such a contraction function has the desirable properties. As before, we can start with the following lemma.

LEMMA 4.7   Any full meet contraction function satisfies $(K^- 1)$–$(K^- 6)$.[6]

Another property of full meet contraction functions that is of some interest is the following *intersection condition:*

$(K^- I)$ For all A and B, $K^-_{A \& B} = K^-_A \cap K^-_B$.

It is easy to show that full meet contraction functions satisfy condition $(K^- I)$. In fact, we have the following representation theorem.

THEOREM 4.8   Any contraction function that satisfies $(K^- 1)$–$(K^- 6)$ and $(K^- I)$ can be generated by a full meet contraction function.

These results seem to justify the use of full meet contraction as a formal model of the intuitive notion of contraction. However, the drawback of full meet contraction is just the opposite of the drawback of maxichoice contraction—full meet contraction in general results in contracted belief sets that are far *too small.* The following result is proved in Alchourrón and Makinson (1982).

LEMMA 4.9   If K^-_A is defined by means of a full meet contraction and $A \in K$, then $B \in K^-_A$ iff $B \in K$ and $-A \vdash B$.

In other words, if we contract K with respect to A in this way, we are left with the propositions of K that are also logical consequences of $-A$. This then has the following consequence.

COROLLARY 4.10   If a revision function $*$ is defined from a full meet contraction $-$ by means of the Levi identity, then, for any A such that $-A \in K$, K^*_A will contain only A together with its logical consequences.

Despite these negative results, the operation of full meet contraction is of some interest because it provides a definite *lower bound* of any contraction operation that satisfies $(K^- 1)$–$(K^- 6)$. Supporting this claim, we have a result from Alchourrón et al. (1985).

LEMMA 4.11   For any contraction function $-$ that satisfies $(K^- 1)$, $(K^- 3)$, and $(K^- 5)$, the set K^-_A includes the full meet contraction $\bigcap(K \perp A)$ for any K and A.

4.4 Partial Meet Contraction Functions

We have seen that using only *one* of the maximal subsets in $K \perp A$ when defining the contraction K_A^- yields a contraction set that is too large and that using *all*, in the sense of full meet contraction, yields a contraction set that is too small. Given this, it is natural to investigate the consequences of using only *some* of the maximal subsets in $K \perp A$ when defining K_A^-.

To make this idea more precise, a *selection function S* can be used to pick out a nonempty *subset* $S(K \perp A)$ of $K \perp A$, if the latter is nonempty, that puts $S(K \perp A) = K$ in the limiting case when $K \perp A$ is empty. The contraction function can then be defined as follows:

(Def Part) $K_A^- = \bigcap S(K \perp A)$.

Such a contraction function is called a *partial meet contraction function*. The intuitive idea is that the selection function S picks out the maximal subsets in $K \perp A$ that are *epistemologically most entrenched*. Thus a proposition B is in K_A^- iff it is an element of all the epistemologically most entrenched maximal subsets of K. I return to a detailed discussion of the notion of epistemic entrenchment later in this chapter.

It should be noted that the concept of partial meet contraction includes as special cases maxichoice contraction and full meet contraction. Maxichoice contraction is partial meet contraction with $S(K \perp A)$ a singleton; full meet contraction is partial meet contraction with $S(K \perp A)$ the entire set $K \perp A$.

The first task now is to check that all partial meet contraction functions satisfy the basic postulates.

LEMMA 4.12   Every partial meet contraction function satisfies postulates (K^-1)–(K^-6).

In fact, we can also prove the converse of this lemma and show that the postulates (K^-1)–(K^-6) *fully characterize* the class of partial meet contraction functions.[7]

THEOREM 4.13   Let $-$ be a contraction function. For every belief set K, $-$ is a partial meet contraction function *iff* $-$ satisfies postulates (K^-1)–(K^-6) for contraction over K.

Assuming that the postulates (K^-1)–(K^-6) are indeed fundamental postulates for any rational contraction function, from this theorem we have strong support that we concentrate on partial meet contraction functions when looking for the most reasonable method of representing contractions of belief sets.

In the definition of a partial meet contraction function, the selection function S is assumed as given. But if we want to look at a specific contraction method, we want to know how one determines which elements of $K \perp A$ are the epistemologically most entrenched. The simplest way of doing this is to assume that there is an *ordering* of entrenchment of all the maximal subsets of K that can be used to pick out the top elements of $K \perp A$. This ordering of the maximal subsets should be independent of which sentence we are retracting; in other words, we want the ordering to be the same for different choices of A. Technically we do this by introducing the notation $M(K)$ for the *union* of the family of all the sets $K \perp A$, where A is any proposition in K that is not logically valid. Then it is assumed that there exists a relation $\leqslant$ of $M(K)$. When $K \perp A$ is nonempty, that is, when not $\vdash A$, this relation can be used to define a selection function S:

(Def S) $S(K \perp A) = \{K' \in K \perp A : K'' \leqslant K' \text{ for all } K'' \in K \perp A\}$.

This identity is called the *marking-off identity*, because $\leqslant$ marks off $S(K \perp A)$ as the most entrenched maximal subsets of K that fail to imply A. If the selection function S is defined by the marking-off identity from some $\leqslant$, we say that S is *relational* over K; and, furthermore, the contraction function generated from *some* such S is said to be a *relational partial meet contraction function*. "Some," because a single partial meet contraction function may, in general, be determined by two distinct selection functions.

So far I have not assumed any particular properties of $\leqslant$, but technically it can be any binary relation. However, it is still possible to show that this way of defining the selection function has some consequences for the properties of the generated contraction function.

LEMMA 4.14   Any relational partial meet contraction function satisfies postulate $(K^- 7)$.

It is easy to construct examples of partial meet contraction functions that do not satisfy $(K^- 7)$, which shows that the set of relational contraction functions is a proper subset of the set of all partial meet contraction functions.

The most interesting case is, of course, when $\leqslant$ is indeed an ordering relation. A minimal requirement for this is that $\leqslant$ be *transitive*. When this is the case, we say that the corresponding selection function S is *transitively relational* and that the contraction function generated from *some* such S is a *transitively relational partial meet contraction function*.

Requiring transitivity of $\leqslant$ has the following consequence for the generated contraction function.

LEMMA 4.15   Any transitively relational partial meet contraction function satisfies $(K^- 8)$.

Again, it is possible to construct examples of relational partial meet contraction functions that do not satisfy $(K^- 8)$, which shows that relationality does not entail transitivity.

The following representation theorem is the central result of this section.

THEOREM 4.16   Let K be any belief set, and let $-$ be a contraction function defined over K. Then $-$ is a transitively relational partial meet contraction function *if and only if* $-$ satisfies $(K^- 1)$–$(K^- 8)$.

Because the collection $(K^- 1)$–$(K^- 8)$ has been independently motivated in chapter 3, this theorem gives us a strong reason to focus on transitively relational partial meet contraction functions as an ideal representation of the intuitive process of contraction.

If we really want $\leqslant$ to be an ordering and not only a partial ordering, $\leqslant$ must be *connected* as well as transitive; that is, it must hold that either $K' \leqslant K''$ or $K'' \leqslant K'$ for all subsets K' and K'' that are possible maximal subsets of K, that is, elements of the set $\bigcup_{A \in K}(K \perp A)$. We say that the selection function S is *connectively relational* iff it is based on some connected relation $\leqslant$ and that a partial meet contraction function is connectively relational iff it is determined by some selection function that is so.

Perhaps surprisingly it follows from theorem 4.17 that imposing connectivity as well as transitivity on the relation $\leqslant$ adds nothing at all to the properties of the contraction functions.

THEOREM 4.17   Let K be any belief set, and let $-$ be a partial meet contraction function over K. Then $-$ is transitively relational iff it is transitively and connectively relational.

This result shows that, for any contraction function defined over a belief set K satisfying $(K^- 1)$–$(K^- 8)$, there is some ordering of the maximal subsets in $K \perp A$. The epistemological interpretation of such an ordering is the topic of sections 4.6 and 4.7.

4.5 Grove's Systems of Spheres

Grove (1986) presents an alternative model of revision functions, using a system of "spheres," that in form is similar to the "sphere" semantics for counterfactuals proposed by Lewis (1973b). By means of the Harper identity this model can, of course, also be used to represent contraction functions. Grove also shows that the spheres model is directly related to the construction in terms of partial meet contraction functions.

Instead of using the sets in $K \perp A$, Grove focuses on the set **M** of all maximal consistent extensions of **L**. If you wish, this can be seen as the set of possible worlds that can be described in **L**. Any belief set K can be
• represented by the subset $[K]$ of **M** that consists of all maximal sets where all the sentences in K are included. This is in analogy with the construction presented in section 2.4. Formally:

(Def $[K]$) $[K] = \{M \in \mathbf{M}: K \subseteq M\}$.

As a special case of this definition we have $[K_\perp] = \varnothing$. Note also that for any formula A we can use the same definition to construct the set $[A]$ of elements in **M**, where A is included.

Conversely, for any subset S of **M**, it is easy to show that the set K_S of formulas included in all elements of S [thus $K_S = \bigcap(M \in S)$] is a belief set. If $S = \varnothing$, we put $K_S = K_\perp$. Thus there is a correspondence between the set **K** of all belief sets and **M**. However, note that for any belief set K there are in general many subsets S of **M** such that $K_S = K$.

A *system of spheres centered on* $[K]$ is a collection **S** of subsets of **M** that satisfies the following conditions:

(S1)   **S** is totally ordered by $\subseteq$; that is, if S and S' are in **S**, then $S \subseteq S'$ or $S' \subseteq S$.

(S2) $[K]$ is the $\subseteq$-minimum of **S**; that is, $[K] \in \mathbf{S}$, and, if $S \in \mathbf{S}$, then $[K] \subseteq S$.

(S3)   **M** is in **S** (and so the largest element of **S**).

(S4)   If A is a sentence and there is any sphere is **S** intersecting $[A]$, then there is a smallest sphere in **S** intersecting $[A]$.

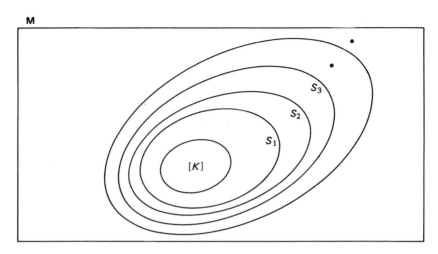

Figure 4.1
A possible worlds representation of a system of spheres centered on K.

A system of spheres centered on $[K]$ can be represented figuratively [cf. Segerberg (1986a); figure 4.1]. A similar representation is used by Lewis (1973b) to provide a semantics for his counterfactual logics. The most important difference is that here the system of spheres is centered on a *belief set K*, or rather its representation $[K]$, whereas Lewis's systems of spheres are always centered around a *single* possible world (that is, an element of **M**). As it turns out, Lewis's systems are not at all appropriate for modeling revision functions.

For any sentence A condition (S4) ensures that, if $[A]$ intersects any sphere at all in **S**, there is some sphere S_A that intersects $[A]$ and is smaller than any other sphere with this property. If $[A]$ does not intersect any sphere, which occurs only if $[A] = \emptyset$ according to (S3), then we take S_A to be **M**. The set $C(A) = [A] \cap S_A$ is the set of "closest" elements in **M** to $[K]$ in which A is an element. This set is marked as the hatched area in figure 4.2. The key idea in Grove's model is that the revision K_A^* of K by A can be represented by the set $C(A)$ of "worlds." To show that this is an appropriate representation, he proves the following two theorems.[8]

THEOREM 4.18   Let **S** be any system of spheres in **M** centered on $[K]$ for some belief set K. If, for any A, K_A^* is defined to be $K_{C(A)}$, then the resulting revision function satisfies (K*1)–(K*8).

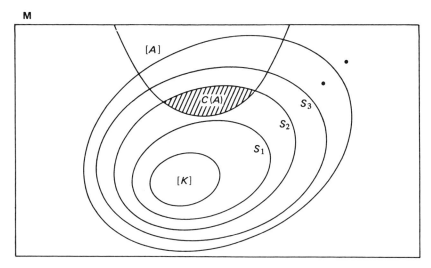

Figure 4.2
A possible worlds representation of the set $C(A)$.

THEOREM 4.19   Let $*$ be any revision function satisfying $(K*1)$–$(K*8)$. Then for any (fixed) belief set K there is a system $\mathbf{S}$ of spheres that is centered on $[K]$ and that satisfies $K_A^* = K_{C(A)}$ for all sentences A.

Thus a revision function can be represented by a family of systems of spheres, one for each belief set K. It should be noted that there need not be any relation between the systems of spheres around two different belief sets.

The same approach can be used to model contraction functions: If we define K_A^- to be generated from $[K] \cup C(A)$, then it is easy to prove, by means of the Harper identity (Def $-$), theorems corresponding to theorems 4.18 and 4.19. So the contraction functions generated in this way are exactly the contraction functions satisfying (K^-1)–(K^-8).

Grove also investigates the relation between the spheres model and the representations in terms of meet contraction functions. He concludes that the representations are "dual" to each other. Let me elaborate a bit on this relationship.

Suppose that K is a belief set and that A is a sentence such that $A \in K$ and not $\vdash A$. Let us look at an element K' of $K \perp A$ and ask what corresponds to $[K']$. As $K' \subseteq K$, it follows that $[K] \subseteq [K']$. Furthermore, $[K']$

must contain at least one world in $[-A]$, for otherwise we would have $A \in K'$. However, $[K']$ cannot contain more than one element of $[-A]$, for suppose that both M and M', where $M \neq M'$, belong to $[K'] \cap [-A]$. Then there must be some sentence B such that $B \in M$ but $B \notin M'$. But then neither $A \lor B$ nor $A \lor -B$ is in K', which contradicts the assumption that $K' \in K \perp A$.

Conversely, for each element $M \in [-A]$, the set $[K] \cup \{M\}$ determines a maximal subset of K that does not entail A. Thus we have made the smallest possible change to $[K]$ to ensure that the result is not contained in $[A]$.

Because we are considering only sentences A that are elements of K (the case where $A \notin K$ is not interesting), there is a *one-to-one correspondence* between the sets in $K \perp A$ and the elements of $[-A]$. We can now use this mapping to say something about the relation between different meet contraction constructions and the corresponding systems of spheres.

First, maxichoice contraction takes K_A^- to be some K' in $K \perp A$, which corresponds to defining $[K_A^-] = [K] \cup \{M\}$ for some single world M in $[-A]$. In terms of spheres this corresponds to the assumption that $C(A)$ is a singleton when it is not empty. This is what Lewis (1973b) calls the "Stalnaker assumption."

Second, full meet contraction is the opposite extreme that takes K_A^- to be $\bigcap(K \perp A)$, which corresponds to $[K_A^-] = [K] \cup [-A]$. In terms of spheres this produces the "coarsest" system possible: The system contains only two spheres, namely, $[K]$ and $\mathbf{M}$ itself.

Finally, partial meet contraction corresponds exactly to systems of spheres intermediate between the two extremes: K_A^- is defined as the intersection of a subset of $K \perp A$. This corresponds to defining $[K_A^-]$ as the union of a number of sets of the form $[K] \cup \{M\}$ where $M \in [-A]$, which is the same as the union of $[K]$ with some subset of $[-A]$.

4.6 Epistemic Entrenchment

It is now time to turn to the concept of epistemic entrenchment. This is a notion that is taken to apply to single sentences in **L**. It is the epistemic entrenchment of a sentence in an epistemic state that determines the sentence's fate when the state is contracted or revised. The two key ideas are:

(i) It is possible to determine the relative epistemic entrenchment of the sentences in a belief set K *independently* of what happens to K in contractions and revisions.

(ii) When a belief set K is contracted (or revised), the sentences in K that are given up are those with the *lowest* epistemic entrenchment.

The fundamental criterion for determining the epistemic entrenchment of a sentence is how useful it is in inquiry and deliberation. Certain pieces of our knowledge and beliefs about the world are more important than others when planning future actions, conducting scientific investigations, or reasoning in general. To give an example of the scientific case, in modern chemical theory, knowledge about the combining weights is much more important for chemical experiments than knowledge about the color or taste of the substances. This difference of entrenchment is reflected in that, if chemists for some reason changed their opinion concerning the combining weights of two substances, this would have much more radical effects on chemical theory than if they changed their opinion concerning the tastes of the two substances.

This example also shows that the epistemic entrenchment of different sentences are, in general, *not* connected with their probabilities. If I have full belief in a sentence, that is, if it is accepted in my belief set, then I judge it to be maximally probable; but I do not regard all sentences that I accept as having equal epistemic entrenchment. Levi (1983) emphasizes the same point:

> In evaluating contraction strategies, we will be led to make discriminations between those items in the corpus to be contracted which are more vulnerable to removal from the corpus and those which are not. In this sense, we can talk of differences within the corpus with respect to grades of corrigibility. It is tempting to correlate these grades of corrigibility with grades of certainty or probability. According to the view I advocate, that would be a mistake. All items in the initial corpus L which is to be contracted are, from X's initial point of view, certainly and infallibly true. They all bear probability 1. (p. 165).

Here Levi uses "corpus L" as I use "belief set K" and "grades of corrigibility" roughly as I use "degrees of epistemic entrenchment."

Rather than being connected with probability, the epistemic entrenchment of a sentence is tied to its explanatory power and its overall informational value within the belief set. For example, *lawlike* sentences generally have greater epistemic entrenchment than accidental generalizations. This is not because lawlike sentences are better supported by the available evidence (normally they are not) but because giving up lawlike sentences means that the theory loses more of its explanatory power than giving up accidental generalizations.[9]

The epistemic entrenchment of a sentence is dependent on the belief state in which it occurs. Different belief sets may thus be associated with different orderings of epistemic entrenchment; even if the sets of sentences contained in the belief sets overlap, the orderings of epistemic entrenchment need not agree on the common parts. In relation to the chemistry example, it can be noted that, according to earlier phlogiston theory, qualitative facts (for example, facts about the color and taste of substances) were more important than quantitative knowledge (for example, facts about combining weights), whereas after Lavoisier and Dalton, the quantitative properties were thought of as more fundamental and qualitative properties considered much less important [see Kuhn (1970)]. On my view of epistemic entrenchment a change of paradigm typically involves a radical change of the ordering of epistemic entrenchment, and, vice versa, a substantial change of the degrees of epistemic entrenchment of the theses in a scientific field is a strong indication of what Kuhn calls a "scientific revolution."

I take the notion of epistemic entrenchment to be more fundamental than the notion of a contraction or a revision function. My goal in this section is to present a set of postulates for epistemic entrenchment that serves as a basis for a construction of such functions. However, one might go in the other direction, starting from a contraction function and using this to define an ordering of epistemic entrenchment.[10] As mentioned earlier, the idea for such a definition would be that the sentence that is the more difficult to retract is the epistemologically more entrenched. Formally this can be achieved by looking at $K_{A \& B}^{-}$, which is the belief set most similar to K where not both A and B are accepted. Unless both A and B are logically valid, at least one of these sentences must be given up in $K_{A \& B}^{-}$. If B is given up in $K_{A \& B}^{-}$, this is a clear indication that A is epistemologically at least as entrenched as B. More technically the following equivalence is desirable:

$(C \leqslant) \quad B \leqslant A \quad$ iff $\quad B \notin K_{A \& B}^{-}$.

I return to this equivalence in section 4.8.

I now return to the problem of axiomatizing the relation of epistemic entrenchment. Here I do not assume that one can quantitatively measure degrees of epistemic entrenchment; instead I formulate some postulates for the qualitative properties of epistemic entrenchment. Because I regard this notion as more fundamental than the notion of a contraction function, reference to such functions must not be made in the postulates.

If A and B are sentences in $\mathbf{L}$, the notation $A \leqslant B$ is used as a shorthand for 'B is at least as epistemologically entrenched as A'. The strict relation $A < B$, representing 'B is epistemologically more entrenched than A', is defined as '$A \leqslant B$ and not $B \leqslant A$'. Note that the relation $\leqslant$ is defined only *in relation to a given K*—different belief sets may be associated with different orderings of epistemic entrenchment.

The first postulate requires $\leqslant$ to satisfy a minimal requirement on an ordering relation:

(EE1) For any A, B, and C, if $A \leqslant B$ and $B \leqslant C$, then $A \leqslant C$. (Transitivity)

When a belief set is revised or contracted, some of the previously accepted sentences must be given up. The ordering of epistemic entrenchment can be used to determine which sentences to retract by requiring that the epistemologically least entrenched sentences be given up first so that the loss of information is minimal, in accordance with the criterion of informational economy.

A special case of this is formulated in the second postulate, which requires that, if a sentence is logically stronger than another, then it is epistemologically less entrenched:

(EE2) For any A and B, if $A \vdash B$, then $A \leqslant B$. (Dominance)

The justification for this postulate is that, if A entails B and either A or B must be retracted from the belief set K, then it is a smaller change to give up A and retain B rather than to give up B, because then A must also be retracted if we want the revised theory to be closed under logical consequences.

At a first glance this seems to go against the criterion of informational economy, because when A entails B, the informational value of A is greater than that of B. However, when giving up A, not all of the informational value of A is lost in the contracted states of belief—sometimes the content of B can be retained. If B is given up, A must also be given up; so in this case more of the informational value of K is lost. This argument shows that postulate (EE2) conforms with the criterion of informational economy. In fact, lacking a more precise definition of informational value, (EE2) seems to be all that can be postulated for a *qualitative* account of epistemic entrenchment.

The third postulate perhaps looks innocent but turns out to be quite powerful:[11]

(EE3)   For all A and B in K, $A \leqslant A \& B$ or $B \leqslant A \& B$. (Conjunctiveness)

The rationale for this postulate goes as follows: If one wants to retract $A \& B$ from the belief set K, this can be achieved only by giving up either A or B. This means that the informational loss incurred by giving up $A \& B$ is the same as the loss incurred by giving up A or that incurred by giving up B. Note that it follows already from (EE2) that $A \& B \leqslant A$ and $A \& B \leqslant B$.

Another way of motivating the postulates for epistemic entrenchment, and (EE3) in particular, is to regard $\leqslant$ as generated from Spohn's degrees of firmness, as presented in section 2.5. The idea is that A is epistemologically less entrenched than B if A has a lesser degree of firmness than B. Formally this amounts to the following characterization:

(4.1) $A \leqslant B$ iff $k(-A) \leqslant k(-B)$.

Here k is Spohn's ordinal conditional function. It is easy to see that, if $\leqslant$ is defined in this way, it will satisfy (EE1)–(EE3). This simple result lends further support to postulate (EE3).

One consequence of (EE3) that should be noted here is that (EE3) implies that the ordering is *connected*.[12]

LEMMA 4.20   Suppose that the ordering $\leqslant$ satisfies (EE1)–(EE3). Then it also has the property that for any A and B either $A \leqslant B$ or $B \leqslant A$. (Connectivity)

When explaining the postulates, I have tacitly assumed that the relevant sentences are *in* K, the belief set under consideration. However, for generality, it is nice to have $\leqslant$ defined for all sentences in **L**. If a sentence is not contained in K, it is not entrenched in K at all and is thus minimal in the ordering $\leqslant$. Formally this can be expressed as follows:

(EE4)   When $K \neq K_{\perp}$, $A \notin K$ iff $A \leqslant B$ for all B. (Minimality)

Note that this postulate also follows from (4.1) because, if $A \notin K$, then $k(-A) = 0$.

Conversely the most entrenched sentences are those that are logically valid, because they will never be given up. And because we have assumed that all other sentences can be given up, we know that only the logically valid sentences can be maximal in $\leqslant$. Thus:

(EE5)   If $B \leqslant A$ for all B, then $\vdash A$.

Note that the converse of (EE5) follows from (EE2) because, if $\vdash A$, then $\vdash B \to A$ for all B.

This completes the set of postulates for epistemic entrenchment. It will be clear in what follows why (EE1)–(EE5) can be regarded as a complete set of postulates for the ordering of epistemic entrenchment. Before turning to connections between the ordering of epistemic entrenchment and other concepts, I present three simple consequences of the postulates.

LEMMA 4.21   Suppose that the ordering $\leqslant$ satisfies (EE1) and connectivity. Then it satisfies (EE3) iff, for any A, B, and C in K, if $C \leqslant A$ and $C \leqslant B$, then $C \leqslant A \& B$.

LEMMA 4.22   Suppose that the ordering $\leqslant$ satisfies (EE1)–(EE3). Then, for all A, B, and C in K, if $B \& C \leqslant A$, then $B \leqslant A$ or $C \leqslant A$.

LEMMA 4.23   Suppose that the ordering $\leqslant$ satisfies (EE1)–(EE3). Then $A < B$ iff $A \& B < B$.

4.7   The Origins of Epistemic Entrenchment

Before discussing the connections between the ordering $\leqslant$ of epistemic entrenchment and the model of contraction functions presented in sections 4.4 and 4.5, I make some remarks on the place of the orderings in a more comprehensive epistemological theory.

I briefly present two fundamentally different approaches to the problem of the origins of epistemic entrenchment. The first can be dubbed the *information-theoretic approach*. The basic idea here is that different sentences have different informative value. Because information is valuable, it is rational to minimize the loss of information when giving up sentences in a contraction of a state of belief. This requirement is proposed by Harper (1977) and Levi (1977b, 1983), but in these papers the authors do not explain how the loss of information is to be evaluated. However, if one could evaluate the loss, the degree of epistemic entrenchment could then be identified with the quantity of information that would be lost if the sentence were retracted from the state of belief.

The most important theories of how information is to be measured in states of belief are intimately connected with Bayesian statistics. A fundamental assumption here is that states of belief can be represented by probability measures defined over the relevant sentences (this representation is discussed in the next chapter). The information-theoretic concepts are then defined with the aid of these probabilities. A good survey of this approach can be found in Williams (1980).

It is, however, by no means clear how such a theory of information can be helpful for constructing contractions and revisions. As mentioned in the previous section, the sentences that are accepted in a state of belief are regarded as certain and thus have probability 1. If the status of some of these sentences is changed so that they are no longer accepted, a minimal change would be to assign these sentences probability values that are close to 1. Such an assignment is, however, unrealistic as a model of a contraction of a state of belief because, when the belief in a sentence is retracted, it is in general not assigned such a high probability value. In chapter 5 the problem of determining contractions of probability functions is discussed. A set of postulates parallel to those in chapter 3 is presented, and some construction ideas are investigated. Such a representation can then be connected with information-theoretic considerations, but much of this remains to be done.

The second approach to the problem of the origins of epistemic entrenchment can be called the *paradigm approach*. A common ingredient of many modern metatheories of scientific research is that certain statements of a scientific theory are never called into question. Kuhn (1970) speaks of "symbolic generalizations" that form a part of the paradigm of a science. Lakatos (1970) introduces the "core" of a research program that is surrounded by a "protective belt" of auxiliary hypotheses. If the research program encounters problems, that is, when it needs to be revised, the sentences in the core are never rejected but perhaps some parts of the protective belt are changed. Sneed (1971) and Stegmüller (1976) also speak of the core and the extended core of a theory. In their structuralist view of scientific theories, the core of the theories contains among other things a set of fundamental axioms that are "immune" to falsification. In addition to the core, the extended core of a theory contains a set of special laws that may be introduced, tested, and also rejected while the core is kept constant.

All these metascientific theories thus present a rudimentary hierarchy among the sentences of a scientific theory. This hierarchy can be interpreted as a rough sorting of these sentences into degrees of epistemic entrenchment, the most entrenched being the sentences that are included in the paradigm or the core of a theory.

However, when determining the finer structure of the ordering of epistemic entrenchment, neither information-theoretic nor metascientific considerations are of any great help. References to accepted theories may be useful when separating laws from accidental generalizations, but I suspect that theoretical considerations will in many cases not give any guidance as to which of two sentences is the epistemologically most entrenched. In these cases one must rely, in general, on *pragmatic factors*. For example, when a person contracts her state of belief in a debate or when giving an explanation, the *conversational context* may be a crucial factor in determining the current epistemic entrenchment of the sentences under consideration. The role of pragmatic factors in explanatory contexts is discussed in chapter 8.

Levi considers the informational value of believing a sentence where this value is determined partly by such pragmatic aspects. He says that "informational value is construed as independent of truth value and as partially dependent on the demands of the inquiries which X regards as worth pursuing at the time. Thus the simplicity, explanatory power and the subject matter of the hypotheses contribute to their informational value" (1977b, pp. 427–428). Levi here presents an account of informational value as context dependent, where the context includes more than the agent's beliefs.

These considerations concerning the origins of the ordering of epistemic entrenchment are far from conclusive. I have only indicated some possible ways of approaching this fundamental epistemological problem, but further investigations are needed. It is conceivable that our intuitive judgments of epistemic entrenchment cannot be explained on the linguistic level in terms of the epistemic status of the sentences that express our beliefs but that more fundamental prelinguistic notions are necessary for a fuller understanding of such judgments.

Formally it has been assumed that the ordering $\leqslant$ is dependent on the belief set K under investigation. A topic that has not been discussed so far is to what extent the ordering $\leqslant$ may change when the state of belief changes. If we briefly return to the paradigm approach to the problem of the origins of the ordering of epistemic entrenchment, it may be argued that a paradigm shift, as Kuhn describes it, involves a radical shift in the ordering of epistemic entrenchment and conversely that a paradigm shift may be *detected* by such a change of the ordering. Following this lead, one may then wonder whether there are such changes and what kinds of changes would occur during a period of "normal science." If the criterion $(C \leqslant)$ is combined with the results in chapter 7, it follows that changes of epistemic entrenchment can be detected with the aid of the *counterfactual conditionals* we are willing to assert, given various states of belief. This operational method gives us, however, little understanding of the underlying factors that determine these changes of epistemic entrenchment.

4.8 Constructing Contraction and Revision Functions from the Ordering of Epistemic Entrenchment

The main purpose of introducing the notion of epistemic entrenchment is to show how it can be used to construct appropriate contraction and revision functions. This is the topic of this section. The construction starts from Grove's model, as presented in section 4.5.

Recall that Grove's model used a system of spheres that was assumed to satisfy postulates (S1)–(S4). Apart from the system of spheres, Grove also introduces a model that is based on an ordering of the sentences in **L**. Let us call this ordering $\leqslant_G$. Like the ordering of epistemic entrenchment, this ordering is dependent on a given epistemic state K. He uses this ordering to define a *revision function* $*$ in the following way:

$(C \leqslant_G)$ $B \in K_A^*$ iff $A \& B <_G A \& -B$.

The interpretation is that a sentence B is included in K_A^* if the sentence $A \& B$ is "closer" to K than the sentence $A \& -B$. Note that, although the ordering of epistemic importance basically applies to sentences that are *in* K, the ordering $\leqslant_G$ has its main force for sentences that are *inconsistent* with K. Thus Grove's interpretation of the ordering $\leqslant_G$ is, at least on the surface, quite different from the interpretation of the ordering $\leqslant$ of epistemic entrenchment. [Grove's ordering is, in fact, closely related to Lewis's (1973b) ordering of "comparative possibility."]

Grove introduces the following postulates for $\leqslant_G$:

$(\leqslant_G 1)$ $\leqslant_G$ is connected.

$(\leqslant_G 2)$ $\leqslant_G$ is transitive.

$(\leqslant_G 3)$ If $\vdash A \to B \lor C$, then $B \leqslant_G A$ or $C \leqslant_G A$.

$(\leqslant_G 4)$ $-A \notin K$ iff $A \leqslant_G B$ for all B.

$(\leqslant_G 5)$ $\vdash -A$ iff $B \leqslant_G A$ for all B.

With the aid of these postulates, Grove is then able to prove the following two theorems that connect the ordering $\leqslant_G$ with revision functions.[13]

THEOREM 4.24   Let $*$ be a revision function that satisfies $(K*1)$–$(K*8)$. Then for any K there is a relation $\leqslant_G$ on $\mathbf{L}$ such that, for all B, $(C \leqslant_G)$ is satisfied and such that $\leqslant_G$ fulfills $(\leqslant_G 1)$–$(\leqslant_G 5)$.

THEOREM 4.25   Let $\leqslant_G$ be any relation on $\mathbf{L}$ satisfying $(\leqslant_G 1)$–$(\leqslant_G 5)$. Then there is a revision function $*$ such that $(C \leqslant_G)$ is satisfied and such that $(K*1)$–$(K*8)$ are fulfilled.

The proofs of these theorems are not repeated here. However, it can be noted that Grove utilizes his sphere representation of revision functions for the proofs. Using a given system $\mathbf{S}$ of spheres (see section 4.5), it is not difficult to see how a relation $\leqslant_G$ can be defined: Let $A \leqslant_G B$ hold if and only if $S_A \subseteq S_B$. It is then easy to verify that this relation satisfies $(\leqslant_G 1)$–$(\leqslant_G 5)$. The converse construction, that is, defining a system of spheres with the aid of an ordering $\leqslant_G$, is in contrast trickier.

What we want, however, is not a representation theorem based on $\leqslant_G$ but one in terms of the ordering $\leqslant$ of epistemic entrenchment. Given Grove's representation results, this can be obtained in an indirect way if we can find some way of connecting the two orderings. To get some idea of what such a connection should look like, note that the ordering of epistemic importance basically applies to sentences that are *in K* and that it is used to determine which sentences should be *retained in K_A^-*, whereas the ordering $\leqslant_G$ has its main force for sentences that are *inconsistent* with K and is used to determine which sentences should be *included in K_A^**. Given this comparison, it is not difficult to see how Grove's $\leqslant_G$ can be used to construct an ordering of epistemic entrenchment. The intuitive idea is that, if B is in K and we want to know whether B should be in K_A^-, we apply the Harper identity and look at $-B$ to check whether it is in K_A^* (which is determined by Grove's method). Formally the following definition does the job:

(Def $\leqslant$)   For all A, B in **L**, $A \leqslant B$ iff $-A \leqslant_G -B$.

The following two lemmas provide the connection between the properties of $\leqslant_G$ and $\leqslant$.

LEMMA 4.26   If $\leqslant_G$ satisfies $(\leqslant_G 1)$–$(\leqslant_G 5)$, then $\leqslant$ introduced by (Def $\leqslant$) satisfies (EE1)–(EE5).

LEMMA 4.27   If $\leqslant$ satisfies (EE1)–(EE5), then $\leqslant_G$ introduced by means of (Def $\leqslant$) satisfies $(\leqslant_G 1)$–$(\leqslant_G 5)$.

These lemmas show that the two set of postulates are equivalent in the sense that they introduce the same relational structure on the sentences in **L**.

For the final piece of comparison, we repeat the following test, which relates $\leqslant$ to a contraction function:

(C$\leqslant$) $B \leqslant A$ iff $B \notin K_{A \& B}^{-}$.

This test should be related to Grove's criterion that relates $\leqslant_G$ to a revision function:

(C$\leqslant_G$) $A \& B <_G A \& -B$ iff $B \in K_A^*$.

The following two lemmas show that, given the Harper and Levi identities, these two criteria are in fact equivalent.

LEMMA 4.28   Assume that $\leqslant_G$ and $*$ satisfy (C$\leqslant_G$). Then $\leqslant$ introduced by (Def $\leqslant$) and $-$ introduced by (Def $-$) satisfy (C$\leqslant$).

LEMMA 4.29   Assume that $\leqslant$ and $-$ satisfy (C$\leqslant$). Then $\leqslant_G$ introduced by (Def $\leqslant$) and $*$ introduced by (Def $*$) satisfy (C$\leqslant_G$).

By putting theorems 4.24 and 4.25 together with lemmas 4.26–4.29 and the results in chapter 3, we obtain the grande finale.

THEOREM 4.30   A contraction function $-$ satisfies (K^-1)–(K^-8) iff $\leqslant$ satisfies (EE1)–(EE5), where $B \leqslant A$ iff $B \notin K_{A \& B}^{-}$ for all A and B in **L**.

The main purpose of introducing the notion of epistemic entrenchment is to show how it can be used in the process of constructing well-behaved contraction functions (and thereby also revision functions). Half of theorem 4.30 guarantees that, if we start with an ordering $\leqslant$ that satisfies postulates (EE1)–(EE5), we can with the aid of (C$\leqslant$) determine a contraction function that satisfies (K^-1)–(K^-8).

Conversely the other half of theorem 4.30 shows that, for any contraction function that satisfies $(K^- 1)$–$(K^- 8)$, we can determine, again by means of $(C \leqslant)$, an ordering of epistemic entrenchment that satisfies (EE1)–(EE5). Or in simpler words, for any well-behaved contraction function [or revision function, by means of (Def $-$)], there exists an ordering of epistemic entrenchment that generates the function. I believe that theorem 4.30 justifies the conclusion that the concept of epistemic entrenchment is a useful tool when studying the dynamics of epistemic states.

4.9   Safe Contractions

I next turn to a presentation of yet another approach to the problem of constructing contraction functions. The approach was introduced by Alchourrón and Makinson (1985) and is called *safe contraction*. Their contraction procedure can be described as follows: Let K be a belief set, and suppose that we want to contract K with respect to A. Alchourrón and Makinson postulate a "hierarchy" $<$ over K that is assumed to be acyclical (that is, for no $A_1, A_2, \ldots, A_n$ in K is it the case that $A_1 < A_2 < \ldots < A_n < A_1$). Given such a hierarchy, we say that an element B is *safe* with respect to A iff B is not a minimal element (under $<$) of any *minimal* subset K' of K such that $K' \vdash A$. Equivalently, every minimal subset K' of K such that $K' \vdash A$ either does not contain B or else contains some C such that $C < B$.

Intuitively the idea is that B is safe if it can never be "blamed" for the implication of A. Note that, in contrast to the earlier constructions, this definition uses minimal subsets of K that *entail* A rather than maximal subsets of K that do *not* entail A. It should be noted that the hierarchy $<$ over K can possibly be seen as an ordering of epistemic entrenchment. However, Alchourrón and Makinson do not give any epistemological interpretation of the hierarchy.

The set of all elements of K that are safe with respect to A is written K/A. The *safe contraction* of a belief set K (modulo a hierarchy $<$) can then be defined as the set of all logical consequences of K/A, that is, $K_A^- = Cn(K/A)$. The basic result in Alchourrón and Makinson (1985) is their observation 3.2:

THEOREM 4.31   Any safe contraction function satisfies $(K^- 1)$–$(K^- 6)$.

An immediate consequence of this theorem and theorem 4.13 is the following.

COROLLARY 4.32   Every safe contraction function over a belief set K is a partial meet contraction function over K.

Alchourrón and Makinson then investigate the consequences of imposing further restrictions on the hierarchy $<$. A first notion is the following: $<$ *continues up* $\vdash$ over K iff for all A, B, C in K, if $A < B$ and $B \vdash C$, then $A < C$. The following result concerning this restriction is of interest.[14]

THEOREM 4.33   Let K be any belief set. Any safe contraction function generated by a hierarchy $<$ that continues up $\vdash$ over K satisfies (K⁻7).

The second restriction on $<$ is similar: $<$ *continues down* $\vdash$ over K iff for all A, B, C in K, if $A \vdash B$ and $B < C$, then $A < C$. The consequences for the properties of the contraction function are similar.[15]

THEOREM 4.34   Let K be any belief set. Any safe contraction function generated by a hierarchy $<$ that continues down $\vdash$ over K satisfies (K⁻7).

A third restriction on $<$ is the following: $<$ is *virtually connected* over K iff for all A, B, C in K, if $A < B$, then either $A < C$ or $C < B$. With the aid of this notion the following theorem can now be proved.[16]

THEOREM 4.35   Let K be any belief set. Any safe contraction function generated by a hierarchy $<$ that is virtually connected and continues up *or* down $\vdash$ over K satisfies (K⁻8).

In another article, Alchourrón and Makinson (1986) prove some representation results for the case when K is a *finite* belief set (in the sense that the consequence relation $\vdash$ partitions the elements of K into a finite number of equivalence classes). The following results correspond to their theorems 1 and 2.

THEOREM 4.36   Let K be a finite belief set. Then $-$ is a safe contraction function generated by a hierarchy $<$ that continues up and down $\vdash$ over K iff $-$ is a relational partial meet contraction function over K.

THEOREM 4.37   Let K be a finite belief set. Then $-$ is a safe contraction function generated by a hierarchy $<$ that continues up and down $\vdash$ over K and is virtually connected iff $-$ is a transitively relational partial meet contraction function over K.

However, it is an open problem whether these representation results can be extended to the case when K is infinite. [Note that the implication from left to right in theorem 4.37 follows also in the infinite case from theorems 4.33 (or 4.34), 4.35, and 4.16.]

4.10   Two Further Application Areas: Logical Databases and Legal Codes

As a conclusion to this chapter, I briefly discuss two problem areas where the techniques presented may be useful. The first area concerns problems connected with updating logical databases and the second problems of derogating and revising legal codes.

Simply speaking, a database is a structured collection of items of information. Here I confine myself to databases in which these items can be identified with certain propositions or sentences. A logical database is then a database that satisfies certain logical closure conditions.[17] Consequently a logical database can be seen as a model of an epistemic state.

The ability of the database user to modify the content of the database is fundamental to all database management systems. Such modifications are called *updates* within computer science. It is clear that changes corresponding to expansions, revisions, and contractions of epistemic states are all important update types for databases.[18] In order to bring out this connection, I borrow an example from Fagin et al. (1983, p. 353).

Consider for example a relational database with a ternary relation SUPPLIES, where a tuple $\langle a, b, c \rangle$ means that supplier a supplies part b to project c. Suppose now that the relation contains the tuple $\langle$Hughes, tiles, Space Shuttle$\rangle$, and that the user asks to delete this tuple. A simple-minded approach would be to just go ahead and delete the tuple from the relation. However, while it is true that Hughes does not supply tiles to the Space Shuttle project anymore, it is not clear what to do about the three other facts that were implied by the above tuple, i.e. that Hughes supplies tiles, that Hughes supplies parts to the Space Shuttle project, and that the Space Shuttle project uses tiles. In some circumstances it might not be a bad idea to replace the deleted tuple by three tuples with null vales:

$\langle$Hughes, tiles, NULL$\rangle$,

$\langle$Hughes, NULL, Space Shuttle$\rangle$,

and

$\langle$NULL, tiles, Space Shuttle$\rangle$.

... The database is not viewed merely as a collection of atomic facts, but rather as a collection of facts from which other facts can be derived. It is the interaction between the updated facts and the derived facts that is the source of the problems.

If we identify a logical database with a belief set, which seems quite natural,[19] the problem of updating the database can be solved by using appropriate contraction and revision functions [or one of these if either (Def *) or (Def −) is assumed]. Using the results of section 4.8, this means that, if only an ordering of epistemic entrenchment [satisfying (EE1)–(EE5)] of the items in the database can be provided, theorems 4.30, 4.17, and 4.16 taken together entail that a satisfactory contraction function (and thus also a revision function) can be constructed.

Fagin et al. (1983) present closely related procedures, although they do not develop a full theory of contractions and revisions.[20] They introduce the notion of a *tagged sentence* consisting of a pair $\langle i, A \rangle$, where A is a sentence and i a natural number representing the *database priority* of A (p. 358). The intention is that, the lower the tag, the higher the priority. They then define a logical database as a finite set of tagged sentences. When defining the update of a database, they require that the sentences with the highest tags be deleted first. This procedure is illustrated by an example of a revision of a small database.

Even if Fagin et al. do not develop their theory in full generality, it is obvious that their "database priorities" can be identified with degrees of epistemic entrenchment and that their ideas for constructing updates are essentially the same as the constructions of contraction functions. Perhaps Spohn's degrees of firmness, as presented in section 2.5, come even closer to their intended interpretation.

This connection between contractions and revisions of epistemic states and updates of logical databases may be fruitful, as databases have a formal structure that goes beyond the structure required of a belief set and this additional structure can be used to introduce *further postulates* for the ordering of epistemic entrenchment (or, equivalently, further postulates on the contraction function). Such postulates, in general, increase the connections between the degrees of epistemic entrenchment of the sentences in the database and consequently *reduce* the amount of information about the sentences that need to be fed into the database by the user. For example, not all tags in the system need to be specified as inputs, but many of them can be derived with the aid of the additional postulates.

Another way of modeling the dynamics of databases is provided by Foo and Rao (1986). Their databases are construed as a set of rules in PROLOG, in which certain sentences are considered to be "negative" information (that is, known to be false); these sentences are used to derive negated statements (instead of defining negation as finite failure as in standard PROLOG). They then provide constructive methods for expanding, contracting, and revising the databases that they show to fulfill conditions that are analogous to the conditions presented in chapter 3. Instead of an ordering of epistemic entrenchment, they work with "strata" of information. However, it is clear that the formal structure of these strata is closely related to the structure of an ordering of epistemic entrenchment.

The second application concerns changes in legal codes. A legal code, or a norm system, has basically the same formal structure as a belief set, for it consists of a set of propositions together with their logical consequences.[21] Legal codes are not static but change over time. Most commonly new rules are added. This type of change, of course, corresponds to the expansion of a belief set. But sometimes norms are retracted—a kind of change that corresponds to contraction. Among legal theorists this process is called a *derogation* of the code. Finally, a new law may be added that contradicts the earlier code. This process, which corresponds to a revision of a belief set, is called an *amendment* of the legal code. In the legal context we can, in parallel with the Levi identity for belief sets, think of an amendment as a composite process of a derogation of old material from the system followed by addition of new norms.

For both derogations and amendments one encounters the same logical problems as those for contractions and revisions of belief sets. These problems are presented in a precise way by Bulygin and Alchourrón (1977) and by Lewis (1979) under the name of "a problem about permission." To give a simple illustration of the derogation problem, I borrow an example from Hilpinen (1981). Suppose that a father has commanded that

(4.2)   The children may watch TV only if they eat their dinner.

(4.3)   The children may eat their dinner only if they do their homework.

A consequence of these norms is that

(4.4)   The children may watch TV only if they do their homework.

This norm is thus also included in the norm system. Now suppose that the norm system is changed by the addition of the following permission by the father:

(4.5) Today, the children may watch the TV without doing their home-
       work.

In the new norm system, (4.4) is of course no longer a valid command, but
(4.2) and (4.3) cannot both be valid either. Which of these commands is
derogated by the father's permission (4.5)?

Again, the problems about derogations and amendments of legal codes
would be solved if appropriate contraction and revision functions were
available. And because a legal code corresponds to a belief set, all the results
of section 4.8 are also applicable in this case. Once these parallels between
the structure of legal codes and the structure of belief sets have been noticed,
the obvious solution to the problems about change of legal codes is to
utilize an ordering of *deontic entrenchment* among the set of laws or norms.
This ordering is then applied in the same way that the ordering of epistemic
entrenchment was applied for contractions and revisions of belief sets.

A rudimentary form of deontic ordering can be determined in a legal
code by its hierarchical systems of sections, including, for example, con-
stitutional laws, criminal laws, and local regulations. Because the full body
of a legal code often indicates conflicting verdicts, an important task for
jurists is to specify in this terminology the ordering of deontic entrenchment
in greater detail. Bulygin and Alchourrón (1977) discuss the application of
a *Normenordnung* and the consequences of gaps in this ordering. In fact,
the creation of precedents is an established way of determining such an
ordering. Closely related formal problems are investigated by Alchourrón
and Makinson (1980), who also assume an ordering of the underlying code,
which they call a "hierarchy of regulations."

One difference that merits attention—the difference between databases
and legal codes on the one hand and belief sets on the other—is that a
database or a legal code is often generated from a *finite set* of propositions,
that is, the written code. And a change of the system always consists in a
change in this generating set of propositions. Makinson (1985a, p. 357)
argues that the intuitive processes of contraction and revision are always
applied to finite *bases* for belief sets (databases or legal codes). And he points
out that, when *maxichoice* contractions (and revisions) are applied to such
bases rather than to entire belief sets (databases, legal codes), they do not
yield the inflated sets that are the consequences of lemma 4.5 and its
corollary.[22]

I hope to have shown that the problems concerning updating databases and amending and derogating legal codes show great formal similarities to the problems of contracting and revising belief sets. Clearly a contribution to a solution within one problem area will be helpful with regard to problems in the others. However, if the languages and the formal structures of the three areas are studied in greater detail, the parallel may break down. Nevertheless, I believe that the similarities between the problem areas are great enough to merit further studies.

5 The Dynamics of Probabilistic Models

5.1 Bayesian Models and Their Dynamics

Bayesianism comes in two parts. The first part of the doctrine is that epistemic states can be represented by *probability functions* defined over the sentences of an appropriate language. This part is generally defended by the Dutch book theorem or some related coherence argument. In the main part of this chapter I assume this representation of states of belief. The second part is *conditionalization*, which is described later in this section.

Probability functions are denoted by P with various sub- and superscripts. They are defined over the language $\mathbf{L}$ and, as before, we assume that $\mathbf{L}$ is governed by a logic that includes classical propositional logic and is identified by its consequence relation $\vdash$. It is also assumed that $\vdash$ is compact. It is convenient to introduce the *absurd* probability function $P_\perp$, which is defined by $P_\perp(A) = 1$ for all A in $\mathbf{L}$. The class of all probability functions, including $P_\perp$, is denoted by $\mathbf{P}$. Assumptions concerning what is included in $\mathbf{P}$ are explicitly noted when they are used. A sentence A is said to be *accepted* in a state of belief represented by a probability function P if and only if $P(A) = 1$.

The second part of the Bayesian doctrine is that rational changes of belief can be described by conditionalization of probability functions whenever this process is defined, that is, whenever the information to be added is consistent with the given probability function. This means that conditionalization of a probability function P corresponds to an *expansion* of the state of belief represented by P. The conditionalization of P on A is denoted P_A^+, because it turns out that it is a generalization of expansions of belief sets. The process is defined as follows:

(Def $+$) P_A^+ is the probability function representing the conditionalization of P on the sentence A iff, for every sentence B, $P_A^+(B) = P(B/A) = P(B\,\&\,A)/P(A)$ whenever $P(A) > 0$. When $P(A) = 0$, we conventionally define P_A^+ to be $P_\perp$.

The convention entails that the identity $P(B) = P(A) \cdot P_A^+(B) + P(-A) \cdot P_{-A}^+(B)$ holds even if $P(A) = 0$. It can be noted that, as defined here, conditionalization is a function from $\mathbf{P}$ and $\mathbf{L}$ to $\mathbf{P}$, which is what we want to have if conditionalization is to be an expansion function.

In this way we can define expansions of states of belief within the

Bayesian tradition. As mentioned in sections 1.4 and 1.5, several forms of epistemic changes other than expansions, contractions, and revisions are of interest when epistemic states are modeled by probability functions. Explicit constructions for some such changes can be found in the literature.[1] The best known of these changes is Jeffrey conditionalization [see Jeffrey (1965)], which represents changes induced by inputs of the form 'the probability of A is x' ($x > 0$). Given that the present epistemic state is represented by P and that the updated state is to be represented by P', Jeffrey defines the result of such an input [which can be described as the constraint that $P'(A) = x$] by the following equation:

(Def J)   For all B, $P'(B) = x \cdot P(B/A) + (1 - x) \cdot P(B/-A)$.

As is easily seen, traditional conditionalization is a special case of (Def J) corresponding to the input $P'(A) = 1$.

However, neither the traditional conditionalization process nor Jeffrey conditionalization helps us with the problems of how to define contractions and revisions of probability functions. The main goal in this chapter is to formulate *postulates* for such contractions and revisions and investigate their consequences and interrelations. After doing this, I suggest some explicit *constructions* of the contraction process. However, before turning to contractions and revisions of probability functions, let us discuss in greater detail the problem of defining expansions of probability functions.

5.2   Why Conditionalize? Some Representation Results

In this section I discuss the arguments for using conditionalization as a representation of expansions of belief. As a preliminary, I show a way of characterizing the conditionalization process with the aid of some postulates. These postulates also turn out to be useful when investigating contractions and revisions. For the project we need a concept of a *mixture* of two probability functions P and P': $(P a P')$ is the a-mixture of P and P' defined by the equation $(P a P')(A) = a \cdot P(A) + (1 - a) \cdot P'(A)$ for all A, where $0 \leqslant a < 1$ and P and P' are both nonabsurd. In the limiting cases we define $(P a P_\perp) = P$ and $(P_\perp a P) = P$ for all probability functions P. Given the concept of a-mixture it is easy to show that conditionalization satisfies the following properties:

(P$^+$1)   If A and B are disjoint, that is, $\vdash -(A \,\&\, B)$, then $P^+_{A \vee B} = P^+_A a\, P^+_B$, where $a = P(A)/P(A \vee B)$.

(P$^+$2) $P^+_A(A) = 1$.

(P$^+$3)   If $\vdash A$, then $P^+_A = P$.

(P$^+$4) $P^+_A = P_\perp$ iff $P(A) = 0$.

In fact, we can show that properties (P$^+$1)–(P$^+$4) characterize the conditionalization process in the following sense.

LEMMA 5.1   Conditionalization is the only function from **P** × **L** to **P** satisfying (P$^+$1)–(P$^+$4).

This lemma gives us a simple representation theorem for conditionalization. Postulates (P$^+$2)–(P$^+$4) are just trivial regularity conditions, and (P$^+$1) is of course the essential postulate. The following is a verbal interpretation of (P$^+$1): If one's state of belief can be represented by an a-mixture $P a P'$, this can be seen as believing in state P with probability a and in state P' with probability $1 - a$. Thus (P$^+$1) says that learning that $A \vee B$ in state P, where A and B are disjoint, is the same as learning A with probability $P(A)/[P(A) + P(B)]$ and learning B with probability $P(B)/[P(A) + P(B)]$. As will be seen, similar ideas turn up in the postulates for contractions and revisions of probability functions.

Formulating postulates that characterize conditionalization is only an indirect way of motivating the process; it would be preferable to give more direct arguments. A lucid presentation of the arguments in favor of conditionalization has been given by Teller (1976). Apart from frequency arguments and Savage-type arguments in terms of changes of preferences, Teller devotes most of his work to a Dutch book argument due to David Lewis and to a *qualitative* condition on changes of belief that (almost) characterizes conditionalization [in comparison, the central postulate (P$^+$1) is quantitative].

The Dutch book argument rests on the assumption that the agent's belief function P represents his betting rates so that, for any proposition B, $P(B)$ is the price for which he would be indifferent between buying and selling the bet '1 if B; 0 otherwise'. The argument then shows that, if the agent knows that his belief function will be P' if he learns that A is true, that is, expands by A, and if P' is not identical with P^+_A, then a bookie who knows no more or less than the agent can induce the agent to buy and sell bets on which he will have a net loss whatever happens.[2] However, the proof rests on the additional assumption that there is a set of mutually exclusive and jointly exhaustive propositions (to which A belongs) that specify in full detail all the alternative courses of experience, that is, all possible expansions the agent might undergo when he is in the belief state represented by P. Unfortunately Teller does not discuss the force of this assumption. In my opinion it is quite restrictive, and, as a consequence, Teller's version of Lewis's argument shows only that conditionalization is the appropriate expansion method in the limited class of situations that satisfy this assumption.

Teller's qualitative condition, which he sees as a way of defending the conditionalization process, will be of some interest later, so let us translate it into the present terminology. Let us, for an arbitrary expansion method defined on probability functions, denote the expansion of P by A by P_A^+. Then the condition is

(P^+T) (i) $P_A^+(A) = 1$.

(ii) For all B and C, if $B \vdash A$ and $C \vdash A$ and $P(B) = P(C)$, then $P_A^+(B) = P_A^+(C)$.

Or, in words, when we want to expand our belief function P by A and we take any two propositions B and C, each of which logically implies A, if B and C are believed equally before the expansion, then they are also believed equally after the change.

Teller (1976, pp. 220–223) shows that, under some additional assumption concerning the richness of the domain of the beliefs represented by P, the only expansion method that satisfies condition (P^+T) is conditionalization. He then presents some arguments in support of condition (P^+T).

5.3   Imaging

Thus there seem to be strong, even if not conclusive, arguments in favor of using conditionalization as the correct representation of expansions of probability models. Are there any alternative representations? So long as one uses probability functions as representations of states of belief, there is, so far as I know, only one other expansion method suggested, namely, Lewis's (1976) *imaging*. Lewis introduced this method not to argue that imaging should be used instead of conditionalization but to show that Stalnaker's (1970) analysis of the probabilities of conditional sentences cannot be described by conditionalization but that it can be represented in terms of imaging.

In fact, the imaging method is a general revision method because it gives nontrivial results when $P(A) = 0$, where A is the new information to be accommodated for. However, even in the case of proper expansions, where $P(A) > 0$, imaging and conditionalization in general produce different results.

In order to introduce the imaging process, we must first present some of Lewis's ontological assumptions concerning possible worlds. Lewis assumes for mathematical simplicity that there are only finitely many possible worlds. Rather than using probability functions defined over sentences, he assumes that they are defined over the class of possible worlds so that each world W has a probability $P(W)$ and these probabilities add up to 1. From the probabilities of worlds one can then obtain probabilities of sentences by summing the probabilities of the worlds in which a sentence is true. In this way one can determine a probability function defined over sentences, which may be taken to represent a state of belief in the Bayesian sense. More precisely, Lewis's framework of possible worlds gives him a more fine-grained representation of states of belief, from which the Bayesian states can then be reconstructed.

Lewis also makes the assumption, central to Stalnaker's semantics for conditionals, that for each world W and each sentence A there is a *unique* world W_A that is the world most *similar* to W where A is true, if there are any worlds at all where A is true. For any probability function P defined on the set of possible worlds and for any sentence that is true in some world, Lewis then defines a probability function that he calls the *image* of P on A, here denoted $P_A^\#$, by putting $P_A^\#(W)$ for all worlds W equal to the sum of $P(W')$ for all worlds W' such that W_A' is identical with W. In simpler terms, the image of a probability function can be computed by shifting the original probability of each world W' over to W_A'.

Why should we be interested in imaging as a representation of expansions (or, more generally, revisions) of probability functions? When we revise our beliefs in the light of new knowledge, we do not want to change our system of beliefs more than is necessary in order to maintain a coherent state of belief. For a proposition A such that $P(A) \neq 0$, both conditionalization on A and imaging on A can be held to revise P as little as possible to make A accepted. Lewis gives the following argument:

Imaging P on A gives a minimal revision in this sense: unlike all other revisions of P to make A certain, it involves no gratuitous movement of probability from worlds to dissimilar worlds. Conditionalizing P on A gives a minimal revision in this different sense: unlike all other revisions of P to make A certain, it does not distort the profile of probability ratios, equalities, and inequalities among sentences that imply A. (Lewis 1976, p. 311)

It is clear that Lewis's description of conditionalization is closely related to Teller's analysis.

Because imaging is an interesting alternative to conditionalization, I now turn to an investigation of its properties. As a beginning, I show that we can dispense with some of the assumptions that Lewis makes when describing the imaging process without giving up the basic idea. First, I present a generalization of Lewis's process that does not rely on the assumption that for every world there is a unique most similar A-world. Second, I give a characterization of the generalized form of imaging in terms of a homomorphism condition that does not presuppose any kind of possible world semantics. I then use these results to highlight some of the properties that distinguish conditionalization from imaging.

In any possible world W a proposition is either true or false. This information about the status of propositions may equally well be represented by a (degenerate) probability function P such that, for all sentences A, $P(A) = 1$ if A is true in W and $P(A) = 0$ if A is false in W. In such a case we say that P corresponds to W. Lewis calls such a probability function opinionated because "it would represent the beliefs of someone who was absolutely certain that the world W was actual and who therefore held a firm opinion about every question" (Lewis 1976, p. 314). In mathematical jargon an opinionated probability function is nothing but a characteristic function.

Lewis believes that possible worlds are more or less similar to each other. Imaging can be seen as a method of using this similarity between possible worlds when defining minimal revisions of probability functions. The starting point for Lewis's definition is the correspondence between truth in possible worlds and probability in opinionated probability functions. Let P^i be an opinionated probability function, and let $P_A^{i\#}$ denote the minimal revision of P^i that raises the probability of A to 1. Because Lewis makes the assumption that for any possible world W^i there is a unique most similar A-world W_A^i (if there are any A-worlds at all), he can simply say that, if P^i is the opinionated probability function that corresponds to W^i, then $P_A^{i\#}$ is the probability function corresponding to W_A^i.

The next step is to extend this way of revising opinionated probability functions to a revision method that applies to all probability functions. Because Lewis "pretends" for mathematical simplicity that there are only finitely many possible worlds, it can be shown that any probability function over these worlds can be seen as a weighted sum of opinionated probability functions.

In order to elaborate this further, we need a preparatory argument. If P^i and P^j are nonidentical opinionated probability functions, then there is some sentence S^{ij} such that $P^i(S^{ij}) = 1$ and $P^j(S^{ij}) = 0$. By taking the conjunction of such S^{ij}'s for any P^i in a finite class of opinionated probability functions, one can find a sentence S^i such that $P^i(S^i) = 1$ but $P^j(S^i) = 0$ for all $P^j \neq P^i$. In analogy with section 2.2 such a sentence S^i is called a *determiner* for P^i.

If it is assumed that there are only finitely many opinionated probability functions $P^1, \ldots, P^n$ (corresponding to a finite set of possible worlds), then a set of determiners $S^1, \ldots, S^n$ for these functions can be used to fix the weights when representing an arbitrary probability function as a linear combination of opinionated functions. The determiners can be seen as identifying descriptions of the corresponding worlds, and they have the property that for any probability function P and any sentence B either $P(B \, \& \, S^i) = P(S^i)$ or $P(B \, \& \, S^i) = 0$. From this it follows that $P(B/S^i) = P^i(B)$, and then it is easy to show that $P(B) = \sum_i P(S^i) \cdot P^i(B)$ for all sentences B. Hence the values $P(S^i)$ function as weights in this sum. These weights are unique, and one can show that they add up to 1.

With the aid of this terminology, we can now define Lewis's imaging process in a precise manner. Let P be an arbitrary probability function, and let $P^i, \ldots, P^n$ be the opinionated probability functions with determiners $S^i, \ldots, S^n$ such that, for all sentences B, $P(B) = \sum_i P(S^i) \cdot P^i(B)$. Let us call a proposition A *possible* if $P^j(A) = 1$ for some probability function P^j. For any possible A the *image* $P_A^\#$ of P on A is defined by $P_A^\#(B) = \sum_i P(S^i) \cdot P_A^{i\#}(B)$ for all sentences B, where $P_A^{i\#}$ as before is the probability function corresponding to W_A^i. Or, in other words, if P is a linear combination of $P^1, \ldots, P^n$ [with weights $P(S^1), \ldots, P(S^n)$], then $P_A^\#$ is a linear combination of the revised opinionated functions $P_A^{1\#}, \ldots, P_A^{n\#}$ with the same weights as for P.

On this account the assumption that to each world W^i there is a unique "closest" A-world W_A^i is equivalent to the assumption that the revision $P_A^{i\#}$ of an opinionated probability function P^i is also opinionated. To some extent this condition seems ad hoc. It is a probabilistic version of condition (3.18). The epistemological interpretation of an opinionated probability function is that it represents the beliefs of a person who has a firm opinion about every question. If such a person, as a result of an unexpected (!) observation or as a hypothesis, adds a sentence A that contradicts her earlier beliefs, then the condition requires that she has a firm opinion about every question also in the resulting revised state of belief. This makes heavy demands even on a *besserwisser*.

I now show that it is possible to retain the idea that the revision of a probability function is a weighted sum of revised opinionated probability functions without assuming that the revision of an opinionated function is also opinionated. In pictorial terms one can say that, instead of moving all the probability assigned to a world W^i by a probability function P to a unique ("closest") A-world W^j, when imaging on A, one can introduce the weaker requirement that the probability of W^i be distributed among *several* A-worlds (that are "equally close"). In other words, instead of having $P_A^{i\#}(S^j) = 1$ for only one j, a more general form is to have $P_A^{i\#}(S^j) > 0$ for several j's such that W^j is an A-world, that is, $P^j(A) = 1$. An obvious requirement is $\sum_j P_A^{i\#}(S^j) = 1$. The new probability of a world W^j after this more general form of imaging can then be computed by summing the portions of probability moved over to it, that is, $P_A^{\#}(S^j) = \sum_i P(S^i) \cdot P_A^{i\#}(S^j)$, where S^j is a determiner for W^j (or P^j). The final step in the definition of the image $P_A^{\#}$ of P on A then consists in putting, for any sentence B, $P_A^{\#}(B) = \sum_j P_A^{\#}(S^j) \cdot P^j(B)$ in the same way as before. The method of revision defined in this way is called *general imaging*. Lewis's imaging is the special case when, for every P^i, $P_A^{i\#}(S^j) = 1$ for some j.

It should be noted that not only are imaging and general imaging capable of describing expansions of states of belief, but they are also general *revision* methods, because there is nothing in the definition of the general image of P on A that presumes $P(A) > 0$. Thus imaging is a more general method of describing belief changes than conditionalization.

5.4 A Representation Theorem for Imaging

In the generalization of Lewis's imaging process that has been described here, the role of the possible worlds has been taken over by the opinionated probability functions. One assumption has been that there are only finitely many such functions so that every probability function can be described as a weighted sum of these. I now present a characterization of general imaging that avoids the finiteness assumption, all applications of opinionated probability functions, and thereby also possible worlds.

The object of study is a *probabilistic revision function*, which is a function from the set **P** of all probability functions and all sentences in **L** to probability functions in **P**. The revision of a probability function P with respect to a sentence A is denoted P_A^*. General postulates for probabilistic revision functions are introduced in section 5.8. Here we need only the assumption that $P_A^*(A) = 1$.

For any P an opinionated probability function P^i that has the property that, if $P(A) = 1$, then $P^i(A) = 1$ for all A is called a *completion* of P. It is assumed that for any P in **P** the completions of P are also in **P**. Recall that lemma 2.3 entails that for any P the set K of sentences A such that $P(A) = 1$ forms a belief set. For any completion P^i of P the set of sentences A such that $P^i(A) = 1$ can be seen as a maximally consistent extension of K. We say that a sentence A is *possible* iff there is some probability function P in **P** such that $P(A) > 0$.

A main problem concerning a probabilistic revision function is what can be said in general about the relation between P and P_A^*. One answer to this problem is that P_A^* is an extension of the conditionalization process. Another answer that can be given under the assumptions is that P_A^* comes from P by imaging on A.

The following property, which is central to my discussion, does not define the relation between P and P_A^* explicitly, but it says something about how these functions are related.[3]

(Hom)   A probabilistic revision function $*$ is said to be *homomorphic* iff, for all probability functions P in the model, if A is possible, then for all functions P' and P'' in the model and all a such that $P = P' a P''$ it holds that $P_A^* = P_A'^* a P_A''^*$.

An interpretation of the requirement that a probabilistic revision function be homomorphic would be that, if a state of belief represented by P can be seen as a mixture of two states of belief represented by P' and P'', then the revision of P by A, that is, P_A^*, is a mixture *with the same proportions* of the revisions of P' and P'' with respect to A, that is, $P_A'^*$ and $P_A''^*$. A more general condition would be to make the same requirement for mixtures of any finite number of probability functions. However, it is easy to show that this more general requirement of homomorphism can be derived from the form presented here.

It is important to note that the formulation of the condition (Hom) does not refer to opinionated probability functions (or possible worlds). In particular, the condition does not rely on the presumption that a probabilistic revision function contains only a finite number of opinionated probability functions.

There is, however, a close connection between homomorphism and imaging. Let us call a probabilistic revision function that is defined for only a finite number of opinionated probability functions a *finite revision function*. The following theorem shows that the requirement of homomorphism, which is applicable not only in the finite case, is a way of characterizing general imaging, which is defined for finite probabilistic revision functions only.

THEOREM 5.2   A finite probabilistic revision function $*$ is homomorphic iff $P_A^* = P_A^\#$; that is, P_A^* comes from P by general imaging on A for all probability functions P in the model and for all possible propositions A.

5.5   Imaging versus Conditionalization

How are imaging and conditionalization related? If we restrict ourselves to the case with finitely many opinionated probability functions, then the two processes can be pictured in the following way. The image of P on a proposition A is formed by shifting the original probability assigned to a possible world W_i where A is false [or, in other words, an opinionated function P_i such that $P_i(A) = 0$] over to a world where A is true [an opinionated function P_j such that $P_j(A) = 1$] or, in the general case, to several such worlds. Probabilities are moved around but not created or destroyed; so the probabilities of worlds (opinionated functions) still sum to 1. The conditionalization of P on A is formed by cutting off all worlds where A is false [opinionated functions P_i such that $P_i(A) = 0$] and then magnifying the probabilities of the A-worlds so that these probabilities add up to 1. The magnification is done on the same scale for all A-worlds [by multiplying by $1/P(A)$ in order to have $P(A) = 1$]; thus the ratios between the probabilities assigned to these worlds remain the same.

With this figurative description it should be clear that imaging and conditionalization do, in general, yield different results. This can be proved more strictly by exploiting the correspondence between homo-morphic probabilistic revision functions and revisions by general imaging. I show that conditionalization in very special cases only satisfies the condition of homomorphism.

This result is a consequence of a more general result that is connected with the following property.[4]

(Pres)   A probabilistic revision function $*$ is said to be *preservative* iff, for all probability functions P and for all propositions A and B, if $P(A) > 0$ and $P(B) = 1$, then $P_A^*(B) = 1$.

The epistemological interpretation of this property is that, if a sentence B is accepted in a state of belief (represented by P) and if A is consistent with what is accepted in this state, then, if A is later accepted as knowledge, B should still be accepted. Requiring that a probabilistic revision function be preservative amounts essentially to the same as (K*4) in chapter 3. This connection is investigated in section 5.8.

It follows immediately from the definitions that, if the revision method is an extension of conditionalization, that is, if $P_A^* = P_A^+$ for all P and A such that $P(A) > 0$, then the probabilistic revision function is preservative. The requirement that a probabilistic revision function be preservative seems to be endorsed, more or less explicitly, by all Bayesian traditionalists. However, it should be noted that, when general imaging was defined, it was not assumed that the revisions should be preservative.

The general result is that on pain of triviality, *probabilistic revision functions cannot be both homomorphic and preservative*. The idea of the proof can be given quite easily in terms of general imaging. Assume that revisions are made by general imaging. Let P be a probability function that assigns positive probabilities to some pairwise disjoint sentences A, B, and C. When one forms the general image of P with respect to $B \vee C$, the probabilities of the A-worlds are moved to B-worlds or C-worlds. Assume that some amount of probability is moved from the A-worlds to some C-world. Then consider a probability function P' that assigns positive probabilities to A-worlds and B-worlds only. Thus $P'(A \vee B) = 1$ and $P'(B \vee C) = P'(B) > 0$. If the belief-change model under consideration is preservative, then $P_{B \vee C}'^{\#}(A \vee B)$ should equal 1. But when the image of P' with respect to $B \vee C$ is formed, some amount of probability is moved from the A-worlds to some C-world. This means that $P_{B \vee C}'^{\#}(A \vee B)$, which is equal to $P'^{\#}_{B \vee C}(B)$, is less than 1, violating the assumption that the probabilistic revision function is preservative.

Before this sketch can be translated into a strict proof, the ground must prepared with some technical matters. First, in the given proof sketch it was assumed that there are *at least* three pairwise disjoint propositions that are assigned positive probabilities by *some* probability function in the probabilistic revision function. Any such probabilistic revision function is said to be *nontrivial*. [Two propositions A and B are said to be disjoint iff $\vdash -(A \& B)$.]

Second, it must be guaranteed that there is such a probability function as P' in the domain of the probabilistic revision function. This assumption is not completely innocent, because a probabilistic revision function that fulfills it does, in general, include more probability functions than are required by the general assumption for probabilistic revision functions.

Let us say that a probabilistic revision function $*$ is *rich* iff, for all probability functions P in **P** and for all pairs of disjoint sentences A and B such that $P(A) > 0$ and $P(B) > 0$, there is *some* a, $0 < a < 1$, such that the mixture function $P' = P^*_A \, a \, P^*_B$ is also in the domain of $*$ (Teller 1976).[5]

In order to give a better understanding of this property, I show how it can be connected with two other properties of probabilistic revision functions. Let us say that a probabilistic revision function $*$ is an *extension of conditionalization* iff $P^*_A = P^+_A$ for all P in **P** and for all sentences A such that $P(A) > 0$. It is now easy to show that , if $*$ is an extension of conditionalization, then $*$ is rich, because, if A and B are disjoint and a is taken to be $P(A)/[P(A) + P(B)]$, then the probability function $P' = P^+_A \, a \, P^+_B$ is identical with $P^+_{A \vee B}$ [compare this with postulate (P$^+$1)]. A second way of guaranteeing that a probabilistic revision function $*$ is rich is to assume that it is convex; that is, for all P and P' in **P**, all a-mixtures of P and P' are also in M. This assumption seems to be natural in some contexts.[6]

After this technical digression, the precise version of the theorem can now be formulated.

THEOREM 5.3   There is no nontrivial and rich probabilistic revision function that is both homomorphic and preservative.

Because it has been shown that, if $*$ is an extension of conditionalization, then $*$ is rich, the theorem has the following immediate corollary.

COROLLARY 5.4   If a probabilistic revision function is nontrivial and an extension of conditionalization, then it is not homomorphic.

The combination of theorems 5.2 and 5.3 shows that the most interesting probabilistic revision functions that are based on imaging or general imaging (that is, those functions that are nontrivial and rich) are not preservative. In particular, a probabilistic revision function that is an extension of conditionalization cannot be described by *any* imaging process unless the function is trivial.

5.6   Preservative Imaging

In the light of theorem 5.3, it should be noted that it is possible to construct another method of revising beliefs that retains the basic idea behind the imaging process but that also is preservative. The new method is called *preservative imaging*. I owe the idea behind the construction to Isaac Levi. The method is defined for finite probabilistic revision functions. Assume for the principal case that $P(A) > 0$. When determining the preservative image $P_A^{\#\,p}$ of P on A, *only* the opinionated functions P^i such that $P(S^i) > 0$ (S^i is the determiner for P^i) are assigned positive probabilities after the revision. This requirement guarantees that the revision is indeed preservative. Let S be the disjunction of all the S^i's for which $P(S^i) > 0$. Figuratively, when forming the preservative image of P on A, the probability of an opinionated function P^i is moved to the "closest" opinionated function (or functions) where both S and A are true. Because we have assumed that $P(A) > 0$, there is always at least one such opinionated function. More formally, the revised probabilities of the opinionated functions are defined by putting

$$P_A^{\#\,p}(S^j) = \sum_i P(S^i) \cdot P_{A\,\&\,S}^{i\,\#\,p}(S^j).$$

The rest of the definition is as before. In the limiting case when $P(A) = 0$, we conventionally put $P_A^{\#\,p} = P_\perp$.

It is important to note that preservative imaging is *not* a special case of general imaging, for probabilistic revision functions that are revised by preservative imaging are in general not homomorphic, which, as we have seen, is a characteristic property of general imaging.

Levi has shown (personal communication) that it is possible to construct nontrivial probabilistic revision functions that are extensions of conditionalization and where the revision can also be described as a case of preservative imaging. This shows that there is no conflict of the sort established in theorem 5.3 between conditionalization and preservative imaging.

Because there are strong reasons in favor of the requirement that a probabilistic revision function be preservative, theorem 5.3 and the considerations in this section indicate that the only interesting form of imaging is preservative imaging. However, Lewis's main reason for introducing the imaging process was not that it has certain properties but that it provides some understanding of how probabilities of *conditional sentences* may be determined. I return to this topic in chapter 7.

5.7 Contractions of Probability Functions

I have now investigated two possibilities of modeling *expansions* of probability functions, namely, conditionalization and imaging. (Imaging is in fact a revision method.) Because preservative expansions are strongly supported by other arguments, the results of the preceding sections indicate that the appropriate expansion method is conditionalization, and this method is assumed in the remainder of this chapter.

My aim in this section is to show how *contractions* of probability functions can be described. In parallel to postulates (K^-1)–(K^-8) for belief sets, I now introduce a number of postulates for contractions of probability functions that can be motivated by similar arguments. Formally the contraction process can be represented as a function from $\mathbf{P} \times \mathbf{L}$ to $\mathbf{P}$. The value of such a contraction function when applied to arguments P and A is called a *contraction of P with respect to A*, and it is denoted P_A^-. This gives us the first postulate:

(P$^-$1)   For all probability functions P and all sentences A, P_A^- is a probability function.

The second postulate is a requirement of "success" simply requiring that A not be accepted in P_A^- unless A is logically valid (in which case it can never be retracted):

(P$^-$2) $P_A^-(A) < 1$ iff not $\vdash A$.

It should be noted that this postulate does not say anything about the magnitude of $P_A^-(A)$, but this number functions as a *parameter* when determining the contraction P_A^-. This leaves open a large number of possibilities for an explicit construction of a contraction function. None of these possibilities will be ruled out by the remaining postulates. If $P_A^-(A) = a$, P_A^- is called an *a-contraction* of P with respect to A.

The third postulate requires that the contraction P_A^- be dependent only on the content of A, not on its linguistic formulation:

(P⁻3)   If $\vdash A \leftrightarrow B$, then $P_A^- = P_B^-$.

In order to cover the trivial case when A is already not accepted in P, that is, when $P(A) < 1$, the following postulate is needed:

(P⁻4)   If $P(A) < 1$, then $P_A^- = P$.

So far, the postulates have only stated some mild regularity conditions. The next "recovery" condition is more interesting:

(P⁻5)   If $P(A) = 1$, then $(P_A^-)_A^+ = P$.

Recall that $(P_A^-)_A^+$ is the conditionalization of P_A^- on A. Postulate (P⁻5) requires that, if A is first retracted from P and then added again (by conditionalization), then one should be back in the original state of belief. The rationale for this is, as before, that the contraction of P with respect to A should be *minimal*—unnecessary losses of information should be avoided. Postulate (P⁻5) then guarantees that as much as possible of the old beliefs is retained. Of course, (P⁻5) is a generalization of (K⁻5).

An immediate consequence of (P⁻2) and (P⁻5) is that, if $\vdash A$, then $P_A^- = P$. More substantial is the following lemma.

LEMMA 5.5   For all B, if $P_A^-(B) = 1$, then $P(B) = 1$.

This lemma shows that the set of sentences accepted in P_A^- is a *subclass* of the set of sentences accepted in P [and a proper subclass iff $P(A) = 1$ and not $\vdash A$]. Note that it follows immediately from this result that, if $P(A) = 1$, then $P_A^-(A) > 0$ (unless $P = P_\perp$).

The next lemma will be useful when the connections between contractions and revisions are established:

LEMMA 5.6   If $P \neq P_\perp$, then $P_A^- = P a (P_A^-)_{-A}^+$ [where $a = P_A^-(A)$ when $P(A) = 1$ and $a = 1$ otherwise].

Postulates (P⁻1)–(P⁻5) are called the *basic postulates* for contraction. The final postulate concerns the connection between P_A^- and $P_{A \& B}^-$:

(P⁻ 6)   If $P^-_{A \& B}(-A) > 0$, then $P^-_A(C/-A) = P^-_{A \& B}(C/-A)$ for all C.

In order to give a motivation for this postulate, we first repeat one of the arguments that was discussed in sections 5.2 and 5.3 as a justification for conditionalization: Unlike all other changes of P to make A certain, conditionalization does not distort the probability ratios, equalities, and inequalities among sentences that imply A.[7] In other words, the probability proportions among sentences that imply A are the same before and after conditionalization.

Contraction can be regarded as "backward" conditionalization, so a similar argument should be applicable to this process as well. More precisely, when contracting P with respect to A, some sentences that imply $-A$ receive nonzero probabilities, and, when contracting P with respect to $A \& B$, some sentences that imply $-A$ or some sentences that imply $-B$ (or both) receive nonzero probabilities. If, in the latter case, some sentences that imply $-A$ receive nonzero probabilities, that is, if $P^-_{A \& B}(-A) > 0$, then the two contractions should give the same proportions of probabilities to the sentences implying $-A$; that is, $P^-_A(C/-A)$ should be equal to $P^-_{A \& B}(C/-A)$ for all C. But this is exactly the content of (P⁻ 6). As will be seen in theorem 5.8, (P⁻ 6) is a generalization of (K⁻ 7) and (K⁻ 8) taken together.

The force of (P⁻ 6) can be illuminated by showing that, given the basic postulates, it is equivalent to both of the following two postulates:

(P⁻ D)   If $P^-_A(-A \& -B) > 0$, then $P^-_A(C/-A \& -B) = P^-_{A \vee B}(C/-A \& -B)$ for all C.

(P⁻ M)   If $P^-_A(-A \& -B) > 0$ and $P(A) = 1$, then $P^-_{A \vee B}(C) = P(C)[a\, P^-_A\, C/-(A \vee B)]$ for all C [where $a = P^-_{A \vee B}(A \vee B)$].

Admittedly these postulates are not perspicuous, but they will be useful in the discussions.

LEMMA 5.7   Given the basic postulates, (P⁻ 6), (P⁻ D), and (P⁻ M) are mutually equivalent.

Next I want to connect the set of postulates for probabilistic contractions with the analysis of contractions based on belief sets as presented in section 3.5. Recall that a belief set is a set K of sentences that contains all logically valid sentences and is closed under logical consequences. Let $\mathbf{K}$ denote the set of all belief sets. As before we let K^+_A denote the expansion of K with respect to A. Similarly, K^-_A denotes the contraction of K with respect to A. The following is a summary of the set of postulates presented in chapter 3:

(K⁻1) K_A^- is a belief set.

(K⁻2) $K_A^- \subseteq K$.

(K⁻3)   If $A \notin K$, then $K_A^- = K$.

(K⁻4)   If not $\vdash A$, then $A \notin K_A^-$.

(K⁻5)   If $A \in K$, then $K \subseteq (K_A^-)_A^+$.

(K⁻6)   If $\vdash A \leftrightarrow B$, then $K_A^- = K_B^-$.

(K⁻7) $K_A^- \cap K_B^- \subseteq K_{A \& B}^-$.

(K⁻8)   If $A \notin K_{A \& B}^-$, then $K_{A \& B}^- \subseteq K_A^-$.

We now define *the belief set K associated with P* as the set of sentences A such that $P(A) = 1$. It is easy to show that this set is indeed a belief set. We adopt the convention that, if K is the belief set associated with P, then K_A^- denotes the set associated with P_A^-. The essential connection between probability functions and belief sets is then given by the following theorem.

THEOREM 5.8   If a contraction function from $\mathbf{P} \times \mathbf{L}$ to $\mathbf{P}$ satisfies (P⁻1)–(P⁻5), then the contraction function from $\mathbf{K} \times \mathbf{L}$ to $\mathbf{K}$, defined by the associated belief sets, satisfies (K⁻1)–(K⁻6), and if (P⁻6) is satisfied, the corresponding contraction function satisfies (K⁻7) and (K⁻8).

5.8   Revisions of Probability Functions

In order to give a probabilistic interpretation of the revision process, I proceed in the same way as with contractions, presenting a set of postulates. As before, the revision process is represented by a function from $\mathbf{P} \times \mathbf{L}$ to $\mathbf{P}$. The value of such a *revision function*, when applied to arguments P and A, is called *the revision of P with respect to A*, and it is denoted P_A^*. The first postulate thus is

(P*1)   For all probability functions P and all sentences A, P_A^* is a probability function.

The second postulate is again a requirement of "success" to the effect that A indeed be accepted in the revised state of belief:

(P*2) $P_A^*(A) = 1$.

The third postulate is parallel to (P⁻3):

(P*3)   If $\vdash A \leftrightarrow B$, then $P_A^* = P_B^*$.

The fourth postulate says that, unless $-A$ is logically valid, P_A^* is a consistent state of belief:

(P*4) $P_A^* \neq P_\perp$ iff not $\vdash -A$.

The fifth postulate is based on the idea that, when revising P with respect to A, we want the change to be the minimal change needed to accept A. I assume for the rest of the chapter that, when A is consistent with P, that is, when $P(A) > 0$, the minimal change of P necessary to accept A is to conditionalize on A. Or, in the terminology of section 5.6, the revision function $*$ should be an extension of conditionalization:

(P*5)   If $P(A) > 0$, then $P_A^* = P_A^+$.

These five postulates are called the "basic postulates for revisions." They are complemented with one more postulate, connecting P_A^* with $P_{A \& B}^*$. The idea, again based on the minimality of changes, is that the revision of P to include both A and B, that is, $P_{A \& B}^*$, should be the same as the expansion of P_A^* by B, that is, $(P_A^*)_B^+$, whenever the expansion process can be applied without causing contradictions, that is, when $P_A^*(B) > 0$ [compare this with the motivation for (K*7) and (K*8)]:

(P*6)   If $P_A^*(B) > 0$, then $P_{A \& B}^* = (P_A^*)_B^+$.

This postulate can be illustrated with the aid of the same figure as in section 3.3. The only difference is that instead of having K's that are sets of possible worlds generating belief sets, we now have P's that are probability functions defined over the sets of possible worlds and that generate probability values of sentences.

In order to grasp the power of the postulate, first note that some of the basic postulates can be replaced with weaker ones if (P*6) is assumed: Postulate (P*2) is equivalent to the requirement that $P_A^*(A) > 0$, given (P*6); and (P*5) becomes equivalent to the trivial assumption that $P_A^* = P$ whenever A is logically valid. This means that (P*5) is, in essence, the special case of (P*6) when $\vdash A$.

The following requirement, which essentially is a consequence of (P*6), gives us an interesting way of identifying revisions [see expression (3.13)]:

(P*I)   If $P_A^*(B) = 1$ and $P_B^*(A) = 1$, then $P_A^* = P_B^*$.

LEMMA 5.9   If a revision function satisfies (P*1)–(P*6), it also satisfies (P*I).

The set of postulates (P*1)–(P*6) is essentially equivalent to Popper's axiomatization of conditional probability functions.[8] The principal difference is that Popper does not assume that the language has any underlying logic but builds logic into his postulates. It is possible to rewrite the present set of postulates also in this way, but I have chosen to presume a given logic for the language in order to simplify the presentation.[9]

Next I show that (P*6) is equivalent to the following requirement, which is a generalization of the mixture postulate (P⁺1) for expansions:

(P*M)   If $\vdash -(A \ \& \ B)$, then $P^*_{A \lor B} = P^*_A \ a \ P^*_B$ [where $a = P^*_{A \lor B}(A)$].

LEMMA 5.10   Given postulates (P*1)–(P*5), (P*6) is equivalent to (P*M).

The following simple consequence of the postulates will be useful in the next section.

LEMMA 5.11 $P^*_A = (P \ a \ P^*_A)^+_A$ (for any a).

Also, the postulates for probabilistic revisions are connected with the associated postulates for revisions of belief sets. If K is the belief set corresponding to the probability function P, then K^*_A denotes the belief set associated with P^*_A. The following is a summary of the set of postulates for revisions of belief sets given in chapter 3:

(K*1) K^*_A is a belief set.

(K*2) $A \in K^*_A$.

(K*3) $K^*_A \subseteq K^+_A$.

(K*4)   If $-A \notin K$, then $K^+_A \subseteq K^*_A$.

(K*5) $K^*_A = K_\perp$ iff $\vdash -A$.

(K*6)   If $\vdash A \leftrightarrow B$, then $K^*_A = K^*_B$.

(K*7) $K^*_{A \ \& \ B} \subseteq (K^*_A)^+_B$.

(K*8)   If $-B \notin K^*_A$, then $(K^*_A)^+_B \subseteq K^*_{A \ \& \ B}$.

As for contractions, it can be shown that postulates (P*1)–(P*6) are indeed generalizations to the probabilistic case of the postulates for belief sets.

THEOREM 5.12   If a revision function from $\mathbf{P} \times \mathbf{L}$ to $\mathbf{P}$ satisfies (P*1)–(P*5), then the revision function from $\mathbf{K} \times \mathbf{L}$ to $\mathbf{K}$ defined from the associated belief sets satisfies (K*1)–(K*6), and if (P*6) is satisfied, the corresponding revision function also satisfies (K*7) and (K*8).

5.9 From Contractions to Revisions and Vice Versa

In chapter 3 we saw how revisions of belief sets could be defined with the aid of contractions (and expansions) and vice versa. In this section I pursue a parallel project for revisions and contractions of probability functions. Levi advances the thesis that revisions can be analyzed as a series of contractions and expansions (see section 3.6). In the terminology of probability functions, this idea can be formulated more precisely as follows: In order to arrive at the revision P_A^* for a probability function P and a proposition A, one first contracts P with respect to $-A$ and then expands P_{-A}^- by A. Levi's thesis can thus be expressed by the identity

(Def P*) $P_A^* = (P_{-A}^-)_A^+$.

This identity gives us a definition of probabilistic revisions in terms of contractions and expansions.

As before, the crucial test of this definition is whether the defined revision function has the desired properties. This is established in the following theorem.

THEOREM 5.13   If a contraction function satisfies $(P^-1)–(P^-5)$, then the revision function generated by (Def P*) satisfies $(P*1)–(P*5)$, and, if the contraction function also satisfies (P^-6), then the revision function satisfies $(P*6)$.

This theorem shows that (Def P*) yields an appropriate revision function. I now turn to the converse problem of defining contractions in terms of revisions. The idea is that the beliefs in a contraction P_A^- can be described as a *mixture* of what is believed in P and what would be believed in the revision of P with respect to $-A$, that is, P_{-A}^*. This suggests the following definition:

(Def P$^-$) $P_A^- = P\,a\,P_{-A}^*$, where $1 > a$ iff $P(A) = 1$ and $a = 1$ otherwise.

In other words, P_A^- is a compromise between the states of belief represented by P and P_{-A}^*, where a is a measure of the degree of closeness to the beliefs in P. Note that for a given revision function (Def P$^-$) yields different contraction functions depending on the choice of a. Because it follows that $P_A^-(A) = a$, the choice of a determines that P_A^- is an a-contraction of P.

Again, we must check that (Def P$^-$) produces a contraction function with the right properties. And here also we have the following comforting result.

THEOREM 5.14   If a revision function satisfies (P*1)–(P*5), then the contraction function generated by (Def P⁻) satisfies (P⁻ 1)–(P⁻ 5), and, if the revision function also satisfies (P*6), the contraction function satisfies (P⁻ 6).

These two theorems show that (Def P*) and (Def P⁻) give satisfactory results. Next I show that the two definitions are, in a precise sense, *interchangeable*. First, lemma 5.6 entails that, if (Def P*) is applied in (Def P⁻), the resulting identity $P_A^- = P a (P_A^-)_{-A}^+$ shows that reconstructing a contraction in this way gives the original function back, as one would hope. Second, lemma 5.11 entails that, if (Def P⁻) is applied in (Def P*), the resulting identity $P_A^* = (P a P_A^*)_A^+$ shows that this reconstruction of the revision function also gives the original function back (this result is independent of the choice of a). These results, together with theorems 5.13 and 5.14, show that postulates (P⁻ 1)–(P⁻ 6) are essentially equivalent to postulates (P*1)–(P*6) and that either the contraction or the revision process can be taken as primitive.

5.10   Construction of Probabilistic Revision Functions

I next turn to the second strategy for tackling the problems of how probabilistic contraction and revision functions are to be described, namely, explicit *constructions*. I suggest some ways of defining a *revision* function and analyze their properties. The corresponding contraction functions are then assumed to be given by (Def P⁻). The concepts and results of this section are to a large extent inspired by van Fraassen (1976b) and Spohn (1986). There are obvious parallels with the constructions of contractions of belief sets discussed in chapter 4.

The first and most general construction idea assumes that, when constructing the revision P_A^* for a given probability function P and given sentence A, one uses a *selection function* that picks out an appropriate probability function.

(Def S)   A function S from $\mathbf{P} \times \mathbf{L}$ to $\mathbf{P}$ is a *(revision) selection function* iff (i) $S(P, A)(A) > 0$; (ii) $S(P, A) \neq P_\perp$ iff not $\vdash - A$; (iii) if $S(P, A)(B/A) > 0$ and $S(P, B)(A/B) > 0$, then $S(P, A) = S(P, B)$.

The idea here is that, if A and B are "compatible" in the sense stated in the antecedent of (iii), then the same probability function is selected for both of them.

To emphasize that S picks out a probability function, $S(P, A)$ is also denoted P_A^S. (Def S) may now be used to define a revision function:

(Def S*)   For all P and A, $P_A^*(C) = P_A^S(C/A)$ for all C.

This definition may not look very much like a constructive definition because it does not say anything about how the selection function is obtained. However, we can prove the following theorem.

THEOREM 5.15   If a revision function $*$ is generated from a selection function by means of (Def S*), then it satisfies (P*1)–(P*6).

Now a more interesting construction would give a recipe for how the selection function is determined. The second constructive step is to use a *well-ordering* to do the job (analogous to the ordering of maximal sets exploited in chapter 4). The ordering can be interpreted as an ordering of closeness [analogous to the similarity between possible worlds used by Lewis (1973b)], so that there is always a closest probability function where any given sentence A has positive probability.

(Def O)   A set $O(P)$ of probability functions is an *ordinal family for P* iff there is a well-ordering $<$ on $O(P)$ such that (i) P is the first element in the ordering and $P_\perp$ is the last; and (ii) for all A there is some P^a in $O(P)$ such that $P^a(A) > 0$ and $P^a \neq P_\perp$ iff not $\vdash -A$.

Given an ordinal family $O(P)$ for each probability function P, we can then define a revision function $*$ as follows:

(Def O*)   For all A, $P_A^*(C) = P^a(C/A)$, where P^a is the *first* function in $O(P)$ such that $P^a(A) > 0$.

LEMMA 5.16   Any revision function obtained from (Def O*) can be generated from some revision selection function by means of (Def S*).

COROLLARY 5.17   Any revision function generated from (Def O*) satisfies (P*1)–(P*6).

The drawback of using selection functions or ordinal families when defining revision functions is that these representations may use a great many probability functions. We would like to use a minimal family of probability functions in the construction of the revision function. An analogous problem in linear algebra is to find a minimal base for representing the vectors in a vector space. One way of ensuring that a base is minimal is to find an *orthogonal* set of vectors as a base. Also in probability theory there is a corresponding concept:

(Def !)   The probability functions P and P' are *orthogonal*, denoted $P \mathbin{!} P'$, iff there is some A such that $P(A) = 1$ while $P'(A) = 0$.

It is trivial that orthogonality is symmetrical, that is, $P \mathbin{!} P'$ iff $P' \mathbin{!} P$. For further properties of !, see Domotor (1983).

Let us now say that a revision selection function is orthogonal iff for any A and B either $P_A^S \mathbin{!} P_B^S$ or $P_A^S = P_B^S$. I now show that all revision functions that satisfy a completeness condition can be generated by an orthogonal revision selection function. To do this, we first need some auxiliary concepts.

(Def $\geqslant$*)   Suppose that $*$ is a revision function. We say that A (weakly) *dominates B in P*, denoted $A \geqslant^* B$, iff $P_{A \vee B}^*(A) > 0$.

LEMMA 5.18   If the revision function $*$ satisfies (P*1)–(P*6), then $\geqslant^*$ is connected and transitive for any P.

COROLLARY 5.19   The relation $=^*$ on $\mathbf{L}$, defined by $A =^* B$ iff $A \geqslant^* B$ and $B \geqslant^* A$, is an equivalence relation.

This corollary shows that $\geqslant^*$ partitions $\mathbf{L}$ into equivalence classes. Let $[A]$ denote the equivalence class containing A. We say that an equivalence class $[A]$ is *complete* iff there is an element A' in $[A]$ such that $P(A'/A) = 1$ for all A in $[A]$. In this case we say that A' is a *determiner* for $[A]$. This condition is equivalent to requiring that the (infinite) disjunction of the elements in $[A]$ is also in $[A]$. We can then formulate the following partial representation theorem.

THEOREM 5.20   Suppose that the revision function $*$ satisfies (P*1)–(P*6) and that the equivalence classes on $\mathbf{L}$ generated by $\geqslant^*$ are complete for all P. Then $*$ is generated by an orthogonal selection function.

The condition of completeness appealed to in this theorem is no doubt quite restrictive. However, my conjecture is that it cannot be dropped altogether. It remains an open question whether all revision functions satisfying (P*1)–(P*6) can be generated by an orthogonal revision selection function.[10]

Spohn (1986) has shown that a stronger representation theorem can be proved if it is assumed that all involved probability functions are σ-additive. In the terminology of this chapter it turns out that we can have both ordinality and orthogonality. The relevant notion, adapted from Spohn (1986), is the following:

(Def DO)   A class $\{P^a\}_{a<y}$ of probability functions is a *dimensional ordinal family for P* iff (i) $\{P^a\}_{a<y}$ is an ordinal family for P, and (ii) for all $b < y$ there is an A_b such that $P^b(A_b) = 1$ but $P^a(A_b) = 0$ for all $a < b$.

It follows immediately from the definition that all functions in a dimensional ordinal family are orthogonal to each other. By (i) we can also use (Def O*) to generate a revision function. It follows from corollary 5.17 that any revision function generated from a dimensional ordinal family satisfies (P*1)–(P*6). The objective is now to prove the converse of this result for the case when all probability functions in the class are σ-additive.

In order to formulate this concept, we need the assumption that **L** is complete, that is, closed, under infinite disjunctions and conjunctions (see section 2.2).

(Def σ)   A probability function is σ-*additive* iff for any class $\{A_i\}_{i<w}$ of propositions in **L**, $P(A_\vee) = \sup_f(P(A_f))$, where A_f is a finite disjunction of elements from $\{A_i\}_{i<w}$ and where $A_\vee$ is the (infinite) disjunction of the entire class $\{A_i\}_{i<w}$.

LEMMA 5.21   If the revision function $*$ satisfies (P*1)–(P*6) and if all probability functions are σ-additive, then, for any P, $>^*$ is a well-ordering. ($A >^* B$ means, of course, $A \geqslant^* B$ but not $B \geqslant^* A$.)

The final step for the representation theorem is then to use this well-ordering to construct a dimensional ordinal family.

THEOREM 5.22   If the revision function $*$ satisfies (P*1)–(P*6) and if all probability functions are σ-additive, then $*$ is generated by a dimensional ordinal function.

In summary, the last result, together with corollary 5.17, shows that, if the language is rich enough to allow the probability functions to be σ-additive, then a revision function satisfies (P*1)–(P*6) iff it is generated by a dimensional ordinal family.

II APPLICATIONS

6 The Dynamics of Belief As a Basis for Logic

6.1 Propositions Defined from Possible Worlds

The proper objects of logic are not sentences but the contents of sentences, that is, *propositions*. Thus, in order to understand what logic is about, one needs a theory of propositions. Nowadays, the best known account of propositions is in terms of possible worlds. On that account a proposition is identified with the set of possible worlds in which it is true. However, because I want to avoid the possible worlds ontology as much as possible, I prefer having a theory of propositions based on more epistemic notions.

The goal of this chapter is to present and develop a definition of propositions in terms of the dynamics of belief. This definition is used as a basis for a reconstruction of propositional logic. The central idea is to identify propositions with certain kinds of expansions of belief. On this interpretation a proposition is characterized by the change it would induce if it were added to an epistemic state. Technically this means that propositions are defined as *functions* with epistemic states as arguments and values.

As a background for the new definition, I briefly discuss the possible worlds account of propositions. This theory of propositions is perhaps best presented in the writings of Robert Stalnaker and David Lewis.[1] Within philosophy of language one traditionally distinguishes the extension from the intension of a linguistic expression. If it is assumed as an ontological basis that there is a given domain W of possible worlds, then precise definitions of what is meant by "extension" and "intension" can be given: The *extension* of an expression is determined relative to a possible world—it is what is denoted by the expression in that possible world; the *intension* of an expression is identified as the *rule* by which the extension is determined. In particular, if one specifies the extension of a sentence to be a truth value, then the intension of a sentence is a function taking possible worlds into truth values. The *proposition* expressed by a sentence is then defined as the intension of that sentence. And if it is assumed that there are only two truth values, an equivalent way of formulating this definition is to say that the proposition expressed by a sentence is a set of possible worlds, namely, the set of worlds in which the sentence has the extension 'true'.

With this definition of a proposition, it is easy to see how the *logic* of propositions can be generated. By using standard set-theoretical operations, we can form composite propositions: The conjunction of two propositions is represented by the intersection of the sets of possible worlds representing the propositions; the disjunction is represented by the union of the sets; the negation of a proposition is represented by the complement relative to W of the set; etc. As is easily seen, this way of constructing the standard logical connectives results in classical truth-functional logic. The underlying reason is simply that the logic of the set-theoretical operations is classical. In this sense we see how the *ontology* used when defining propositions *determines* the logic of propositions.

This way of constructing logic may seem natural—in fact, it is probably how we learned propositional logic in the first place: by using Venn diagrams, etc. In the remainder of this chapter I present an alternative theory of propositions using epistemic states and their dynamics as an ontological basis. As it turns out, the underlying logic is somewhat different.

6.2   Propositions Defined by Changes of Belief

According to the analysis presented in chapter 1, an epistemic state changes only as the result of an epistemic input. Depending on what type of model of an epistemic state is chosen, these inputs may take different forms. In a sense the epistemic inputs can be seen as idealized representations of an agent's perceptual experiences.

Another more abstract way of looking at epistemic inputs is to identify an input with the change it induces in various epistemic states. Formally this idea can be expressed by defining an epistemic input as a function from epistemic states to epistemic states. This definition has the advantage that it makes unnecessary a more precise description of what epistemic inputs are. Consequently we need not discuss the ontology of epistemic inputs. On this approach the only entities that need to be assumed are epistemic states and functions defined on epistemic states.

The guiding idea behind the suggested definition of epistemic inputs is that, when a function representing a certain input A is applied to a given epistemic state K, the value of the function is the state that would be the result of accommodating A to K. On this level of abstraction, if two inputs always produce the same new epistemic state, that is, if the inputs are identical as functions, then there is no reason to distinguish them, but they will be regarded as identical inputs.[2] This way of defining epistemic inputs is analogous to defining events by means of changes of physical states—an event is something that takes one physical state into another.

It should be noted that the definition of an epistemic input as a function from epistemic states to epistemic states, does not presume any particular model of epistemic states. The epistemic states can be regarded simply as points in a space. In this chapter there are absolutely no assumptions about the structure of states of belief. Thus all the models presented in chapter 2 are compatible with the present analysis of epistemic inputs. However, it should be noted that most models of epistemic states in chapter 2 presume some form of logic.

The most important type of input for models of epistemic states is the acceptance of new evidence as certain or "known" in the resulting epistemic state. In the simplest cases the induced changes can be modeled as expansions, and in this chapter I concentrate on expansions, postponing contractions and revisions to section 6.6.

Often an expansion of an agent's epistemic state occurs as a result of the agent's accepting the content of a sentence, that is, a proposition. Thus a proposition that leads to an expansion is a particular kind of epistemic input. Following the general identification of epistemic inputs, we can now formulate the following key definition:

(Def Prop)   A proposition is a function from epistemic states to epistemic states.

This definition is the point of departure for the reconstruction of propositional logic from the dynamics of belief. Functions representing propositions are denoted $A, B, \ldots$ just as before, and the result of applying the function A to an epistemic state K is denoted $A(K)$ (this is a new epistemic state). It is important to keep in mind that *not all* functions defined on states of belief are called propositions. Propositions form a subclass of the epistemic inputs that result in expansions, that is, when new evidence is accepted as certain and in particular as a consequence of linguistic communication. The main task in front of us is to give a more precise characterization of the class of propositions. I do this by introducing a set of postulates that guarantee the existence of operations corresponding to the standard logical connectives. Before this is done, we cannot speak of the logic of propositions.

In passing, I present a simple application of the definition of a proposition. Let A be a proposition, that is, a function defined on epistemic states. A is said to be *accepted as known* in the epistemic state K if and only if $A(K) = K$. In other words, this identity says that, if the function corresponding to the epistemic input A is applied to K, then the resulting state of belief is K itself: Adding A has no effect on K. The relation 'A is accepted in K' will play a central role in the theory to be presented, parallel to the role of the relation 'A is true in the world w' for the possible worlds analysis of propositions.

6.3   Basic Postulates for Propositions

In this section the class of epistemic inputs that can be identified with propositions is characterized by a set of postulates. In order to formulate these postulates, we need, first, a definition of the basic epistemic structure. A *belief model* is a pair $\langle \mathbf{K}, \mathbf{Prop} \rangle$, where $\mathbf{K}$ is a set of epistemic states and **Prop** is a class of functions from $\mathbf{K}$ to $\mathbf{K}$. The elements of $\mathbf{K}$ are called epistemic states, and they are denoted K, K', ... as usual. It should be noted that nothing is assumed about the structure of the elements in $\mathbf{K}$; in particular, they are not assumed to be belief sets. The elements in **Prop** are called propositions. A, B, C, ... are used as variables over **Prop**. The class **Prop** is intended to represent the class of propositions relevant to the epistemic states in $\mathbf{K}$. The goal is to pick out properties of propositions that distinguish them from other forms of epistemic inputs. This is done by a series of postulates, most of which assume that **Prop** has certain closure properties.

The first assumption is that the epistemic inputs corresponding to propositions can be iterated and that the *composition* of two such inputs is also a proposition. The composition of two propositions A and B is denoted $A \& B$. Note that $A \& B$ does not denote a linguistic entity but a *function* from epistemic states to epistemic states. Formally this requirement is expressed in the following postulate:

(P1)   For every A and B in a belief model $\langle \mathbf{K}, \mathbf{Prop} \rangle$, there is a function $A \& B$ that is also in **Prop** such that $A \& B(K) = A(B(K))$ for every K in $\mathbf{K}$.

It follows from this postulate that the composition operation is associative, that is, that $A \& (B \& C)(K) = (A \& B) \& C(K)$ for all A, B, and C in **Prop** and all K in $\mathbf{K}$.

It is also postulated that the composition operation is commutative and idempotent:

(P2)   For every A and B and K in a belief model $\langle \mathbf{K}, \mathbf{Prop} \rangle$, $A \& B(K) = B \& A(K)$.

(P3) For every A and every K in a belief model $\langle \mathbf{K}, \mathbf{Prop} \rangle$, $A \, \& \, A(K) = A(K)$.

Obviously these postulates are not valid for epistemic inputs in general. Often what is important is the order of inputs for which the epistemic state is the result. Similarly, iterations of the same input often have a cumulative effect (this is one thing that distinguishes nagging from informing). However, on the idealized interpretation of propositions—as expansions of knowledge resulting in the acceptance of evidence as certain—these postulates are reasonable requirements. Furthermore, it will turn out that they have a great simplifying effect on the technical derivations.

If A is accepted as known in K, that is, if $A(K) = K$, and $K' = B(K)$ for some B, then it follows from (P2) that A is accepted as known in K' also, because $A(K') = A(B(K)) = A \, \& \, B(K) = B \, \& \, A(K) = B(A(K)) = B(K) = K'$. Consequently epistemic changes represented by propositions in a belief model are *monotonic* in the sense that, once a proposition is accepted as known, it will be accepted in all later epistemic states (so long as the epistemic inputs are propositions). This is of course as it should be, for my aim is to model propositional inputs resulting in expansions of belief. However, when dealing with contractions and revisions in the final section of this chapter, (P2) can, of course, not be assumed to be valid.

We can now introduce a relation of *logical consequence* between propositions: A proposition B is a consequence of a proposition A in a belief model $\langle \mathbf{K}, \mathbf{Prop} \rangle$ iff $B(A(K)) = A(K)$ for all K in $\mathbf{K}$. An equivalent way of formulating this is to say that B is a consequence of A iff B is accepted as known whenever A is accepted as known. With the aid of this fundamental notion, we can define further logical concepts: A proposition D is said to be a *strongest* (resp. *weakest*) proposition in a class of propositions iff all propositions in the class are consequences of D (resp. have D as a consequence). It follows from (P2) that, if a class has a strongest (or weakest) proposition, then it is unique as a function. To see this, assume that both A and B in the same class of propositions are strongest. Then B is a consequence of A, that is, $B(A(K)) = B \, \& \, A(K) = A(K)$ for all K in $\mathbf{K}$. Similarly, because A is a consequence of B, we know that $A(B(K)) = A \, \& \, B(K) = B(K)$ for all K in $\mathbf{K}$. But then it follows from (P2) that $A(K) = B(K)$ for all K in $\mathbf{K}$, so A is identical with B. That there is a unique weakest proposition in a class, if any, is shown in a similar way.

To simplify the notation, I henceforth use $A = B$ to mean that $A(K) = $

$B(K)$ for all K in $\mathbf{K}$. This simplification is unproblematic so long as the discussion concerns only one belief model at a time.

For mainly technical reasons the identity function, here denoted by $\top$, is assumed to be a proposition:

(P4)   The identity function $\top$, defined by $\top(K) = K$ for all K in $\mathbf{K}$, is in any belief model $\langle \mathbf{K}, \mathbf{Prop} \rangle$.

This function will play a central role when the *logic* of propositions is discussed. Let us say that a proposition A is a *tautology* in the belief model $\langle \mathbf{K}, \mathbf{Prop} \rangle$ iff $A = \top$, that is, $A(K) = \top(K)$ for all K in $\mathbf{K}$. A central question is then, What propositional forms are tautologies in all belief models? However, before a substantial answer to this question can be given, some further postulates are necessary.

The next postulate is a formal characterization of the information obtained when one learns that one thing *implies* another (or is *equivalent* to another). The idea behind the postulate can be expressed as follows: If one comes to accept the proposition 'if A, then B' as certain, then this knowledge may not directly influence one's behavior, but one will be *disposed* to accept B if A is later accepted as certain. A similar account can be given for a proposition of the form 'A if and only if B'. In order to describe this kind of change of belief in a formal manner, I borrow a concept from category theory:[3]

(P5)   For every A and B in a belief model $\langle \mathbf{K}, \mathbf{Prop} \rangle$, the class of functions D that satisfy the equation $A \mathbin{\&} D = B \mathbin{\&} D$ has a weakest element.

A function D that satisfies the equation in (P5) is in category theory called an *equalizer* of A and B. In the present context the name suits well because if D is accepted, it will equalize the further information that can be obtained from A or B. We know already that for any propositions A and B there is a unique equalizer of A and B. The proposition postulated in (P5) can thus be given a well-defined name: The equalizer of A and B is denoted $A \leftrightarrow B$. From this we define the proposition $A \rightarrow B$ that corresponds to the information that A implies B by the following equation:

(Def $\rightarrow$) $(A \rightarrow B)(K) = (A \leftrightarrow (A \mathbin{\&} B))(K)$ for all K in $\mathbf{K}$.

I have now introduced enough postulates to be able to start investigating which propositions are tautologies in the sense defined. When determining which propositional forms are tautologies in all belief models, the following lemma is extremely helpful:

LEMMA 6.1   For any belief model $\langle \mathbf{K}, \mathbf{Prop} \rangle$ and any propositions A, B, and C in $\langle \mathbf{K}, \mathbf{Prop} \rangle$, $B \& A = C \& A$ iff $(B \leftrightarrow C) \& A = A$.

COROLLARY 6.2   For any belief model $\langle \mathbf{K}, \mathbf{Prop} \rangle$ and any propositions A and B in $\langle \mathbf{K}, \mathbf{Prop} \rangle$, $A = B$ iff $A \leftrightarrow B = \top$.

With the aid of this corollary it is now possible to determine some propositional forms that are tautologies in all belief models. It is easy to show that all instances of the following proposition schemas are tautologies in all models:

(6.1) $(A \& B) \to A$.

(6.2) $(A \& B) \to B$.

(6.3) $(A \to B) \to ((A \to C) \to (A \to (B \& C)))$.

(6.4) $(A \to (B \to C)) \to ((A \to B) \to (A \to C))$.

(6.5) $A \to (B \to A)$.

Recall that the formulas (6.1)–(6.5) are not sentences but functions defined on epistemic states. It is also easy to show that modus ponens preserves tautologies in the sense that, if A and $A \to B$ are tautologies in a belief model, then B is also a tautology in that model. These facts are significant when answering the question of which logic is determined by the postulates for propositions.

6.4   Negation and Disjunction

So far the postulates that have been introduced concern only composition of propositions, corresponding to conjunction, and equalizers, corresponding to equivalence (or implication). I now turn to postulates for propositions corresponding to negation and disjunction.

The negation of a proposition is defined by first assuming the existence of a falsity proposition:

(P6)   In every belief model $\langle \mathbf{K}, \mathbf{Prop} \rangle$ there are a constant function $\bot$ and a belief state $K_\bot$ such that $\bot(K) = K_\bot$ for all K in $\mathbf{K}$.

$K_\bot$ is called the *absurd epistemic state*. With the aid of (P2) it is easy to show that $\bot$ is the only constant function in **Prop**: Assume that $*$ is a function and K_* an epistemic state such that $*(K) = K_*$ for all K in **K**. It then follows from (P2) that $K_* = *(\bot(K)) = \bot(*(K)) = K_\bot$. The interpretation of the proposition $\bot$ is then given by the fact that it is accepted as known only in the absurd epistemic state $K_\bot$. Furthermore $K_\bot$ is an *attractor state* in the sense that no further propositional input can lead out of it, because for any A in **Prop**, $A(K_\bot) = A(\bot(K)) = \bot(A(K)) = K_\bot$.

As is standard in propositional logic, the negation $-A$ of a proposition A can now be defined as the proposition $A \to \bot$.

From (P6) it follows that all propositions of the following form are tautologies in all belief models:

(6.6) $\bot \to A$.

The postulate for disjunction is in the same style as the postulate concernining equalizers. The rationale for the postulate is that, when one first obtains the information that A or B and then later comes to accept A as known, the net effect is the same as merely adding A to what one accepts (and analogously for B). This is one property that is used to characterize the disjunction of two propositions. The other property is that the disjunction is the strongest proposition with the property mentioned. Formally this is expressed as follows:

(P7)   For every A and B in a belief model $\langle$**K**, **Prop**$\rangle$, the class of functions D that satisfy both the equations $D \& A = A$ and $D \& B = B$ has a strongest element.

Using the result of the previous section, we know that there is a unique strongest function satisfying the equations. This function is called the disjunction of A and B, and it is denoted $A \lor B$.

With the aid of (P7) and the earlier postulates it is now easy to establish that all propositions of the following forms are tautologies in all belief models:

(6.7) $A \to (A \lor B)$.

(6.8) $B \to (A \lor B)$.

(6.9) $(A \to C) \to ((B \to C) \to ((A \lor B) \to C))$.

6.5 Completeness Results

I have now introduced postulates for operations of propositions that correspond to each of the standard sentential connectives. In this section

I present some technical results that answer the question of which logic is determined by these postulates.

The propositional schemata (6.1)–(6.9) are not sentences in a formal language but functions defined on epistemic states. Given the postulates (P1)–(P7) there is, of course, an obvious correspondence between the propositions in a belief model and the sentences in a standard propositional language ($\top$ and $\bot$ are sentential constants in this language). This entails that we can consider the propositions that are tautologies in a given belief model as a class of sentences and then ask how the formulas that are included in all such classes can be axiomatized. Let us say that a logic **L** is *determined* by a class of belief models **M** iff for any propositional schema S all substitution instances of S (interpreted as functions in belief models) are tautologies in all belief models in **M** exactly when all instances of S (interpreted as formulas in a propositional language) are theorems in **L**.

If interpreted as sentence schemata, the formulas (6.1)–(6.9), together with modus ponens as the only inference rule, constitute an axiomatization of *intuitionistic* propositional logic [see Segerberg (1968)]. All instances of these schemata are tautologies in all belief models, and, as was mentioned earlier, modus ponens preserves tautologies. This means that the logic determined by postulates (P1)–(P7) includes the intuitionistic propositional logic. In fact, I now show that the logic determined by these postulates is *exactly* the intuitionistic logic. This is accomplished by showing that belief models are equivalent to the *algebraic semantics* of intuitionistic logic, that is, that of pseudo-Boolean algebras.[4]

(Def PBA)   A *pseudo-Boolean algebra* (PBA) is a pair $\langle \mathbf{B}, \leqslant \rangle$, where **B** is a nonempty set and $\leqslant$ is a partial ordering on **B** such that for any two elements a and b of **B**: (i) the least upper bound $a \cup b$ exists; (ii) the greatest lower bound $a \cap b$ exists; (iii) the pseudo-complement $a \Rightarrow b$ of a relative to b, defined to be the largest x in **B** such that $a \cap x \leqslant b$, exists; (iv) a least element, 0, exists.

The element 1 in a PBA is defined as $0 \Rightarrow 0$.

In order to establish the proper correspondence between belief models and pseudo-Boolean algebras, let us first suppose that we have a PBA $\langle \mathbf{B}, \leqslant \rangle$. I show how to construct an equivalent belief model. Let $\mathbf{K} = \mathbf{B}$. For any a in **B**, the function P^a is defined by $P^a(x) = a \cap x$ for any x in **B**. Let **Prop** be the class of such functions P^a. That this definition of the model

$\langle \mathbf{K}, \mathbf{Prop} \rangle$ is satisfactory is shown in the following lemma:[5]

LEMMA 6.3 $\langle \mathbf{K}, \mathbf{Prop} \rangle$ is a belief model that satisfies (P1)–(P7) and, for any a in $\mathbf{K}$, $a = 1$ iff $P^a = \top$.

In order to establish the converse correspondence, let us next assume that we have a belief model $\langle \mathbf{K}, \mathbf{Prop} \rangle$. We construct an equivalent PBA. The objects in $\mathbf{B}$ are the *ranges* of the functions in $\mathbf{Prop}$; that is, $a \in \mathbf{B}$ iff there is some function A in $\mathbf{Prop}$ such that a is the range of A. The range of A is denoted C_A. Note that it follows from (P3) that $K \in C_A$ iff $A(K) = K$. The ordering relation $\leqslant$ is defined to be standard set inclusion $\subseteq$.

LEMMA 6.4 $\langle \mathbf{B}, \leqslant \rangle$ is a PBA such that $A = \top$ iff $C_A = 1$.

In the construction of the PBA for this lemma, the only information about the elements in $\mathbf{Prop}$ that is used is their ranges. That this is sufficient may be surprising, but it can be shown that the propositions in $\mathbf{Prop}$ can be identified with their ranges in the following sense: If two propositions have the same range in a belief model $\langle \mathbf{K}, \mathbf{Prop} \rangle$, then they are identical as functions in $\langle \mathbf{K}, \mathbf{Prop} \rangle$. To see this, assume that A, $B \in \mathbf{Prop}$ and that $C_A = C_B$. Then for any K in $\mathbf{K}$, $B(K) \in C_A$ and $A(K) \in C_B$. It follows from (P2) and (P3) that $A(K) = B \& A(K) = A \& B(K) = B(K)$ for all K in $\mathbf{K}$ and hence that $A = B$. This way of identifying propositions brings out the close connection between the constructions in lemmas 6.3 and 6.4.

We have now arrived at the central theorem of this chapter.

THEOREM 6.5   The class of all belief models satisfying (P1)–(P7) determines the intuitionistic propositional logic $\mathbf{I}$.

The philosophical interest of this theorem depends on the strength of the arguments in favor of postulates (P1)–(P7). When formulating these postulates, I have given each of the traditional sentential connectives an independent interpretation (except, of course, for the interdefinability of equivalence and implication). When I formulated the postulates, I aimed at capturing the informational force of the connectives by choosing characteristic functional equations.

It is interesting to note that, if we pick out the postulates for propositions that concern $\&$ and $\rightarrow$ (or $\leftrightarrow$) only, that is, (P1)–(P5), then it follows from the so-called separation theorem for intuitionistic logic that the logic determined by these postulates is axiomatized by the propositional schemata that contain only these connectives, that is, (6.1)–(6.5).[6] Similarly, the logic generated by (P1)–(P6), which concerns &, →, and −, is axiomatized by the formulas that concern these connectives only, that is, (6.1)–(6.6); and the logic generated by (P1)–(P5) and (P7) (&, →, and ∨) is axiomatized by (6.1)–(6.5) together with (6.7)–(6.9), which incidentally is an axiomatization of Johansson's minimal logic [see Segerberg (1968, p. 30)].

In order to arrive at *classical* propositional logic, we need one more postulate for the class of propositions in a belief model. The following additional requirement on equalizers is easy to understand given the interpretation of propositions as corresponding to the acceptance of new evidence in an epistemic state:

(P8)   For every A and B in a belief model $\langle \mathbf{K}, \mathbf{Prop} \rangle$, $A \leftrightarrow B = (-A) \leftrightarrow (-B)$.

Or in other words, the information that, if added to a state of belief, equalizes A and B also equalizes $-A$ and $-B$.

We can now prove the following theorem.

THEOREM 6.6   The class of all belief models that satisfy (P1)–(P8) determines the classical propositional logic $\mathbf{C}$.

Alternatively (P8) may be replaced by the following postulate.[7]

(P9)   For every A, B, and C in a belief model $\langle \mathbf{K}, \mathbf{Prop} \rangle$, $A \leftrightarrow (B \leftrightarrow C) = (A \leftrightarrow B) \leftrightarrow C$.

This postulate, which requires that the equalizer ↔ be associative, is perhaps more in line with the interpretation in terms of category theory. To see that (P9) also generates classical logic, it is sufficient to replace both B and C with ⊥: By means of the definition of negation, (P9) then reduces to $A = --A$.

As a simple application, let us return to expansions of belief sets as presented in section 3.2. If we, for any *sentence* A in such a system of belief sets, define a *function* A^+ by the equation $A^+(K) = K_A^+$, it is easy to show that the resulting class of functions (with the obvious structure of connectives) satisfies postulates (P1)–(P8) and thus forms a *model* of these postulates. This model, however, does not give us anything new because the definition of belief sets already presumes a relation ⊢ of logical consequence that satisfies classical propositional logic.

6.6   Propositions Corresponding to Contractions and Revisions

So far, only propositions corresponding to epistemic inputs leading to expansions of an epistemic state have been considered. The main aim of this section is to introduce propositions defined as epistemic inputs leading to contractions or revisions. To a large extent the analysis is based on the results in chapter 3.

In line with (Def Prop) an epistemic input leading to a contraction is conceived of as a function from epistemic states to epistemic states. To be more precise, if the epistemic input is 'delete A' (contract with respect to A), then the corresponding proposition is the function that takes K into K_A^- for any K in **K**. Let us denote this function by $\bar{A}$.

We can then formulate the following definition:

(Def Prop⁻)   A contraction-extended belief model is a triple $\langle \mathbf{K}, \mathbf{Prop}, \mathbf{Prop}^- \rangle$, where (i) $\langle \mathbf{K}, \mathbf{Prop} \rangle$ is a belief model satisfying (P1)–(P8); (ii) **Prop⁻** is a class of functions from K to K such that $\mathbf{Prop} \subseteq \mathbf{Prop}^-$; (iii) for each A in **Prop** there is an $\bar{A}$ in **Prop⁻** (not in **Prop**, unless $A = \top$).

We can now supplement this definition with some postulates for the contraction functions A, corresponding to the postulates (K^-1)–(K^-6) in chapter 3. The content of (K^-1) is a consequence of (ii) and (iii) in the definition. Postulate (K^-2) can be reformulated as

(6.10)   For all K in **K** and for any B in **Prop**, if $B(\bar{A}(K)) = \bar{A}(K)$, then $B(K) = K$.

Or in other words, if B is accepted as known in $\bar{A}(K)$, it is also accepted as known in K. Postulates (K^-3), (K^-4), and (K^-5) become, respectively (conventionally put $\bar{\top} = \top$):

(6.11)   If $A(K) \neq K$, then $\bar{A}(K) = K$.
(6.12)   If $A \neq \top$, then $A(\bar{A}(K)) \neq \bar{A}(K)$.
(6.13)   If $A(K) = K$, then $A(\bar{A}(K)) = K$.

The content of (K^-6) is also built into Def Prop⁻ by means of the way of identifying propositions with their corresponding functions.

It follows from (6.11) and (6.12) that, if $A \neq \top$, then $\bar{A} \circ \bar{A}(K) = \bar{A}(K)$ (where "∘" means functional composition), which thus corresponds to (P3)

in the postulates for the class **Prop**. It should be noted that we cannot require the correspondence of (P2) for contraction functions because it is not generally the case that $\bar{A} \circ \bar{B}(K) = \bar{B} \circ \bar{A}(K)$. This fact is, of course, closely connected with the nonmonotonicity of the contraction operation on epistemic states.

Following the ideas in section 3.6, we can now define for each A in **Prop** a revision function A^* with the aid of the contraction function $\bar{A}$:

(Def P*) $A^* = A \circ \overline{-A}$.

From this definition we can then derive the following postulates, which correspond to the contents of postulates (K^*1)–(K^*6) for revisions of belief sets:

(6.14) $A(A^*(K)) = A^*(K)$.

(6.15)   If $-A(K) \neq K$, then $A^*(K) = A(K)$.

(6.16) $A^* = \perp$ iff $A = \perp$.

A consequence of these postulates that is of particular interest for the analysis of conditional sentences in the next chapter is the following lemma.

LEMMA 6.7   If $A \to B$ is accepted as known in $\bar{A}(K)$, then B is accepted as known in $A^*(K)$.

Instead of defining propositional functions corresponding to revisions as in (Def P*), we can of course introduce revision directly:

(Def Prop*)   A revision-extended belief model is a triple $\langle \mathbf{K}, \mathbf{Prop}, \mathbf{Prop^*} \rangle$, where (i) $\langle \mathbf{K}, \mathbf{Prop} \rangle$ is a belief model satisfying (P1)–(P8); (ii) **Prop*** is a class of functions from K to K such that **Prop** $\subseteq$ **Prop***; (iii) for each A in **Prop** there is an A^* in **Prop***.

This time we do not require that A^* not be in **Prop**. We can now supplement this definition with (6.14)–(6.16) as postulates [rather than seeing them as consequences of (Def Prop$^-$)].

However, it should be noted that, starting from revisions, we cannot automatically define contractions by translating (Def $-$) of section 3.6 into the terminology of functions defined on epistemic states. The reason is that I have explicitly avoided making any assumptions concerning the structure of epistemic states. And (Def $-$) presumes that we can form the intersection of two epistemic states. If we are working with belief sets, we know that the intersection of two belief sets is a belief set, but in general it may not be possible to find any operation on a particular model of epistemic states that corresponds to the intersection operation on belief sets. This may be a reason for considering contraction to be a more fundamental process than revision.

6.7   Concluding Remarks

In this chapter I have shown how propositional logic can be constructed from the dynamics of belief. The key idea for the construction is the definition of a proposition as a function representing changes of belief. This forms the conceptual basis for the postulates for propositions. The postulates are of an existential character in the sense that, for each of the operations on propositions that correspond to the sentential connectives, there is a postulate that only assumes the existence of the compound propositions. To wit, these postulates are (P1), (P5), (P6), and (P7). [The postulates (P2) and (P3) are exceptions because they impose further restrictions on the conjunction operation.] These postulates give us an independent interpretation of each of the sentential connectives.

The ontological basis of the construction is meager. The only entities that have been assumed to exist are epistemic states and functions defined on epistemic states. In order to emphasize this further, let me mention some things that have *not* been assumed: First, it is not necessary that there be an object language that expresses the propositions to be studied. In a sense, this chapter shows how to do logic without a language. To be sure, this has been done before; see, for example, the polyadic algebras of Halmos (1962). Second, no (formal) set theory has been used, but all constructions have been expressed solely in terms of functions. Of course, the functions used here can be given a set-theoretical basis, but this does not seem to add anything to our understanding of the underlying structure. Third, it can be noted that the construction does not in any way use the concept of a possible world.

The fact that only some objects (called epistemic states) and functions on these objects have been used reminds one of *category theory*. The concept of an equalizer has in fact been borrowed from that theory. It should be noted here that in this chapter no structure whatsoever has been assumed for the epistemic states.

Mathematically the construction is but a simple exercise in category theory. On the other hand, the construction uses only a small part of the conceptual apparatus of that theory.[8] It is my hope that the construction presented here may be helpful for understanding why intuitionistic logic is the logic of category theory, because theorem 6.5 indicates that intuitionistic logic comes out more naturally in the present setting.

Except for the postulates in section 6.6, all the other postulates are motivated by the suggested interpretation of propositions as representing the addition of new accepted evidence to a state of belief. There are, however, other kinds of epistemic input that do not fit this interpretation and that do not satisfy the postulates introduced here. As discussed in section 1.4, van Fraassen (1980b) presents some other types of inputs for the Bayesian model of epistemic states. He also discusses the problem of how states of belief ought to change in response to these kinds of input. An open question is whether it is possible to formulate postulates of the same kind as those for other kinds of epistemic input. On analogy with the construction here, these kinds of input would correspond to other types of functions on epistemic states. It may turn out that, in order to formulate such postulates, it may be necessary to require that the epistemic states have some additional structure, for example, as in the Bayesian models described in section 2.7.

7 Conditionals

7.1 The Ramsey Test for Conditionals

The starting hypothesis of this chapter is that conditional sentences in various forms are about changes of states of belief. The goal is to investigate whether it is possible to develop an epistemic semantic model for conditional sentences based on the dynamics of belief. My aim is not to provide truth conditions for conditional propositions; rather, I want to formulate *criteria of acceptability* for different types of conditional sentences. These criteria are formulated in terms of changes of epistemic states.

The form of conditional sentence that is central here is 'If A were the case, then C would be the case' or 'If A is the case, then C is (will be) the case', where A may or may not contradict what is already accepted in given epistemic state K. If A contradicts what is accepted in K, the conditional is called a *counterfactual* (relative to K); otherwise it is called an *open conditional* (relative to K). Thus it is not primarily the linguistic form of the antecedent A of a conditional (for example, whether it is formulated in the subjunctive or in the indicative mood) that determines the status but the epistemic attitude toward A. Other forms of conditional statements are discussed in section 7.3.

The epistemic semantics for counterfactuals and open conditionals is based on F. P. Ramsey's test for evaluating a conditional sentence. His test can be described as follows: In order to find out whether a conditional sentence is acceptable in a given state of belief, one first adds the antecedent of the conditional hypothetically to the given stock of beliefs. Second, if the antecedent together with the formerly accepted sentences leads to a contradiction, then one makes some adjustments, which are as small as possible without modifying the hypothetical belief in the antecedent, such that consistency is maintained. Finally, one considers whether or not the consequent of the conditional is then accepted in this adjusted state of belief.[1] The Ramsey test can be summarized by the following rule:

(RT) Accept a sentence of the form 'If A, then C' in a state of belief K if and only if the minimal change of K needed to accept A also requires accepting C.

This test has attracted a great deal of attention as a possible starting point for a formal semantics of conditionals.[2] Ginsberg (1986) argues that a formal semantics for counterfactuals is of great value for many problem areas within AI, in particular, because they form the core of nonmonotonic inferences.

The Ramsey test presumes some method of *revising* states of belief. Given the analysis of belief revisions in chapter 3, we see that it is natural to reformulate the test in a more condensed way:

(RT) $A > C \in K$ iff $C \in K_A^*$.

Note that this formulation presupposes that sentences of the form $A > C$ belong to the object language and that they can be *elements* of the belief sets in a belief revision model. Let us call this extended object language $\mathbf{L}'$. This presupposition is questioned in section 7.4.

More precisely, it is assumed that $\mathbf{L}'$ is the minimal extension of $\mathbf{L}$ closed under the conditional operator $>$ and that the underlying logic, determined by $\vdash$, satisfies the same assumptions as in section 2.2. Because the structure of $\mathbf{L}'$ is thus scanty, it is not possible to fill in any details in the analysis of counterfactuals. In particular, all *temporal* aspects of conditionals are left aside, because there are no means for distinguishing different tenses in $\mathbf{L}'$. For analyses of the logical relations between time and conditionals, see Thomason and Gupta (1980) and van Fraassen (1976a).

7.2   The Logic of Conterfactuals

The concise formulation of the Ramsey test makes it possible to introduce some standard basic semantic concepts that are central for the development of a *logic* of conditional sentences. These concepts are defined in relation to a *belief revision system* that consists of a set $\mathbf{K}$ of epistemic states and a revision function $*$ from $\mathbf{K} \times \mathbf{L}'$ to $\mathbf{K}$. It is assumed that $*$ satisfies (RT) and that the set $\mathbf{K}$ is *closed under expansions*; that is, if $K \in \mathbf{K}$, then $K_A^+ \in \mathbf{K}$ for all A.

(Def Val)   A formula A in $\mathbf{L}'$ is *satisfiable in a belief revision system* $\langle \mathbf{K}, * \rangle$ iff there is some $K \in \mathbf{K}$ such that $K \neq K_\perp$ and $A \in K$. A formula A is *valid in a system* $\langle \mathbf{K}, * \rangle$ iff $-A$ is not satisfiable in the system. A formula A is (logically) *valid* iff A is valid in all belief revision systems.

(Def Val) provides us with a semantic apparatus for conditionals. A closely related semantic approach is the so-called premise semantics developed by Veltman (1976) and Kratzer (1979, 1981). Their approach is compared to the one presented here by Rott (1984).

The main objective of this section is to show how various conditions on the revision function ∗ make different conditional propositions logically valid. We start from minimal assumptions about the revision function and then add conditions on ∗ one by one, basically those presented in chapter 3. It is shown that in most cases these conditions correspond directly to well-known axioms for conditionals.

The first question is, Which formulas are valid in all belief revision models? In the formulation of (Def Val) it is presumed that ∗ is a function taking belief sets as values, which means that (K∗1) is satisfied. This seems to be a minimal assumption for an appropriate definition of validity. The answer to the question is provided by the following axiom system, which I call **CM**:

Axiom Schemata
(A1)   All truth-functional tautologies
(A2) $(A > B) \,\&\, (A > C) \to (A > B \,\&\, C)$
(A3) $A > \top$

Derivation Rules
(DR1)   Modus ponens
(DR2)   If $B \to C$ is a theorem, then $(A > B) \to (A > C)$ is also a theorem.

The following completeness result is proved in Gärdenfors (1978a).

THEOREM 7.1   A formula A is logically valid iff A is a theorem in **CM**.[3]

This theorem forms the basis for additions of further conditions on the revision function ∗. The first condition we want to add is, of course, the basic (K∗2), that is, $A \in K_A^*$. It is then easy to show that this addition corresponds, by means of (RT), to the following axiom scheme:

(A4) $A > A$.

LEMMA 7.2   All instances of (A4) are valid in a belief revision system $\langle \mathbf{K}, * \rangle$ iff the system satisfies (K∗2).

From (A4) and (DR2) the following derived rule can be obtained:

(DR3)   If $A \to B$ is a theorem, then $A > B$ is also a theorem.

Thus, given (A4), (A3) is superfluous.

We next turn to the effects of imposing (K∗3) and (K∗4). Postulate (K∗3) (the requirement that $K_A^* \subseteq K_A^+$) corresponds to the following axiom scheme:

(A5) $(A > B) \rightarrow (A \rightarrow B)$.

LEMMA 7.3   All instances of (A5) are valid in a belief revision system $\langle \mathbf{K}, * \rangle$ iff the system satisfies (K*3).

For reasons that appear in section 7.4, we do not assume the full force of (K*4) but only the following weaker version:

(K*4w)   If $A \in K$ and $K \neq K_\perp$, then $K \subseteq K_A^*$.

This condition corresponds to the following axiom scheme:

(A6) $A \& B \rightarrow (A > B)$.

LEMMA 7.4   All instances of (A6) are valid in a belief revision system $\langle \mathbf{K}, * \rangle$ iff the system satisfies (K*4w).

As regards (K*5) (if not $\vdash -A$, then K_A^* is consistent), it does not seem possible to find a simple correspondence in the object language. The closest we can come is an axiom scheme like this:

(A7) $(A > -A) \rightarrow (B > -A)$.

LEMMA 7.5   If a belief system $\langle \mathbf{K}, * \rangle$ satisfies (K*5), then (A7) is valid in $\langle \mathbf{K}, * \rangle$.

It does not seem possible to prove the converse of lemma 7.5. I return to the status of (A7) later.

The condition (K*6) (if $\vdash A \leftrightarrow B$, then $K_A^* = K_B^*$) corresponds to the following axiom scheme:

(A8) $(A > B) \& (B > A) \rightarrow ((A > C) \rightarrow (B > C))$.

LEMMA 7.6   All instances of (A8) are valid in a belief revision system $\langle \mathbf{K}, * \rangle$ iff the system satisfies (K*6).

We next turn to (K*7) (the condition that $K_{A \& B}^* \subseteq (K_A^*)_B^+$). The appropriate axiom scheme turns out to be the following:[4]

(A9) $(A > C) \& (B > C) \rightarrow (A \vee B > C)$.

LEMMA 7.7   Assume that (A4)–(A8) are valid in the belief revision system $\langle \mathbf{K}, * \rangle$. Then all instances of (A9) are valid in $\langle \mathbf{K}, * \rangle$ iff the system satisfies (K*7).

As direct consequences of lemmas 7.2–7.4, 7.6, and 7.7, one obtains completeness theorems for the axiom systems that are constructed from **CM** by adding various combinations of (A4)–(A6), (A8), and (A9) as axiom schemata.

As regards the final condition (K*8) (if $-B \notin K_A^*$, then $(K_A^*)_B^+ \subseteq K_{A\,\&\,B}^*$), it is not possible to formulate an axiom that corresponds to this requirement. The reason is that this condition entails (K*4) as a special case, and it is shown in section 7.4 that (K*4) cannot, on pain of triviality, be combined with the Ramsey test (RT), which forms the basis for the present logical investigation. Instead, we work with the following weaker form of (K*8):

(K*L)   If $-(A > -B) \in K$, then $(K_A^*)_B^+ \subseteq K_{A\,\&\,B}^*$.

Note that the antecedents of (K*8) and (K*L) correspond to two ways of formulating 'B *might* be accepted if A were accepted'. I return to a discussion of 'might' conditionals in the next section.

The axiom that corresponds to (K*L) is

(A10) $(A > B)\ \&\ -(A > -C) \to (A\ \&\ C > B)$.

LEMMA 7.8   Assume that (A4)–(A8) are valid in the belief revision system $\langle \mathbf{K}, * \rangle$. Then all instances of (A10) are valid in $\langle \mathbf{K}, * \rangle$ iff the system satisfies (K*L).

The axiom schemes (A1)–(A10) and the derivation rules (DR1) and (DR2) are all well known from the logic of conditionals. It is of some interest to compare these axioms with Lewis's (1973b) analysis of counterfactuals. Lewis presents an "official" axiomatization of conditionals, which he calls **VC**. It is easy to show that all axioms and derivation rules presented so far are derivable in **VC**. In fact the converse is also true.

THEOREM 7.9   A formula A is a theorem in **VC** iff it is derivable from **CM** together with the axiom schemata (A4)–(A10).

This theorem and the preceding lemmas are proved in Gärdenfors (1978a, pp. 399–401). There it is also shown that the axiom scheme (A6) can be derived from the remaining axioms. Furthermore, the following axiom scheme is considered:

(A11) $(A > B) \vee (A > -B)$.

If added to Lewis's **VC**, (A11) yields Stalnaker's axiomatization of conditionals. Axiom scheme (A11) corresponds to the following condition on belief revisions:

(K*C)   If K is a maximal belief set, then K_A^* is also a maximal belief set for all sentences A.

This condition is identical with (3.18). Recall that a belief set is said to be maximal iff either A or $-A$ belongs to the belief set for all sentences A.

7.3   Other Kinds of Conditionals

Theorem 7.9 gives us some motivation to proceed with the program of formulating an epistemic semantics for conditionals. The Ramsey test (RT) is formulated for conditionals of the forms 'If A were the case, then C would be the case' and 'If A is the case, then C is (will be) the case'. When interpreting these conditionals in terms of the dynamics of belief, it is natural to associate the subjunctive 'would' with the case when $-A$ is accepted in the current belief set K, whereas the indicative 'is' (or 'will be') corresponds to the case when A is indetermined in K; that is, neither A nor $-A$ belong to K. Thus the semantic analysis of these conditionals provided by the Ramsey test is that counterfactuals are about belief revisions and open conditionals are about belief expansions.

In this section the idea behind the Ramsey test is extended to other forms of conditionals. I first want to consider 'even if' conditionals. The notation $B E A$ is used to represent a sentence of the form 'B would be the case even if A were the case'. The semantic analysis I suggest here is that 'even if' conditionals are about *contractions*.

As a support for this analysis, let us compare it with the analysis given by Pollock (1976, p. 40). He suggests the following definition of E in terms of the conditional connective $>$:

(Def E) $(B E A) \leftrightarrow B \, \& \, (A > B)$.

If (RT) is applied for $>$ in this definition, this analysis amounts to the following criterion of acceptability for 'even if' conditionals:

(7.1) $B E A$ is accepted in a (consistent) belief set K iff B is accepted both in K and in K_A^*.

However, if we next apply the Harper identity for contractions, that is, (Def $-$) in section 3.6, this criterion is equivalent to

(RTE) $B E A$ is accepted in K iff B is accepted in K_{-A}^-.

In this precise sense we can say that 'even if' conditionals are about contractions of belief sets.

As a converse to (Def E) we may take E as primitive and introduce $>$ by means of the Levi identity. This gives us the following definition:

(Def $>$) $(A > B) \leftrightarrow (A \to B) E A$.

This definition also accords with Pollock's analysis. On the basis of it, an axiomatic analysis of 'even if' conditionals can be developed along the same lines as for $>$ in the previous section.[5]

I have argued (Gärdenfors 1979a, 1981) that a slightly stronger criterion than (RTE) is more appropriate. I suggest the following analysis:

(RTE') $B E A$ is accepted in K iff B is accepted in both K_A^* and K_{-A}^*.

If we apply the Ramsey test (RT) to this criterion, we obtain the following alternative definition of E in terms of $>$:

(Def E') $(B E A) \leftrightarrow (A > B) \& (-A > B)$.

Or in words: 'B, even if A' means, on this analysis, 'If A were the case, B would be the case and if $-A$ were the case, B would also then be the case'. A seemingly odd consequence of this definition is that $B E A$ is logically equivalent to $B E - A$. To be sure, there are situations when a person states a sentence of the form 'B would be the case even if A were the case' but where the sentence cannot be replaced by a sentence of the form 'B would be the case even if A were not the case'. However, this is a consequence of the fact that these sentences have different criteria of *assertability*, which does not imply any difference as regards criteria for *acceptability*. In fact, a sentence of the form $B E A$ is normally assertable in a state of belief K only if A is not accepted in K. So, if A is accepted in K, $B E - A$ may be assertable, but $B E A$ is not. However, both sentences may be acceptable in K.

The only case in which the criteria (RTE) and (RTE') give different results is when $A \in K$ (and K is consistent). If $A \in K$, then it follows from (RTE) that $B E A$ is equivalent to $B \& A$, whereas, according to (RTE'), $B E A$ says something more, viz. $B \& A \& (-A > B)$.

In support of the criterion (RTE'), let us imagine that someone says to you, "I am convinced that B would be the case even if A were the case." If you happen to know that A is in fact true but that B is false, then you know that the speaker is wrong. But suppose now that you know that both A and B are true. It seems quite clear that you are not willing to *agree* with the speaker that $B E A$ *unless* you also accept that B would be the case if $-A$ were the case, that is, $-A > B$. On the analysis (RTE), on the other hand, it is sufficient that you accept A and B in order to agree with the speaker.

'Might' conditionals have been treated in a step-parent fashion in the literature. I argue that there is an ambiguity in the use of 'might' conditionals. Lewis (1973b) treats an expression of the form 'if ... might ...' as an indivisible idiom. However, I believe that a sentence of this form can be analyzed in terms of the meanings of 'if' and 'might'.

The standard use of 'may' and 'might' is to express *epistemic* possibility. If I say, "Robert Fischer might win (or might have won) the world championship in chess again," it means that Fischer's winning (or having won) is *compatible* with my knowledge. The obvious acceptability criterion for a sentence of the form 'might A' is that 'might A' is accepted in an epistemic state K iff $-A$ is not accepted in K.

There are cases when 'might' means some kind of possibility to *act*, rather than epistemic possibility. 'Fischer might have come to Moscow' may mean that it was within Fischer's power to come. However, in most cases the epistemic interpretation is intended [see Stalnaker (1984, p. 143)].

After this digression on the ordinary use of 'might', we now return to 'might' conditionals. Let us symbolize a sentence of the form 'B might be the case if A were the case' by $B M A$. Using the Ramsey test for conditionals in combination with the epistemic analysis of 'might', we can say that the primary meaning of $B M A$ is that, if a state of belief K is revised in order to include A, then B is not excluded in the resulting state of belief, that is, $-B$ is not accepted in K_A^*. This leads to the following acceptability condition:[6]

(RTM) $B M A$ is accepted in a (consistent) belief set K iff $-B$ is not accepted in K_A^*.

In order to bring out the power of (RTM), it should be compared to the analysis suggested by Lewis (1973b). He defines the connective M directly from $>$ as follows:

(LM) $(B M A) \leftrightarrow -(A > -B)$.

This definition corresponds to the following acceptability criterion:

(7.2) $B M A$ is accepted in K iff $-(A > -B)$ is accepted in K.

It should be noted that (LM) in combination with the Ramsey test (RT) gives a stronger definition of M than (RTM) because, if $-(A > -B) \in K$, then $-B \notin K_A^*$, but the converse is not true in general. The reason is that the conditions on the revision function that were presented in chapter 3 do not entail that for any sentences A and B either $A > -B$ or $-(A > -B)$ is accepted in a belief set. If (RTM) is used as a characterization of M, then the symbol M cannot be defined explicitly in terms of the conditional connective $>$. So, in this sense, the addition of the symbol M to the object language would strengthen its expressive power in an essential way. Levi (1987b) discusses the consequences of such an addition for the analysis of counterfactuals.

Recall that when the logic for $>$ was developed in the previous section, the condition (K*8) was replaced by the weaker (K*L). The only difference was in the antecedents of the two conditions, and these antecedents correspond to the two interpretations of 'might' given here.

In my opinion the normal meaning of the 'might' conditional is given by (RTM). The difference between this meaning and the stronger provided by (LM) is that, if $A > -B$ is not accepted in a state of belief K, then a later addition of $A > -B$ to K need not conflict with any sentence accepted in K that can be expressed in terms of $>$. Therefore the change with respect to the set of such sentences may be accommodated by an expansion of K. On the other hand, if $-(A > -B)$ is accepted in K, then a later acceptance of $A > -B$ leads to a contradiction among sentences expressible by $>$, and such a change must be accommodated by a proper revision of K.

To give an example in support of (RTM), I may believe that, if I were to play a game of chess against Oscar, I might win the game, simply because I have no information to the contrary. However, I would not regard it as something contradicting my counterfactual beliefs if someone told me that Oscar is a skilled chess player who takes every game seriously, so if I were to play against him, I would lose. Rather, I would learn something new, and this change of belief is best represented by an expansion.[7]

It is only in cases where a purely random factor is involved that one uses the stronger meaning of the 'might' conditional. For example, if I have strong evidence for believing that a particular die is fair, then I will accept the sentence 'If this die were thrown, it might show a six', and I would regard the sentence 'If this die were thrown, it would not show a six' as the negation of the first sentence. This stronger sense of the 'might' conditional is used when there is no piece of additional information consistent with sentences expressible by > that are now accepted that will make it necessary to give up the 'might' conditional.

As a final kind of conditional I briefly mention *necessary implication*. By this I refer to sentences of the form 'If A were the case, then B would necessarily be the case', which we symbolize $A \Rightarrow B$. This kind of conditional can easily be incorporated in the epistemic kind of semantics presented here. The following criterion of acceptability is along the same lines as (RT):

(RTN) $A \Rightarrow B$ is accepted in a belief set K in a belief system $\langle \mathbf{K}, * \rangle$ iff B is accepted in all belief sets in $\langle \mathbf{K}, * \rangle$ in which A is accepted.

This criterion accounts for 'A necessarily implies B'. It is easy to show that the logic for this form of necessary implication is the modal system **S5**.

This ends my outline of an epistemic semantics for conditionals. I have tried to show that various kinds of changes of belief correspond to different kinds of conditionals in a natural way. In my opinion this correspondence gives a better understanding of the meaning of conditionals, their function in arguments, and their logical properties than the semantics based on possible worlds and similarities between possible worlds. Furthermore, the use of epistemic states as an ontological basis for the analysis does not give rise to the ontological problems connected with possible worlds and their properties. However, as will be seen in the next section, the epistemic analysis of conditionals is not without problems.

7.4   The Incompatibility of (RT) and (K*4)

Theorem 7.9 seems to justify the claim that the Ramsey test can be used as a basis for an epistemic semantics of conditionals. However, the list of conditions that have been used to generate the logic of conditionals does not include (K*4) [or the full strength of (K*8)]. An interesting question is whether it is possible to use (RT) together with (K*4) when analyzing the logic of conditionals. With minor qualifications, the answer turns out to be no. In order to put the result as strongly as possible, I will not formulate (K*4) directly. Rather, I start from the following *preservation condition*, which is a nonprobabilistic version of the condition (Pres) in chapter 5:

(K*P)   If a sentence B is accepted in a given state of belief K and if A is consistent with the beliefs in K, then B is still accepted in the minimal change of K needed to accept A.

The rationale for this criterion is, as so many times before, a matter of informational economy: Information is not gratuitous, and we do not want to give up beliefs unnecessarily. As will be seen, the preservation criterion, which is strongly endorsed within the Bayesian tradition, is essentially equivalent to (K*4).

The Ramsey test and the preservation criterion are each of considerable interest for the analysis of the dynamics of belief. The main purpose of this section is to prove that, on pain of triviality, *the Ramsey test and the preservation criterion and inconsistent with each other.*

In order to do this carefully, let us list the assumptions that are necessary: We start with an object language **L**′ including propositional connectives and the conditional operator $>$. (In fact, it is not necessary to assume that **L**′ contains sentences with iterated occurrences of the conditional operator.) The language is governed by a logic that is identified by its consequence relation $\vdash$. Belief sets are closed under deductive consequences and a belief revision system is an ordered pair $\langle \mathbf{K}, * \rangle$, where **K** is a set of belief sets and $*$ is a revision function over **K**.

Note that in **L**′ sentences containing the conditional connective $>$ are treated on a par with sentences without this operator. For future reference this assumption is here stated explicitly:

(0)   Belief sets include sentences containing the conditional connective $<$ as elements.

The Ramsey test is dependent on this assumption:

(RT) $A > B \in K$ if and only if $B \in K_A^*$.

A consequence of (RT) that will be important later is the following *monotonicity criterion*, which was discussed in section 3.3:

(K*M)   For all belief sets K and K' and all sentences A, if $K \subseteq K'$, then $K_A^* \subseteq K_A'^*$.

The proof that (RT) entails (K*M) is trivial: Suppose that $K \subseteq K'$ and that $B \in K_A^*$. By (RT), $A > B \in K$ and hence $A > B \in K'$. By the other half of (RT), we then have $B \in K_A'^*$ as desired. Note that (K*M) is formulated in terms of the revision operation alone and does not refer to the conditional connective. As before, let us say that a sentence A is *consistent with* a belief set K iff $-A \notin K$. The preservation criterion can then be formulated as follows:

(K*P)   If $-A \notin K$ and $B \in K$, then $B \in K_A^*$.

I should also list the conditions on the revision function that are needed for the proof. The first one is well known:

(K*2) $A \in K_A^*$.

Second, we need some way of expressing the idea that K_A^* is the *minimal* change of K needed to accept A. The following very weak criterion is one half of (K*5):

(K*5w)   If $K_A^* = K_\perp$, then $\vdash -A$.

The motivation behind (K*5w) is that a minimal revision of K with respect to A should not lead into the absurd state of belief, unless it is logically unavoidable.

The following properties of expansions [earlier called (3.10) and (3.5)] turn out to be useful in the proof:

(7.3) $K_{A \vee B}^+ \subseteq K_A^+$.

(7.4) $(K_A^+)_B^+ = K_{A \& B}^+$.

Now if $B \in K_A^+$, then $A \to B \in K$; and hence by (K*P), if $-A \notin K$, then $A \to B \in K_A^*$. But then, by (K*2), $B \in K_A^*$. This means that (K*P) and (K*2) entail (K*4), which I repeat here:

(K*4)   If $-A \notin K$, then $K_A^+ \subseteq K_A^*$.

In fact, (K*P) and (K*4) are equivalent, given (K*2).

The final assumption that is needed for the inconsistency result is that the belief revision system is nontrivial. As usual, two propositions A and B are said to be *disjoint* iff $\vdash -(A \& B)$. A belief revision system $\langle \mathbf{K}, * \rangle$ is said to be *nontrivial* iff there are at least three pairwise disjoint sentences A, B, and C and some belief set K in $\mathbf{K}$ that is consistent with all three sentences, that is, $-A \notin K$, $-B \notin K$, and $-C \notin K$.

THEOREM 7.10   There is no nontrivial belief revision system that satisfies all the conditions (K*2), (K*5w), (K*M), and (K*P).[8]

It should be noted that the conditional connective $>$ is used neither in the formulation of the theorem nor in its proof. If $(K*P)$ is replaced by $(K*4)$, then $(K*2)$ is not needed for the proof of the theorem.

COROLLARY 7.11   There is no nontrivial belief revision system that satisfies all the conditions $(K*2)$, $(K*5w)$, (RT), and $(K*P)$.

The theorem and its corollary show that the Ramsey test (RT) and the preservation condition $(K*P)$ [or, equivalently, $(K*4)$] cannot both be rational criteria for belief revisions. Which one is the cause of the inconsistency result?

My present position is that (RT) is the culprit. One way to argue for this is, I believe, to consider $(K*M)$ and its consequences for belief revision systems. In the final section of this chapter, I also criticize (RT) directly as a test for when a conditional should be accepted.

In section 3.3 I advanced some general considerations against the rationality of $(K*M)$. We can here complement this with an example that illustrates the abstract argument in that section: Consider Victoria and her alleged father Johan. Let us assume that Victoria, in her present state of belief K, believes that her own blood group is O and that Johan is her father, but she does not know anything about Johan's blood group. Let A be the proposition that Johan's blood group is AB, and C the proposition that Johan is Victoria's father. If she were to revise her beliefs by adding the proposition A, she would still believe that C, that is, $C \in K_A^*$. But, in fact, she now learns that a person with blood group AB can never have a child with blood group O. This information, which entails $C \rightarrow -A$, is consistent with her present state of belief K, and thus her new state of belief, call it K', is an expansion of K. If she then revises K' by adding the information that Johan's blood group is AB, she will no longer believe that Johan is her father, that is, $C \notin K_A'^*$. Thus $(K*M)$ is violated.

Note that this example does not depend on the presence of any conditionals in K or in K'. In fact, if we assume (RT) and not just $(K*M)$, then Victoria would have believed $A > C$ in K. But then the information that a person with blood group AB can never have a child with blood group O would *contradict* her beliefs in K, which violates our intuitions that this information is indeed consistent with her beliefs in K.

This violation can also be taken as an argument against (RT). The most problematic implication of (RT) is the one saying that, if $B \in K_A^*$, then $A > B \in K$. In a sense, this implication requires that *too many* conditionals be elements of a belief set K because it must contain conditionals related to all possible revisions that K may undergo. Two other examples that go against the Ramsey test and thereby also against (K*M) are presented by Gibbard (1981, pp. 226–229) and Harper (1981, pp. 18–20). Examples like these do not, of course, conclusively refute (K*M), but in my opinion they are sufficient to point out this condition as the cause of the inconsistency result in section 7.3. The case against (K*M) will soon be strengthened because (K*M) will be given independent support from the Bayesian analysis of rationality.

7.5   Weaker Versions of the Ramsey Test

On way of attacking the triviality result would be to argue that the formal version (RT) of the Ramsey test that is used in the derivation of (K*M) does not correspond to the intuitive content of the informal version presented at the beginning of section 7.1. Rott (1986) suggests that the formal version is too strong and that, if it is weakened, the triviality result may be circumvented. In particular, Rott points out the following consequence of (RT), which he deems unacceptable:

(7.5)   If $A \in K$ and $C \in K$, then $A > C \in K$.

This follows from (K*4) [or (K*4w)] and (RT). As is seen in lemma 7.4, (7.5) is closely connected with the validity of the axiom scheme

(A6) $A \& B \to (A > B)$.

For this reason it is interesting to look for weaker versions of (RT) that do not entail (7.5). Here are some candidates:

(7.6) $A > C \in K$ iff $C \in K_A^*$ and $C \notin K$.

This version blocks the derivation of (K*M). A closely related alternative is

(7.7) $A > C \in K$ iff $C \in K_A^*$ and $C \notin K_{-A}^*$.

This principle is called the "strong Ramsey test" in Rott (1986).
    The next version of the Ramsey test is of a slightly different kind:

(7.8) $A > C \in K$ iff $C \in (K_C^-)_A^*$.

The idea behind (7.8) is that, when determining whether you should accept

$A > C$ in K, first retract C from K and then consider whether C is in K_C^- revised to include A.

The following variation on the Ramsey test is even weaker than (7.6)–(7.8):

(WRT)   If $A \vee C \notin K$, then $A > C \in K$ iff $C \in K_A^*$.

This principle takes care of almost all the worries with (7.5) because it says something only about the conditional $A > C$ for the case when we already know that $A \vee C \notin K$ and thus that neither A nor C is in K, and it leaves completely open what happens to the conditional in all other cases.

LEMMA 7.12   (a) Expression (7.6) entails (WRT); (b) expression (7.7) and (K*3) entail (WRT); (c) expression (7.8) and (K$^-$3) entail (WRT).

Unlike the original (RT), none of the weaker Ramsey tests (7.6)–(7.8) and (WRT) entail (K*M), which was used in theorem 7.10. It might therefore be hoped that the weaker versions are compatible with (K*P) and (K*4). However, they all entail the following weak monotonicity principle:

(K*WM)   If $K \subseteq K'$, $A \vee C \notin K'$, and $C \in K_A^*$, then $C \in K_A'^*$.

LEMMA 7.13   (WRT) entails (K*WM).

And even (K*WM) is incompatible with (K*P).

THEOREM 7.14   There is no nontrivial belief revision system that satisfies (K*4), (K*5w), and (K*WM).

COROLLARY 7.15   There is no nontrivial belief revision system that satisfies (a) (7.6), (K*P), (K*2), and (K*5w); (b) (7.7), (K*P), (K*2), (K*5w), and (K*3); (c) (7.8), (K*P), (K*2), (K*5w), and (K$^-$3); (d) (WRT), (K*P), (K*2), and (K*5w).

Peter Lavers has shown that, if (K*WM) is replaced by

(K*WM')   If $K \subseteq K'$, $C \notin K_{-A}^+$, and $C \in K_A^*$, then $C \in K_A'^*$,

then theorem 7.14 holds even if it is assumed only that the underlying logic $-$ is the *minimal logic* (so that the belief sets are only closed under this logic).[9] Of course, (K*WM') is *classically* equivalent to (K*WM).

Theorem 7.14 and its corollary show that the triviality theorem involving the Ramsey test is relatively robust in relation to different formulations of the test. However, (WRT) can be further weakened by requiring that the test only apply when $-A \in K$, that is, when the conditional $A > C$ is truly a *counterfactual*. Thus one may want to consider a principle such as

(7.9) $A > C \in K$ iff $-A \in K$ and $C \in K_A^*$

or, alternatively, the weaker

(7.10)   If $-A \in K$, then $A > C \in K$ iff $C \in K_A^*$.

I have not been able to prove a triviality result for either of these principles. This should come as no surprise, as (7.9) and (7.10) assume that $-A \in K$, whereas (K*P) has $-A \notin K$ in its antecedent. It remains to be seen whether any interesting logic can be produced from one of these principles along the same lines as in section 7.2. However, I believe that (7.9) and (7.10) are too weak to capture the intuitive content of the Ramsey test, which should also apply to open conditionals, that is, when $-A \notin K$. For this reason I do not think that replacing (RT) by (7.9) or (7.10) is a promising way out of the triviality results.

7.6   Discussion of the Inconsistency Result

Theorems 7.10 and 7.14 and their corollaries present us with a dilemma: When investigating belief revision systems, we must give up either the Ramsey test or the preservation condition. In section 7.4 I argued that the Ramsey test is the most problematic, but let us take a closer look at each of the horns of the dilemma.

If we keep the Ramsey test but give up the preservation condition [that is, (K*4)], it is possible to construct a semantics for conditionals based on belief revision systems, as we have seen in section 7.2. It is therefore reasonable to say that the Ramsey test yields an appropriate analysis of the logic of conditionals.

At the other horn of the dilemma, as we have seen in chapters 3 and 4, it is possible to keep the preservation criterion and to add further criteria on rational belief revision systems, in particular (K*8) [which entails (K*4) and thus (K*P)].

The preservation condition also follows from the Bayesian doctrine of belief changes as presented in chapter 5. Recall that within this tradition states of belief are modeled by probability functions and consistent additions of belief are modeled by *conditionalization*.

To see the connection between conditionalization, formulated as (Def +) in chapter 5, and (K*P), recall that we defined the belief set K *associated with* the probability function P as the set of sentences B such that $P(B) = 1$. It was show in theorem 5.12 that the set associated with a probability function is indeed a belief set and that, if K is associated with P and $P(A) > 0$, then the set associated with the conditionalization of P on A is K_A^+, that is, the expansion of K by A. Now, if we let K_A^* denote the belief set associated with P_A^*, condition (K*P) and thereby also (K*4) follows immediately from (P*1)–(P*5) and (Def +).

Stalnaker (1970) discusses how conditionalization can be extended to cover also the case when $P(A) = 0$. In connection with this, he proposes the following way of assigning probabilities to conditionals:

(ST) $P(A > C) = P(C/A)$.

Here it is assumed that the function $P(C/A)$ is defined for all propositions A and that this function defines the belief revisions to be used [that is, $P_A^*(C) = P(C/A)$ for all A and C]. It is clear that, if K_A^* is associated with such a conditional probability function, then (RT) follows immediately as a special case of (ST).

We can now establish a connection between theorem 7.10 and Lewis's (1976) triviality result, which in the present terminology can be formulated like this: There is no nontrivial probabilistic belief revision system that satisfies both conditionalization and (ST). Here the belief revision system is said to be nontrivial iff there are at least three pairwise disjoint sentences A, B, and C such that for some probability function P in the system $P(A) > 0$, $P(B) > 0$, and $P(C) > 0$. The restriction of this assumption to belief sets is exactly the assumption of nontriviality that was made for theorem 7.10.

Theorem 5.3 provides a triviality result that is not dependent on the assumption (Def +) that expansions be made by conditionalization. (Def +) was replaced by the much weaker probabilistic preservation condition (Pres):

(Pres)   If $P(A) > 0$ and $P(B) = 1$, then $P_A^*(B) = 1$.

As is easily seen, this condition is a probabilistic version of (K*P). Theorem 2 in Gärdenfors (1982a) states that, under some mild conditions on the belief revision system, (ST) and (Pres) cannot both be satisfied. In fact, the proof of this result is closely related to the proof of theorem 7.10.

We thus see that theorem 7.10 is an even more general version of Lewis's triviality result.[10] It is much more general because it depends neither on the assumption that expansion should be made by conditionalization nor on the assumption that states of belief should be modeled by probability functions. The conditions (RT) and (K*P) can be formulated for a large class of models of epistemic states and changes of belief, including non-probabilistic models. But as we have seen, they cannot both be satisfied.

Perhaps the real cause of the inconsistency is hidden among the additional assumptions in the theorem or its corollary. Is it possible to save the Ramsey test by using one of the conditions (0), (K*2), or (K*5w) as a scapegoat? I take the nontriviality assumption and condition (K*2) to be beyond doubt. This leaves us with conditions (0) and (K*5w).

As regards (K*5w), it can be noted that, if it is dropped, the remaining conditions are consistent. We can simply take the conditional connective $>$ to be identical with the material implication $\rightarrow$ and then put $K_A^* = K_A^+$ for all belief sets K and all sentences A. But this solution defines K_A^* as the absurd belief set $K_\perp$ as soon as $-A \in K$. The point of (K*5w) is to serve as a buffer against such trivializations of belief revisions.

Then let us turn to condition (0). A possible way to retain both (K*P) and the idea behind the Ramsey test would be to deny that beliefs in conditional sentences belong to the kind of belief sets for which belief revisions are defined. The elements of belief sets can be thought of as things we believe to be true and thus as things that may have truth values. On the other hand, beliefs in conditional sentences can be seen as being about *belief sets and how they will be revised.* And such beliefs lack truth values. Thus conditional sentences will never be elements of belief sets. On this view the Ramsey test may be formulated as follows: A sentence $A > B$ is acceptable in relation to belief set K if and only if $B \in K_A^*$. This formulation does not include $A > B$ as an element of K. As a consequence, the derivation of (K*M) is blocked, and thus the inconsistency result is prevented.

This view of conditional sentences has been advocated by Isaac Levi among others.[11] The main problems with this position are, first, that it does not account for *iterated* conditionals. What kind of belief would a sentence like the following be on this view? 'If this vase breaks if dropped on the floor, then it breaks if thrown against the wall' [see van Fraassen (1976a)]. Furthermore, it is difficult to see how *probabilities* of conditional sentences can be compared to probabilities of nonconditional propositions if these two kinds of sentence are the objects of different kinds of belief. Levi does not treat these problems. Because he claims that conditional sentences lack truth values, he also does not find it meaningful to assign probabilities to them, nor does he allow iterations of conditionals.[12]

It is possible that the position outlined here can be extended to cope with iterated conditionals and to say something interesting about the probabilities of conditionals, but this remains to be seen.

Yet another way out of the inconsistency theorem would be to reject the epistemic framework that has been used here. In particular, it may be claimed that a conditional *sentence* need not express the same *proposition* in all epistemic contexts. On this approach the derivation of (K*M) from (RT) would be blocked. The assumption that $K \subseteq K'$ is the assumption that every sentence in K is in K'. But it does not follow from this that the proposition expressed by the sentence $A > B$ (relative to context K') is accepted in K' just because the proposition expressed by that sentence (relative to K) is accepted in K.[13]

The drawback of this expedient is that it calls for a theory of how the proposition expressed by a given conditional sentence is determined from the epistemic context. Some results in this direction can be found in Adams (1975), Gibbard (1981), and Stalnaker (1984), but we are far from a fully developed theory.

In this connection it should be mentioned that Harper (1976) has developed a probabilistic semantics for conditionals that are relativized to the acceptance context. However, his theory seems to be too general; it says little about how the contents of a sentence of the form $A > B$ in different epistemic contexts are related to each other. And I suspect that, as soon as the contents of conditionals in different epistemic situations are connected by some reasonable conditions, the force of the Ramsey test, even if relativized, will lead to serious problems.

7.7 Conditional Beliefs and Beliefs in Conditionals

The Ramsey test has been a leitmotiv for the analysis of conditionals in this chapter. It can be interpreted as saying that beliefs in conditionals are nothing but conditional beliefs. This notion can be made precise by saying that 'B is believed conditionally on A in an epistemic state K' means that B is accepted in the revision of K with respect to A, that is, $B \in K_A^*$.

One direction of the Ramsey test was criticized in the previous section: If one believes B conditionally on A in K, then one accepts the conditional

$A > B$ in K, that is, $A > B \in K$. The converse direction claims that *all* conditionals that one accepts represent such conditional beliefs. However, this half of (RT) is not without problems. The following troublesome example is borrowed from Stalnaker (1984, p. 105):

Suppose I accept that if Hitler had decided to invade England in 1940, Germany would have won the war. Then suppose I discover, to my surprise, that Hitler did in fact decide to invade England in 1940 (although he never carried out his plan). Am I now disposed to accept that Germany won the war? No, instead I will give up my belief in the conditional. In this case, my rejection of the antecedent was an essential presupposition of my acceptance of the counterfactual, and so gives me reason to give up the counterfactual rather than to accept its consequent, when I learn that the antecedent is true.

The reason why one would give up the counterfactual rather than accept the consequent is that, in the terminology of chapter 4, the negation of the consequent (that Germany did not win the war) has a much higher degree of epistemic entrenchment than the counterfactual. In fact, the second half of the Ramsey test (if $A > B \in K$, then $B \in K_A^*$) requires that for all A and B sentences of the form $A > B$ have higher epistemic importance than both A and B. As Stalnaker's example shows, this requirement is not realistic, and hence we have another argument against using the Ramsey test in its strong form as a basis for a semantics of conditionals.

In summary, the considerations in sections 7.4–7.7 show that the condition (RT) and its variations are too simple for an adequate analysis of conditionals. Apart from theorems 7.10 and 7.14, a number of examples show that the semantics of conditionals is much more complicated. A more sophisticated analysis also requires, besides logical analysis, extensive linguistic and psychological investigations. However, this does not entail that the *epistemic approach*, that is, the strategy of using epistemic states and epistemic dynamics as the foundations for the semantics, fails. On the contrary, I hope to have shown in the earlier sections of the chapter that this is a promising approach.

8 Explanations

8.1 Program

The topics of chapters 8 and 9 are *explanations* and *causal beliefs*. These topics are, of course, closely connected and consequently are analyzed in a similar fashion: The key concept in both analyses is that of *contraction*.

We first turn our attention to the pragmatics of explanations. According to a well-known tradition, an explanation is understood as some kind of *inferential relation* between the sentences included in the explanans and explanandum. Hempel (1965) views both deductive-nomological and inductive-statistical explanations in this way. Focusing on logical methods as the main tool of analysis, as is done in this tradition, is a symptom of what Stegmüller (1983) calls "the third dogma of empiricism": The tools of logic are sufficient for the explication of all fundamental concepts that are relevant for philosophy of science.

In contrast to this dogma, I argue here that it is not sufficient to consider only the explanans and explanandum sentences and their inferential relations when determining whether something constitutes an explanation; the *epistemic circumstances* are of great importance as well. In particular, the *beliefs* of the persons giving (and requesting) an explanation are crucial for the evaluation of a purported explanation. My goal is to present an account of explanations where the connection between the explanans sentences and the explanandum is always evaluated *relative to an epistemic state*.

According to the analysis presented here, the characteristic role of the explanans part of an explanation (the sentences given as the explanation) is to convey some *information* about the explanandum (the fact to be explained). At a first glance, this characterization may seem odd, because when a person wants an explanation of a fact E, he or she normally already knows that E is true. So the information conveyed by the explanans does not change the belief in E that is in the person's present epistemic state, call it K. On the other hand, it is quite clear that the fact that E may be more or less *surprising* or *unexpected*, and the principal effect of a successful explanans is that the surprise at E is *decreased*. As will be seen, this does not preclude that we can also explain facts that are familiar and not surprising at all. However, when asking for an explanation of a well-known phenomenon E, we in a sense pretend that E is surprising. I suggest that this strategy can be explained in terms of contractions.

So how is the surprise value of a sentence E to be measured? My suggestion is that, rather than studying the present epistemic state K, one should consult the *contraction* K_E^-, in which E is not known but which in other respects is as similar to K as possible. If E has just occurred, K_E^- normally corresponds to the person's epistemic state before he learned that E. The surprise value of E is inversely related to the degree of belief associated with E in K_E^-. The central criterion on explanations is that the explanans in a nontrivial way should decrease the surprise value of the explanandum.

Degrees of belief, epistemic states, and contractions of epistemic states are thus central concepts in the analysis. In order to make these concepts more precise, I introduce a probabilistic model of epistemic states. These models are more complicated than those discussed in chapter 5 because they exploit *second-order probabilities*. Essentially, the models consist of (first-order) probability measures defined over properties and (second-order) measures of the belief values of propositions. I believe that the higher degree of complexity is compensated for by the richer representation of epistemic states.

With the aid of these models of epistemic states I formulate my analysis of explanations. This characterization covers both statistical and deductive explanations. The analysis is compared to some other accounts of explanations and it is then applied to some of the examples that have appeared in the literature.

8.2 Background

Before the analysis is presented in greater detail, I would like to compare its main features to some other theories of explanations. Apart from providing a background, this comparison gives some motivation for much of the material.

In all his works on explanations, Hempel assumes that explanations are potential predictions. With respect to deductive explanations, this assumption presents no problems; but when statistical explanations are considered, it has the result that only explanans sentences that make the explanandum highly probable are acceptable. It has been argued by Coffa (1974) and Salmon (1971) that Hempel's assumption stems from an implicit commitment to determinism. However this may be, Hempel believes that, to the extent it is possible to explain a fact, there are sentences that are true and that make the fact highly probable.

A characteristic difference between Hempel's theory and mine is that according to Hempel the explanans should show that the phenomenon described by the explanandum was to be *expected*, whereas I demand only that the explanans should make the explanandum *less surprising*. A classical counterexample to the postulate that explanations are potentially predictive is Scriven's (1959) paresis example. Using the machinery of this chapter, Scriven's example and Hempel's defense against it are analyzed in detail in section 8.5.

Salmon's (1971) theory of explanation accords with mine in that it does not demand that the explanans should make the explanandum highly probable. On the other hand, Salmon does not require that the explanans should *increase* the probability of the explanandum—he is satisfied as soon as the explanans *changes* the probability of the explanandum. Calling an argument that lowers the probability of the explanandum an explanation seems to me to contravene completely any reasonable concept of explanation. If one asks for an explanation of why a phenomenon occurred and the answer makes the occurrence even more unlikely, then one would feel deceived and would even more desire an explanation of why the phenomenon occurred.

Or, in the terminology of another tradition, a person asking for an explanation of a phenomenon expresses a "cognitive dissonance" between the explanandum and the rest of his beliefs. The primary role of the explanans is to eliminate or reduce this cognitive dissonance [see Sintonen (1984)]. The cognitive dissonance is here measured by the surprise value of the explanandum, and the degree of "cognitive relief" corresponds to the reduction in this surprise value provided by the explanans. However, an argument that is an acceptable explanation according to Salmon's theory may lead to an increase in cognitive dissonance.

There are, however, more fundamental differences between Hempel's and Salmon's theories and mine. Most important, my models of epistemic states and changes of belief are more elaborate. In support of my models I later argue that the explanatory status of the examples Salmon presents as counterexamples to Hempel's theory is not so definite as Salmon argues but is to a large extent dependent on what *background beliefs* are assumed.

Another author who violates "the third dogma of empiricism," that is, goes against viewing explanations as inferential relations, is Hansson (1975). He points out that one explanandum sentence may correspond to several explanation-seeking why-questions. For example, the questions 'Why, among all my friends, did John develop cancer?' and 'Why, among

all heavy smokers, did John develop cancer' correspond to the same
explanandum, viz. 'John developed cancer'. Hansson shows that the
appropriateness of different explanans sentences may depend on the why-
question posed. A possible answer to the first question is 'Because John
smoked two packs of cigarettes a day', but this answer seems inappropriate
for the second question.

The phrases "among all heavy smokers" and "among all my friends" in
the example demarcate so-called *reference classes*. Hansson argues that the
reference class is an important part of an explanation-seeking why-
question, and he gives a characterization of explanations in terms of probabilities in a reference class. In my analysis the reference class mentioned
in a why-question is an indication of the knowledge and beliefs one has
when asking the question. I show how my analysis of epistemic states can
be used to find the appropriate reference class for an explanation. Thus the
contents of that part of Hansson's theory are consequences of the theory
presented here.

The theory of explanations that comes closest to the present one is van
Fraassen's (1977; 1980c, ch. 5). He also stresses various pragmatic factors
of explanations, in particular, their dependence on contextual factors.
However, he does not give any account of the structure of the epistemic
states that form the basic contextual elements.

8.3   Second-Order Probabilistic Models of Epistemic States

I now turn to a presentation of the models of epistemic states that are
essential for my analysis of explanations. The ontological basis for the
models is sets of possible worlds, and the semantics of the object language
is defined in relation to such sets. However, the present models are more
complicated than the possible worlds models of section 2.4.

The object language is a first-order language in contrast to the propositional languages that were used earlier. In order to avoid technical complications, I exploit an object language that contains as few components
as possible. I use only two types of sentences: singular sentences and probability sentences. Atomic sentences are built up from predicates and individual constants. For simplicity I assume that all predicates are one-place.
Predicates are denoted Q, R, S, etc., and individual constants are denoted
a, b, c, etc. Singular sentences are defined as atomic sentences or truth-
functional combinations of atomic sentences. Probability sentences take

the form $p(A/B) \geqslant r$. Here A and B are predicates followed by the individual variable x or truth-functional combinations of such expressions, and r is a real number between 0 and 1. Truth-functional combinations of probability sentences are also called "probability sentences." The intended use of the different kinds of sentence is that singular sentences represent "facts," whereas probability sentences represent "general knowledge" and "inductive beliefs."

I deliberately avoid including quantificational sentences in the language. This is done merely to simplify the discussion—quantificational sentences are common ingredients in explanations. Their role is here taken over by sentences of the form $p(Qx/Rx) = 1$. I do not think that limiting oneself to those explanations that can be formulated in this simple object language excludes any of the central features of explanations, and I believe that my analysis can quite easily be extended to more sophisticated object languages.

Before turning to the models of epistemic states I use in explaining explanations, let me say a few words about Hempel's way of modeling knowledge and belief. Hempel is of the opinion that a deductive explanation is a *logical* relation between the explanans and the explanandum and that this relation is independent of the background knowledge. However, for the so-called inductive-statistical explanations, Hempel is forced to evaluate an explanation in relation to some assumed background knowledge in order to formulate his "requirement of maximal specificity" (more about this requirement later). Hempel's models of background knowledge are quite simple; they are described as classes of sentences that are assumed to be consistent and closed under logical deduction. Hempel's models are thus essentially belief sets, as discussed in earlier chapters. However, this way of modeling background knowledge gives a rather one-sided picture because it is impossible to decide whether the sentences not in the class are probable or improbable or, more generally, what degree of certainty one is willing to ascribe to them. And, as will be argued shortly, this is important when evaluating purported explanations involving probabilistic elements.

The first component in the models of epistemic states is a set W of possible worlds (or possible states of the world). Individual possible worlds are denoted u, v, w, etc. Recall that I am in no way a realist about possible worlds, but I regard them as a useful heuristics. The main role of the set W is to introduce a *conceptual* framework for the models of epistemic states.

The interpretation of the set W is that what you accept as knowledge in a given epistemic state is exactly what is true in all worlds in W (see sections 2.4 and 6.1). In a sense the use of possible worlds is a way of describing what you do not know. The more you learn, the fewer states of the world are compatible with what you know.

Two possible worlds can be different in many ways. An individual can have different properties in different worlds. Because I do not know the eye color of the person who just called me on the telephone, I can consequently imagine some states of the world in which she has blue eyes and some states in which she has brown eyes. More generally, two states of the world can differ in their frequency of a certain property among the individuals. I do not know the frequency of albinism among rabbits. I know that the probability of a rabbit being an albino is greater than 0 and I believe that it is less than 0.2, but for all I know, the actual probability could be anything in between. Another way to put this is to say that it is compatible with my knowledge that different possible states of the world may have different proportions of white rabbits.

This aspect of an epistemic state is incorporated as a second component by assuming that for every possible world w in W there is a probability measure P_w that is defined over all subsets of the set of *individuals* in w. For simplicity I assume that the same set of individuals exists in all possible worlds in W. If S is a subset of the set of individuals, $P_w(A)$ represents the probability that an individual belongs to the set S in the world w.

I assume that there is a fixed interpretation I of the object language that for a given possible world tells us, for each individual constant, which individual it denotes and, for each predicate symbol, which individuals have the property it denotes. If Q is a predicate, I put $Q_w = I(Q)$ (the set of individuals in w who has the property Q), and correspondingly $a_w = I(a)$ denotes the individual associated with the individual constant a in the world w.

A sentence of the form Qa is *true in w* iff $a_w \in Q_w$. A sentence of the form $p(Qx/Rx) \geqslant r$ is *true in w* iff $P_w(Q_w/R_w) \geqslant r$. The truth conditions for the connectives are the standard ones. A sentence A is said to be *accepted as knowledge* in an epistemic state K iff A is true in all worlds in the set W that is a part of K. These definitions generate an interpretation function I from sentences to sets of possible worlds. The set of worlds where a sentence A is true is denoted $I(A)$. Note that the truth conditions in these definitions are only heuristic tools, and they imply nothing about the connections with the "actual" world. The key concept is, as in earlier chapters, the acceptability condition.

In general, different worlds have different probability measures. In many cases, however, there are predicates Q (or truth-functional combinations of such predicates) such that $P_w(Q_w) = P_u(Q_u)$ for all possible worlds u and w in W. In such a case the probability of the predicate Q can be said to be *known* in the given epistemic state, because in all possible worlds that are compatible with what is accepted as known, the same proportion of individuals have the property that is described by Q. I know, for example, that the probability of winning some amount of money in the Swedish state lottery is one-sixth. For most properties, however, we are uncertain of their probabilities, and therefore the probability measure of the corresponding set of individuals may vary considerably between different possible worlds.

All worlds that are possible in a certain epistemic state are not equally probable. If I at this moment try to call my friend, I consider it more likely that he is at work than that he is at home. According to my beliefs, it is therefore more probable that the actual world is among those worlds where my friend is at work than among those where he is at home.

In order to measure the probability of different states of the world, I bring in, as a third component of an epistemic state, another probability measure B, which is defined over the set of *subsets* of W. If U is a subset of W, then $B(U)$ is a measure of the probability that the actual world is among those in U. As discussed in chapter 6, propositions are often defined as sets of possible worlds, namely, those states in which the proposition is true. The measure B may therefore be called a *belief function* because it measures the degree of belief in a proposition.

As we have seen, the probability of a property Q can be different in different possible worlds. Using the belief function B, it is possible to determine the probability that a certain property has a certain probability in a given epistemic state. Thus one obtains from the probability measure P_w together with the measure B a *second-order probability distribution* for facts involving an individual having a certain property. For some probabilities we know the probability distribution with almost certainty—an ordinary coin shows a head in 50% of the throws. For other properties the probabilities may be extremely uncertain—at my present stage of knowledge I know little about the probability of a mare giving birth to twin foals, and consequently the possible states of the world should from my point of view show widely spread probabilities of such an event.

Even if you do not know very much about the probability of a certain property, you sometimes have to make a guess. Such a guess is then based on a first-order probability, which is an *amalgamation* of the second-order probability distribution. A particularly simple way of defining such an amalgamation formally is to introduce a first-order probability measure P_V for every subset V of W in the following way:

$$\text{(Def } P_V) \quad P_V(Q) = \sum_{w \in W} P_w(Q) \cdot B(\{w\})/B(V), \quad \text{provided that } B(V) \neq 0.$$

For infinite sets V the sum should be replaced by an integral. I call $P_V(Q)$ the *expected probability* of finding an individual in the set represented by Q, that is, Q_w for different worlds w, given that the set of possible worlds is V. For simplicity P_W is abbreviated P. It should be noted that forming the expected probability is only one way among many possible ways of amalgamating the second-order distribution [see Levi (1987a)].

This ends the description of the models of epistemic states. To sum up, an epistemic state K consists of (1) a set W of possible worlds containing a fixed set of individuals, (2) for each world w a probability measure P_w that is defined over sets of individuals in w, and (3) a belief function B that measures the probability of sets of possible worlds. (For generality I denote these models of epistemic states by K even if they are probabilistic models.) The P_w-measures together with B yield a second-order probability distribution of properties, and from this I have defined the first-order expected probability measure.

It is perhaps of some interest to note that the object language associated with the epistemic states is not rich enough to express all distinctions that are possible to make in the states. In particular, the second-order distributions function as hidden variables in relation to the language.

Using the models of epistemic states introduced here, it is easy to describe *expansions* of beliefs. Suppose that we are given a state K that consists of a set W of worlds, a set of probability measures P_w, and a belief function B. We now want to add to K the content of a sentence A and its consequences. When A is accepted as known, only the worlds in which A is true will become possible, that is, compatible with what is accepted as known. I denote this set of states W_A^+. For all w in W_A^+ the probability measures P_w are unchanged in the expanded model. The new belief function B_A^+ is defined from the old one by the equation $B_A^+(V) = B(V/W_A^+)$ for all subsets V of W_A^+. The degree of belief in a set V of states of the world in the expanded state of belief is thus the same as the degree of belief in V *given* A in the old state. We have thus defined the expanded epistemic state K_A^+ as the triple $\langle W_A^+, P_w : w \in W_A^+, B_A^+ \rangle$.

This definition covers the case of expanding the epistemic state K, that is, when the sentence A is consistent with what is accepted as true in K. Following the constructions presented in chapter 5, it should be easy to see how similar definitions can be provided for contractions and revisions. In order to avoid repetitions, I do not pursue the details of these constructions here.

An essential feature of the present models of epistemic states is that for every combination of predicates there is a measure of its probability. It is true that the measures P_w can be different in different worlds, but the interesting and useful measure is the expected probability.

Although there is for every combination of predicates an expected probability, it is not necessary to *revise* the epistemic state as soon as one wishes to add to the accepted beliefs a probability statement that is in conflict with the present expected probability. What will happen is that the worlds in which the new probability statement is false will no longer be possible, and thus the second-order probability distribution will change from having a large spread to being concentrated on a definite value. Although I would guess that the probability of a mare giving birth to twin foals in 10% (which is thus my present *expected* probability of this kind of event), I would *not* take it as something *contradicting* my beliefs if someone told me that the probability is in fact 1.5%. I am uncertain of the figure 10%, and it is only some kind of average of all probabilities I can conceive of.

One advantage of the present kind of models of epistemic states over Hempel's way of describing knowledge by a set of sentences is that there is both a simple way of modeling expansions of beliefs and a well-defined expected probability of every combination of predicates. If an epistemic state is described simply as a set of sentences and if this set includes a probability sentence for every combination of predicates, then it will be difficult to describe how the set of sentences is changed when further sentences are added. If one, for example, wants to add a probability sentence that is in conflict with some of the earlier ones, it seems difficult to judge how this new probability sentence will influence the epistemic status of the other probability sentences.

8.4   An Analysis of Explanations

With the aid of the suggested models of epistemic states, a characterization of explanations is now within reach. The analysis is restricted to the simplest situations in which the explanandum is a singular sentence. I formulate some necessary conditions for explanations. The central idea is that the explanans should increase the belief value of the explanandum in a nontrivial way. The belief value of a sentence is defined in terms of a given epistemic state. This state is not the state where the explanation is desired but instead the *contraction* of that state with respect to the explanandum sentence. The definition of the belief value of a sentence is based on the principle of using the "total evidence" when determining single-case probabilities. I also discuss the connections between the belief value and Hempel's requirement of maximal specificity.

Explanations are often considered as answers to why-questions. The primary function of questions is to show that the asker does not know the answer to the question and wants to know the answer. There are of course questions that lack one or both of these characteristics, such as a teacher's questions or rhetorical questions, but these are not used in a normal way. My aim is to clarify what kind of information one wishes to obtain when asking an explanation-seeking why-question.

When you ask a question of the type 'Why E?' you normally accept as known that E is true. The reason for asking is that you did not (or pretend that you did not) *expect* E to be true. If it were possible to conclude from the "rest" of your knowledge that E is (or would become) true, then you would have no need for an explanation.

We can now distinguish two epistemic states in connection with an explanation of a sentence E. In the first situation, which here is called K, you accept E as true but you do not know why. In the second, you assume that you do not know whether E or not but otherwise your beliefs are as similar to those in K as possible. This means that the second epistemic state should be identified with K_E^-, that is, the *contraction* of K with respect to E. A typical case is that K_E^- is the epistemic state you were in before you discovered that E and expanded your state to K. [Recall that one of the axioms, to wit (P^-5), for contractions of probability functions is that $(P_E^-)_E^+ = P$.] I claim that suggested explanation should be evaluated in relation to the epistemic state K_E^- rather than in relation to K.

When judging an explanation of E, I thus start from a state of belief in which E is not accepted as known. A natural measure of the degree of expectation of a sentence E in an epistemic state K is $B(I(E))$, where $I(E)$ is the set of worlds where E is true. Because we are focusing on K_E^-, a central problem is how to determine the value of $B_E^-(I(E))$ in this state of belief, where B_E^- is the belief function in K_E^-. Because we have assumed that E is a singular sentence, the belief value of which is dependent on the probability statements accepted in K_E^-, this problem is essentially the classical problem of single-case probabilities translated into the present framework of epistemic states. Here I present a tentative solution to this problem that relies on Reichenbach's principle of using the narrowest reference class. However, instead of any form of "objective" probability measure, this principle is formulated in terms of the "subjective" expected probability measure P, which can be defined in any state as belief.

In order to determine the single-case probability of an explanandum sentence of the form Qa, we first make an assumption concerning the connection between the expected probability measure P and the belief function B with respect to Qa:

(SCP) Let K be an epistemic state with possible worlds W, belief function B, and a defined measure P of expected probability. Let R be the strongest predicate for which it is accepted as true in K that Ra, that is, for which $I(Ra) = W$. If nothing else of relevance to Qa is known about a, then $B(I(Qa)) = P(Q/R)$.

This assumption says that the proportion of worlds in which Qa is true, that is, $B(I(Qa))$, is indeed what can be expected of an individual a with property Q given that a has property R. R is here assumed to be the narrowest reference class to which a is known to belong. For example, if you already know that Qa, then R_w will always be a subset of Q_w, and it then follows that $B(I(Qa)) = P(Q/R) = 1$, which is the correct value. It is also easy to check that the assumption (SCP) does not violate the requirement that B be a probability measure over the set of possible worlds. $B(I(Qa))$ is called the belief value of the sentence Qa in K. To avoid cluttering the notation, expressions of the form $B(I(Qa))$ will in the remainder of the chapter be abbreviated $B(Qa)$ when there is no risk of confusion.

Note that the condition (SCP) is quite weak and to some extent undetermined because of the proviso that "nothing else of relevance to Qa is known about a." It may, for example, not be fully accepted that a has a property S, that is, the belief value of Sa is less than 1, but it may nevertheless be very likely that Sa, and this may influence the judgment of $B(Qa)$. In order to make the condition more precise, we need an analysis of "relevance." The traditional definition is that Sa is relevant to Qa iff $B(Qa) \neq B(Qa/Sa)$. For a criticism of this definition and an alternative analysis, see Gärdenfors (1978b).

The condition (SCP) is applied to an explanandum sentence E in the contracted epistemic state K_E^-. If you are in state K_E^- where the belief value of E is less than 1 and if you then discover that E is true (that is, you change your epistemic state to K), then to some extent E comes as a surprise; the bigger the surprise, the smaller the belief value E had in K_E^-, and the need for an explanation arises. It is precisely in these situations that the question 'Why E?' has the normal function of an explanation-seeking question. An appropriate answer to such a question—an explanation worthy of the name—should change the state of belief so that the belief value of the explanandum *increases*. However, in order to accept something as an explanation, we do not require that the belief value of the explanandum be high (close to 1), as Hempel requires, but that the belief value be higher than before we had the information that the explanans sentences contribute.

In order to avoid explanations of the type 'E, because E', which increase the belief value of E (but in a trivial and noninformative way), I require that the explanans convey information that is relevant relative to the beliefs in the initial state of belief K in which one knows that E. Formally this requirement amounts to that the explanans E should not be derivable from the beliefs in K.

These considerations lead us to the following necessary conditions for an explanation:

(EXP) An explanation of a singular sentence E relative to a state of belief K (where $E \in K$) consists of (i) a conjunction T of a finite set of probability sentences and (ii) a conjunction C of a finite set of singular sentences that satisfy the requirements that (iii) $B_E^-(E/T \& C) > B_E^-(E)$, where B_E^- is the belief function in the state K_E^-, and (iv) $B(T \& C) < 1$ (that is, $T \& C \notin K$).

In a less precise way, (EXP) can be rephrased by saying that explaining E (in a given state of belief K) amounts to finding an answer to the question 'If I did not know that E, what acceptable sentences T or C could be used to raise the probability of E (diminish the surprise of E) without begging the question?' This formulation brings out a connection linking counterfactuals, explanations, and the dynamics of belief.

In (EXP), we can distinguish *three* different states of belief, viz. K, K_E^-, and $(K_E^-)_{T \& C}^+$. K_E^- is the state relative to which the belief value of the explanandum E, before it is known to be true, is determined [with the aid of (SCP)]. $(K_E^-)_{T \& C}^+$ is the epistemic state that arises from K_E^- when the explanans $T \& C$ is added. The central clause (iii) in (EXP) compares the belief value of E in this state with the belief value of E in K_E^-. The sentence E is not accepted as known in $(K_E^-)_{T \& C}^+$ unless $T \& C$ constitutes a deductive explanation of E. It is important for the following discussion to keep the distinctions between these three epistemic states in mind. It should also be noted that both K_E^- and $(K_E^-)_{T \& C}^+$ are *hypothetical* epistemic states that are used only for the evaluation of (iii) in (EXP). It is thus not meaningful to say that either of these situations *precedes* K in time.[1]

In fact, there is a fourth epistemic state that is relevant, namely $K_{T \& C}^*$, which is the resulting state adopted by the individual if she accepts the explanation $T \& C$. Normally $T \& C$ is consistent with K, in which case this fourth state is simply $K_{T \& C}^+$. However, (EXP) does not exclude the case when $T \& C$ contradicts the beliefs in K, in which case the explanation leads to a genuine revision of the initial epistemic state K.[2]

Levi (1987a) also suggests an epistemically relativized analysis of explanations in terms of contractions and revision. However, there is nothing corresponding to condition (iii) in (EXP) in his analysis because he works with a different concept of acceptance than what is used here.

I do not require that the conjunction T of probability sentences or the conjunction C of singular sentences be nonempty. It is thus possible that an explanans consists merely of a singular sentence. The probability sentence, which in principle is required to change the belief value of the explanandum, may be a sentence that is already known in the epistemic state K. If I wonder why Victoria is tanned although it is winter here, the answer that she has recently spent a week on the Canary Islands is in my opinion a satisfactory explanation because I already know that most people who go to the Canary Islands return tanned.

In a similar way it is possible that an explanans consists only of a probability sentence, viz., in those cases where the relevant singular sentences are already included in the epistemic state. If I ask why Mr. Johansson, whom I know well, has been taken ill with lung cancer, it is a satisfactory explanation to learn that a substantial percentage of those who work with asbestos develop lung cancer, because I already know that Mr. Johansson has been manufacturing asbestos mats for twenty-five years.

It is well known that commonplace explanations often consist only of a single sentence—a probability sentence (a universal sentence) or a singular sentence. Such explanations have been considered *elliptic* in previous theories of explanation, and it has been found necessary to supplement them with further sentences. Because I assume an underlying epistemic state, my characterization of explanations, in accordance with practice, shows that it is possible to accept as fully satisfactory an explanans that consists of a single sentence.

It seems as if there may be cases of explanations in which the explanans sentences T & C already are included in K, and thus condition (iv) of (EXP) is violated. For example, in answer to the question 'Why did Victoria leave Oscar?' it is perfectly acceptable to give the explanation 'Because he got so fat', even though it is already commonly known that Oscar got very fat recently. (I am grateful to Hans Rott for raising this point, as well as for providing the example.) However, even if the answer 'Because he got so fat' is what is *uttered* as an explanation, the *tacit consequence* that Victoria was disgusted by Oscar's corpulency is the proper explanans, and this fact is *not* included in K and thus it does not violate condition (iv). This is but one type of example of how the main function of a speech act is to convey an unspoken presupposition. This function is not peculiar to explanations but occurs in various kinds of communicative contexts.

8.5   Applications of the Analysis

In this section I use the machinery that was introduced in sections 8.3. and 8.4 to analyze some of the best-known examples from the literature. I also discuss some of the general problems that have arisen in connection with different theories of explanation.

As a paradigm case I have selected Scriven's famous paresis example. To a great extent my analysis of this example is parallel to Hansson's (1975). His arguments are, however, based on an analysis of why-questions, whereas my stepping stones are epistemic states.

The facts behind Scriven's example are that paresis develops only in patients who have been syphilitic for a long time, but only a small number of syphilitic patients ever develop paresis. Furthermore, no other factor is known to be relevant for the development of paresis. Now Scriven maintains, quite contrary to Hempel's theory, that the fact that a certain person has been suffering from syphilis, together with the general statements about paresis, explains why that person developed paresis. The more general rule that Scriven is exemplifying is that, if a property R is the only known cause of the property Q, then one can, by pointing out that a certain individual has the property R, explain why he has Q, independently of how probable Q is given R.

Hempel (1965, pp. 369–370) defends his theory by a counterexample that he claims has the same logical structure as the paresis example: No one wins the first prize in the Irish sweepstakes without buying a ticket, but only a small number (in fact only one) of those who have bought tickets wins the first prize. Hempel argues that it is not possible to explain why someone wins the prize by pointing out that she has bought a ticket.

In order to illustrate the differences between these two examples and to make it clear why Scriven's example after all is an explanation and Hempel's is not, we must try to expose the background beliefs that are assumed in the two examples.

I imagine that in the tacit epistemic state K in Scriven's example, there is no property that is expected to be relevant for paresis. The probability in this epistemic state of someone developing paresis is estimated at a very low value, say 0.0001. When an explanation of the fact that Nietzsche developed paresis is requested, there is thus nothing you know about him that could be relevant for the fact that Nietzsche, among all people, developed paresis. Let R be the narrowest reference class to which Nietzsche is known to belong (excluding the fact that he has developed paresis), and let Q be the property of suffering from paresis. The explanandum is thus Qa, where a is an individual constant representing Nietzsche. In $K_{\bar{Q}a}$ we then have $P(Q/R) = P(Q) = 0.0001$, and according to (SCP), it follows that $B_{\bar{Q}a}(Qa) = 0.0001$.

Let S be the property of suffering from syphilis. The explanation suggested by Scriven, now consists of the probability sentences $p(Qx/Sx) = 0.1$ and $p(Qx/-Sx) = 0$, the conjunction of which is T in (EXP) and, unless it is already included in $K_{\bar{Q}a}$, the singular sentence Sa, which is C. We can then apply (SCP) again to derive $B_{\bar{Q}a}(Qa/T \,\&\, C) = 0.1$ and thus the belief value of the explanandum has increased, in accordance with (iii) in (EXP).[3] Scriven's example is therefore approved of as an explanation according to (EXP).

For Hempel's example the situation is somewhat different. Let Q denote the property of winning the first prize in the sweepstakes, and let S be the property of buying a ticket. When explaining why Qa, where a is the winner, it is natural to suppose that in the epistemic state K_{Qa}^- it is accepted as known that everyone who wins the first prize in the sweepstakes has bought a ticket. When you learn that an individual a has won the first prize, you normally do not know anything about a that is relevant for her winning the prize, except that she has bought a ticket. If R is the narrowest reference class to which a is known to belong, then in the epistemic state K_{Qa}^- we have $P(Q) = P(Q/R) = P(Q/R \& S)$, and with the aid of (SCP) we conclude that $B_{Qa}^-(Qa) = B_{Qa}^-(Qa/Sa)$. To point out that a has bought a ticket is thus not a satisfactory explanans for the explanandum Qa because it does not increase its belief value. For these reasons I agree with Hempel in that the only known cause of an event need not be an explanation of the event.

However, I do not consider Hempel's example to be a parallel to Scriven's. The difference derives from what is assumed to be the adequate epistemic state for the explanation. In order to make Scriven's example an explanation, we must assume that one is not cognizant of the law that only those who have been suffering from syphilis develop paresis. An inevitable part of the explanans is then this law. When constructing an underlying epistemic state for Hempel's example, however, the most natural assumption is that the statement 'only those who have bought tickets may win the first prize' is included among the accepted beliefs.

If the assumptions about the underlying beliefs are changed so that one already knows that paresis is necessarily preceded by syphilis, then the information that Nietzsche suffers from syphilis no longer explains why he developed paresis. With *this* assumption about the background beliefs, Hempel's and Scriven's examples are in fact parallel, and neither of them is accepted as an explanation, but this is not the example Scriven had in mind.

The fact that different background beliefs have a crucial effect on Scriven's example can also be demonstrated by considering the why-questions that are relevant in the two situations. This is the strategy employed by Hansson (1975). In the first situation, when you do *not* know that syphilis is a necessary condition for paresis, the natural question is 'Why, among all people, did Nietzsche develop paresis?' In the second epistemic state, where you *do* know that syphilis is necessary for paresis, one asks instead, 'Why, among all syphilitic persons, did Nietzsche develop paresis?' The phrases 'among all people' and 'among all syphilitic persons' indicate which reference classes apply to the individual. In Hansson's theory the reference class is an important part of the why-question and decisive for which explanans sentences are possible for the explanandum mentioned in the question. When you put a question of the form 'Why, among all R, does a have property Q?' the purpose of mentioning R is to point out that you already know that a has the property R and also that you do not know anything more about a that you think is relevant for a's having the property Q (except something you take for granted that everyone knows). In the theory of explanations presented here, there is no explicit need to consider the reference classes mentioned in the why-questions because your knowledge about which properties individuals have is assumed to be baked into the epistemic states. Stegmüller says that "different kinds of *why-questions* are, from this point of view, nothing but *linguistic manifestations of different kinds of epistemic situations*, in which the persons, who put explanation-seeking questions, find themselves" (Stegmüller 1983, p. 952; my translation). For an analysis of the pragmatics of why-questions, see Sintonen (1984).

In connection with this discussion of the role of reference classes I want to add some comments on Hempel's requirement of maximal specificity. The condition on the belief function B that is formulated in (SCP) is a specification of the idea that, when determining the probability of a single event, the total evidence should be taken into consideration. Hempel says that his requirement of maximal specificity is not, as he has earlier argued, "a rough substitute of the requirement of total evidence." The reason is that "this reasoning confounds two different questions. One of these concerns the strength of the evidence for the *assertion that* the explanandum event did occur; the other, the probability associated with an I-S *explanation of why* the explanandum event occurred" (Hempel 1968, p. 121). In the first case, Hempel argues, the requirement of total evidence is applicable. In the second case it is not applicable, he continues, because when seeking an explanation of why E occurred, E is normally included in what you know, and therefore the probability of E given what you know is 1. However, in most cases the explanans confers on the explanandum sentence a probability that is less than 1, and therefore the requirement of total evidence does not apply in this situation.

Hempel discusses only the epistemic state that arises when one has come to know that E is true, viz. K in (EXP). According to my analysis, however, an explanans should be evaluated in relation to K_E^-, which normally is the epistemic state that was at hand before E was accepted. And in relation to *this* state the requirement of total evidence is applicable [as formulated in (SCP)].

Thus I consider Hempel's original justification of his requirement of maximal specificity to be the correct one and the later one as misleading for the reason that he does not distinguish the two relevant epistemic states K and K_E^-. Stegmüller (1983, pp. 958–959) argues that this leads to serious problems for Hempel. The formulation of (SCP) that corresponds to Hempel's requirement of maximal specificity is, of course, different from his, because I use different tools to describe epistemic states.

I next turn to a class of examples that according to Salmon (1971) show that Hempel's theory of explanations is unsatisfactory. One of the examples is the following:

John Jones avoided becoming pregnant during the past year, for he has taken his wife's birth control pills regularly, and every man who regularly takes birth control pills avoids pregnancy. (Salmon 1971, p. 34)

Salmon claims that this is not an explanation: "Men do not become pregnant, pills or no pills, so the consumption of oral contraceptives is not required to explain the phenomenon in John Jones's case (though it may have considerably explanatory force with regard to his wife's pregnancy)" (p. 34). Later, Salmon summarizes the group of examples in the following way:

Each of these explanandum events has a high prior probability independent of explanatory facts, and the probability of the explanandum event relative to the explanatory facts is the same as the prior probability. In this sense the explanatory facts are irrelevant to the explanandum event. (p. 36)

The reason why Salmon's example does not appear to be an explanation to *us* is that we already *know* that men never become pregnant. As Salmon points out, the belief value of the fact that John Jones does not become pregnant does not increase when we learn that he has taken oral contraceptives. If someone did not have this elementary knowledge about the functioning of the human body—for example, a child or an extraterrestial being—then the information that John Jones has consumed oral contraceptives together with the law that nobody who takes oral contraceptives becomes pregnant might provide an explanation of why John Jones did not become pregnant, which is acceptable to such a being.

Thus Salmon's example does not appear to be an explanation to us, not because the logical structure of the explanans sentences is incorrect but because we have common background beliefs that preempt the information of the explanans sentences.

8.6 Some Consequences of the Analysis

A consequence of the requirement (iii) in (EXP) that the belief value of the explanandum should increase is that explanations are not just right or wrong but that there are *degrees* of explanation. The more an explanation increases the belief value of the explanandum, the better it is. Of two explanations of the same explanandum one may increase the belief value of the explanandum much more than the other. In such cases there is a tendency to reject the less informative explanation and no longer call it an explanation. However, had the more informative explanation not been at hand, the other might have been accepted.

Deductive explanations are the best, as they increase the belief value of the explanandum to the maximum value. The reason why deductive explanations are considered definitive is that it is not possible to increase the belief value of the explanandum by further knowledge.

From condition (iii) in (EXP) we obtain a natural measure of the *explanatory power* of an explanans $T \& C$ relative to an explanandum E in an epistemic state K_E^-. The greater the difference between $B_E^-(E/T \& C)$ and $B_E^-(E)$, the greater the explanatory power of $T \& C$ relative to E and the more informative the explanation. Definition (EXP) allows several explanations of a sentence E. Using $B_E^-(E/T \& C) - B_E^-(E)$ as a measure of the explanatory power is thus a way of determining which explanation is the best one.

Condition (iii) in (EXP) does not entail that the probability of E after learning that $T \& C$ should be greater than 0.5 (or any other limit) but only that the explanans *raises* the probability of the explanandum. This feature of (EXP) has been criticized by Schurz (1983, p. 190).[4] To use Schurz's example, if we want to explain why Peter won the first prize in a lottery containing one million tickets, it is not satisfactory to point to the fact that Peter has bought ten tickets, even if this raises the probability from 0.000001 to 0.00001. And if we use the measure introduced, we see that this "explanation" indeed has a very low explanatory value. Even if the explanatory value of this example falls below the level of what can be demanded of an explanation, I do not believe it is possible, in general, to introduce any lower limit on the explanatory value or on the probability of the explanandum after the explanans has been presented. In particular, as the paresis example shows, I do not believe that it can be required that the probability of the explanandum after the explanans has been presented should be greater than 0.5.

In connection with this, one can note that some writers have maintained that there are two kinds of explanations—the so-called how-possibly and why-necessarily explanations [see Dray (1957)]. In my opinion there is no essential difference between these two kinds of explanation, and both are covered by my analysis. When explaining why an event *necessarily* occurred, one starts from an explanandum that has belief value less than 1 (as always), and the explanans then raises the belief value of the explanandum to the maximal value of 1.

When explaining how an event could *possibly* occur, one starts from an explanandum, the belief value of which is close to 0 or even 0. The explanans then raises the belief value of the explanandum, but not always close to 1 as Hempel (1965, p. 428, note 5) argues. In those cases where the explanandum contradicts the beliefs accepted in the epistemic state K, the explanans sentence will induce a *revision* of K. This kind of model is not possible to model on Hempel's approach.[5]

As a consequence of the fact that explanations are always evaluated in relation to an epistemic state, it is possible that an explanans $T \& C$, which has been accepted as an explanation of E relative to a state K, ceases to be an explanation in a state K' that contains more knowledge than K. For example, I may be surprised by the fact that Victoria is tanned in the month of February. If I ask for an explanation and get the answer that Victoria has recently spent a week on the Canary Islands, I accept this as an explanation because I know that most people who have recently been on the Canary Islands are tanned. However, if I later learn that it had been raining on the Canary Islands the week Victoria was there, the old explanation is no longer satisfactory, and I once more lack information on why she is tanned. This is an example of what Rott (1982) and Stegmüller (1983, p. 1011) call a "spurious" explanation.

It seems as if Hempel has assumed that a logical analysis of the sentences occurring in an explanation is sufficient, at least regarding deductive explanations. He compares his analysis to the metamathematical proof theory, where the concept of study does not correspond to the common-place use of proofs but to an idealized form of proof. He says that his models of explanations

are not meant to describe how working scientists actually formulate their explanatory accounts. Their purpose is rather to indicate in reasonably precise terms the logical structure and the rationale of various ways in which empirical science answers explanation-seeking why-questions. The construction of our models therefore involves some measure of abstraction and of logical schematization. (1965, p. 412).

It is my hope that the analysis presented in this chapter shows that Hempel's idealization fails to account for some of the essential features of explanations.[6]

Before Hempel had analyzed statistical explanations, it had been believed that these explanations would turn out to be generalizations of the deductive explanations that Hempel and Oppenheim had analyzed in a seemingly successful way. It turned out, however, mainly because of what Hempel calls "the ambiguity of inductive-statistical explanation," that it would be impossible to characterize such explanations only in terms of relations between the sentences in the explanans and the explanandum. Hempel therefore felt forced to study statistical explanations *relative* to a knowledge situation. A lucid account of the reasons for Hempel's deviation from the kind of analysis used for deductive explanations has been given by Coffa (1974).

If you are in an epistemic state in which you can predict with certainty or almost certainty that E will occur, then if E does indeed occur, you will not need any explanation of this fact. But still, it must be admitted, in situations like this we can also speak of "the explanation" of E. The reason for this is that we can imagine a contraction K_E^- of our present epistemic state in which E is not accepted and then ask what would be an explanation relative to this state. A typical example of this phenomenon is when a teacher asks a pupil for an explanation of a fact E, although the teacher's belief value of E relative to his present epistemic state is very high. In such a situation the teacher *pretends* that he is in an epistemic state where E has a comparatively high surprise value. The poor pupil then has to find out, first, which epistemic state the teacher pretends to be in and, second, which elements from the teacher's actual epistemic state will provide an explanation of E relative to the pretended state of belief. Sintonen (1984) presents further aspects on explanation as a communicative act.

In a similar way several persons can agree on "the explanation" of a fact with which they are already familiar because when they try to put themselves in an epistemic state in which they do not know the explanandum (the contracted epistemic state), they reach similar epistemic states, and therefore the same sentences will work as an explanans. Although such a unanimity in the selection of contracted epistemic states is quite frequent, it is not possible to construct a general theory of explanations on these grounds. One reason for this is that different persons use different contraction functions (recall that different orderings of epistemic entrenchment yield different contractions). So, even if they start from the same state of belief K, they will end up with different contractions K_E^- in relation to which the explanation is to be found. This shows that explanations are highly dependent on the context, which is a feature stressed by van Fraassen (1980c, ch. 5). In the terminology of chapter 4, this context dependency can be explained by the fact that different persons have different orderings of epistemic entrenchment. And even more clearly, in the case when they also start from different epistemic states, it is not surprising that different explanans sentences have varying explanatory values.

As a matter of fact, there are many explanatory situations in which the opinions diverge as to what is "the explanation" of a given fact. When explaining why a particular car accident happened, one person may be satisfied to learn that the tires of the car were worn out; another person, who is familiar with the conditions of the car, may find that heavy rains are the explanation; and a third person may feel enlightened to learn that, whenever a vehicle is driven at high speed on a wet road surface, the friction is considerably reduced.[7]

8.7 Conclusion

What has been attempted in this chapter is to outline the basis for a unified approach to explanations. The main idea has been something that may seem completely trivial—that an explanation should provide relevant information on what is to be explained so that it becomes less surprising. However, when the information conveyed by an explanation is evaluated relative to different epistemic states, this idea has been shown to have far-reaching consequences.

The analysis presented here is *epistemological* because the focus on different epistemic states is illuminating when studying explanations as a form of exchange of information between individuals. And the analysis is *pragmatic* because it contains more than a logical analysis of the sentences occurring in the explanans and in the explanandum and because it clarifies why many arguments from everyday conversations can be accepted as explanations when other theories consider them as elliptical explanations.

In order to simplify the presentation, I have made several assumptions, which must be weakened or eliminated in a more general theory of explanations. First, I have limited myself to explanations of singular sentences, and I have thereby avoided all problems concerning lawlikeness and different levels of comprehensiveness among sentences. Second, I do not claim that my conditions for explanations are sufficient, not even for explanations formulated in the simple object language of this chapter. For example, I have made no attempts to eliminate redundant elements in the explanans sentences.[8]

Finally, but perhaps most important, the models of epistemic states are still rudimentary and only to be regarded as heuristic devices. I believe that, in order to obtain deeper theories of explanations that can also serve as theories of *understanding*, one must develop more sophisticated and psychologically more realistic models of epistemic states and their dynamics.

9 Causal Beliefs

9.1 Background

The final application of the models of epistemic dynamics is an analysis of causal beliefs. Causation has always been thought to be closely related to explanation. Indeed, causal beliefs, like explanations, are analyzed here in terms of contractions. So on the present approach the relationship between causation and explanation is highlighted by reducing both notions to that of contraction.

In modern writings on causation *regularity* theories have dominated the discussions [see, for example, Beauchamp and Rosenberg (1981)]. Typically an event C is said to cause another event E if the fact that E follows C instantiates some regularity or, in other words, if there are true *laws* that together with C and other initial conditions entail E. However, it is difficult to formulate this analysis so that causation itself is not confused with other causal relations. For example, C might be an *effect* of E, which could not, given the laws and the initial conditions, have occurred otherwise than by being caused by E; or C might be an *epiphenomenon* of E, that is, an effect of some genuine cause of E. These problems for regularity theories are discussed by Lewis (1973a) and Mackie (1974).

A different approach to causation is suggested by Lewis (1973a). He analyzes causation in terms of *counterfactuals*. The starting point for his analysis is the idea that 'C causes E' means essentially that 'if C had been absent, E would have been absent as well'. Some philosophers would say that analyzing causation by counterfactuals is circular because understanding counterfactuals presupposes that we understand causation. However, Lewis would deny this because he believes that counterfactuals can be analyzed with the aid of similarities between possible worlds, and such similarities do not depend on any causal relations.

Both the regularity analyses and Lewis's analysis presume a *deterministic* universe. However, it is clear that many commonplace causal statements are *probabilistic*. For instance, if we claim that an excessively fatty diet was the cause of Falstaff's death, we do not mean that the consumption of fat determined Falstaff's death (at a particular point of time) but only that it raised the probability of the event (occurring at that time).

A probabilistic analysis of causation has been suggested by several authors, among which Reichenbach (1956), Good (1961, 1962a), Granger (1969), and Suppes (1970) have been pioneers. The basic idea in their analyses is precisely that *a cause raises the probability of the effect*. However, not all events that raise the probability of another event can be counted as causes. In order to sort out those pairs of events that stand in a causal relation to each other, we must add further conditions. Suppes handles this by distinguishing *genuine* from *spurious* causes as well as *direct* from *indirect* causes.

In this chapter I present an analysis of causal *beliefs* that is intended to apply to deterministic and probabilistic cases. I argue that, because it is normally known that both C and E have occurred when it is claimed that C caused E, it is necessary to return to the *contraction with respect to C* of the given epistemic state when evaluating C's potential influence on E. In this contracted state, I apply only the simple criterion that the occurrence of C raises the probability of the occurrence of E. I hope to show that, by exploiting the properties of contractions, it is possible to avoid many of the problems that have faced earlier theories of probabilistic (and deterministic) causation.

Spohn (1983a) also presents an essentially epistemic analysis that is related to the one presented here. However, he does not refer explicitly to the concept of a contraction. His key notion is that a cause should raise the "modal rank" of the effect. The concept of modal rank is then given both a deterministic and a probabilistic interpretation. In the deterministic case the modal rank of different propositions seems to be essentially the same as the degree of epistemic entrenchment as presented in chapter 4.

9.2   The Information Problem

Among the probabilistic theories of causation, Suppes's theory (1970) has been discussed most extensively. Suppes's epistemology is essentially Bayesian. In particular, he models an epistemic state by a (single) probability function defined over events. For the main part of this chapter I also assume this way of modeling epistemic states.

It has been claimed by several authors that Suppes's account of causation is defective [see, for example, Hesslow (1976), Salmon (1980), and Otte (1981)], and a number of counterexamples have been presented. Some of these examples are discussed in section 9.4. In my opinion a common feature of these examples is that they show that the *information* contained in a single probability function is not sufficient to differentiate genuine from spurious causes or direct from indirect causes. Otte (1981) summarizes his criticism of Suppes as follows:

The basic problem facing a definition of spurious causation which depends solely on probability relations among events seems to be that there is no way of distinguishing between a causal chain and a fork when the probabilities involved are the same. Suppose we have the chain of necessary and sufficient causes $C \rightarrow B \rightarrow A$ and a necessary and sufficient common cause $B \leftarrow C \rightarrow A$. All of the probability relations in this case will be identical, yet in one case B is a genuine cause of A and in another case B is a spurious cause of A. Thus there appears to be no way to distinguish genuine from spurious causes using only probability relations among the events, which is a very serious problem for a probabilistic theory of causality. (p. 180)

Thus the problem for the theory seems to be a problem of insufficient information: A single probability function does not contain enough information to enable us to sort out genuine causal relations from spurious ones. I therefore want to discuss some ways of supplementing a probability function with further information.

Suppes mentions a related problem in his discussion of the definition of "spurious cause in sense one" (Suppes 1970, pp. 23–26). His solution to the problem—the definition of "spurious cause in sense two"—is to introduce a *partition* of the event space in relation to which the causal relations are evaluated. This is one way of taking further information into account when defining causal relations. Suppes's idea of using partitions has been elaborated by Cartwright (1979) and Skyrms (1980) among others. The partitions they use are supposed to be a maximal specification of *causally relevant* background factors. I believe that something like this was also the intended interpretation of the partitions used by Suppes.

One drawback of Cartwright's and Skyrms's proposals is that they are partially circular: In order to distinguish genuine from spurious causes, we must already know the causally relevant background factors. So even if they succeed in avoiding some of the counterexamples that have been presented for Suppes's theory, their definitions are not complete analyses of probabilistic causation. Furthermore, the extra amount of information demanded is quite substantial: In order to determine whether C is a cause of E, *all* causally relevant background factors must be available. It seems clear that we often have determinate beliefs about causal relations between events, even if we do not know exactly which factors are causally relevant to the events in question.

Another way of exploiting additional information and avoiding the alleged counterexamples is to say that, if we only *knew more* about the process between a cause C and an effect E, we would see that each step in the chain of events satisfies Suppes's definitions, even if the direct step from

C to E does not. Or, in other words, if we insert a sufficient number of steps between C and E, the counterexamples will disappear. For example, Rosen (1978) writes in her comment on Hesslow's (1976) thrombosis example (to be discussed in section 9.4):

We wrongly believe that taking the pills always lowers a person's probability of thrombosis because we base our beliefs on an inadequate and superficial knowledge of the causal structures in this medical domain where unanticipated and unappreciated neurophysiological features are not given sufficient attention or adequate weighting. (p. 606)

Salmon (1980) calls this strategy "the method of more detailed specification" (p. 64). It is clear that, if this strategy is to be applied to any causal process, we must assume more or less total information about the process in order to evaluate causal claims. Thus this strategy demands even more additional information than the strategy of using partitions. From a pragmatic point of view, another argument against this strategy is that we frequently form causal beliefs even if we have only a limited knowledge of the intermediate steps of the underlying process.

9.3   An Epistemic Analysis of Causal Beliefs

For me, causality is primarily a *cognitive* concept. My position is Kantian to the extent that I believe that it is a kind of category mistake to try to give a "realistic" or "objective" interpretation of causality, where the causal relation holds among real events, independently of minds having beliefs about the events. Thus I interpret causal claims only *in relation to a given state of belief*. Some further arguments for this position have been given by Spohn (1983a, pp. 382–384), who discusses the advantages of an epistemic interpretation of probabilistic causality and the disadvantages of a realistic interpretation.

Even if I am wrong about the possibility of a realistic interpretation of causality, an analysis of the epistemic interpretation is an important one. The central problem in this project is to delimit the type of information that is used when forming causal beliefs. For me the basic relation to be analyzed is 'In the state of belief P (or K), C is a cause of E', where C and E are beliefs about the occurrence of two *single* events. I comment on causal relations between general events in section 9.7.

My analysis is a combination of two seemingly disparate ideas. The first is the part of the Bayesian doctrine that says that an epistemic state can be represented by a probability function. For the main part of the chapter I take this thesis as unproblematic—at least for beliefs concerning single events.

The second idea derives from Hume's second definition of causality, which says that, if the cause had not been, the effect never had existed (Hume 1748, sect. VII). The relation of this definition to his first definition is discussed in section 9.8. Indeed, Lewis (1973a) took Hume's second definition as the starting point for his counterfactual analysis of causation, using possible worlds and similarities between possible worlds as primitive concepts.

In contrast to Lewis, I give an *epistemic* interpretation of Hume's definition. I believe that this type of interpretation is what Hume intended. In order to cover also nondeterministic cases of causation, I want to work with a probabilistic extension of the definition.[1] The key notion for the definition is that of a *contraction* of a probability function:

(Def Cause)   In the epistemic state represented by the probability function P, C is a cause of E iff (i) $P(C) = P(E) = 1$ and (ii) $P_C^-(E/C) > P_C^-(E)$.

The main point of this definition is to put the contraction P_C^- in focus of the evaluation of a causal belief instead of the original probability function P. According to the first clause of the definition, both C and E are known to have occurred (that is, they both have maximal probability in P), so these values cannot be used for any interesting comparisons. In relation to P_C^- the evaluation is simply the key idea in Suppes's and others' theories: The cause raises the probability of the effect. The difference lies in *which* probability function this test is applied to.

Before proceeding to a discussion of the properties of (Def Cause), let me illustrate the definition with a simple example. Assume that C describes the event that the butcher consumed half a pound of table salt and that E describes the event that he died the night after. Let P be the belief function corresponding to the present state of belief in which it is known that C and E have occurred, that is, $P(C) = P(E) = 1$. If we want to determine whether C caused E, we should, according to (Def Cause), consider the belief function P_C^-, corresponding to the epistemic state in which the belief in C has been retracted but in other respects is as similar to P as possible. This is the hypothetical state in which we assume that we did not know that the butcher ate the salt. Because salt is a poison if consumed in large quantities, the probability that the butcher will die, given that he eats half a pound of salt, increases drastically, that is, $P_C^-(E/C) > P_C^-(E)$, and thus C is a cause of E according to (Def Cause).

It should already be noted here that, unlike Suppes, I do not present a definition of prima facie cause, which must then be complemented by a distinction between spurious and genuine causes. In the next section I try to show that (Def Cause) can handle both the cases of spurious causes discussed by Suppes and the putative counterexamples that his theory has been charged with. Also note that the definition is intended to cover the *deterministic* case as well, that is, the case when all relevant probabilities are 1 or 0. In this case P and P_C^- in the definition can be replaced with K and K_C^-, respectively.

The additional information assumed in (Def Cause), apart from the probability function P representing the given epistemic state, is a probability function P_C^- for each event C. Given the presentation of contractions of probability functions in chapter 5, I believe that from an epistemological point of view the additional information provided by a contraction function is more naturally available than both maximal specifications of causally relevant background factors and total information about the course of events.

When applying (Def Cause) to some problematic examples in the next section, I use the notion of a contraction of a probability function in an informal way and I assume that the formal properties of contractions as presented in chapter 5 are fulfilled. One of the postulates discussed in that chapter is, however, questionable in the present context, namely the "recovery" postulate (P⁻ 5), which can be formulated as follows:

(P⁻ 5)   If $P(C) = 1$, then $P_C^-(E/C) = P(E)$ for all E.

This postulate is one way of formulating the idea that the contraction of P with respect to C should be minimal in the sense that unnecessary losses of information should be avoided. It also makes precise the sense in which contraction is "backward" conditionalization. If this postulate is accepted, then (Def Cause) can be simplified. According to clause (i) of the definition we have, $P(C) = P(E) = 1$. If we apply (P⁻ 5), we know that $P_C^-(E/C) = P(E) = 1$; so this means that clause (ii) of (Def Cause) reduces to the requirement that $P_C^-(E) < 1$.

This consequence of (P⁻ 5) shows that, in the typical case of a probabilistic cause, the postulate is too strong [see the discussion of $(K^- 5)$ in section 3.4]. This claim can also be supported by an example. Assume that we have thrown a die (event C) and that it showed a six (event E). In the probability function P representing the present epistemic state, C and E are accepted as having occurred, that is, $P(C) = P(E) = 1$. The contraction P_C^- is most naturally taken to be identical with the epistemic state present immediately before the throw. [In this state $P_C^-(C)$ may be high, but it is not 1 until the throw has actually been made.] However, $P_C^-(E/C)$ is not 1 as required in $(P^- 5)$ but only $\frac{1}{6}$. On the other hand, the throw C makes E an element of a *homogeneous partition*. The partition consists of the possible outcomes of the throw, and it is homogeneous because no additional information (except for what can be generated from the elements of the partition themselves) can change the probabilities of the elements in the partition.

In general, it is thus more natural to require something like the following weaker version of $(P^- 5)$:

$(P^- 5w)$ In P_C^-, C makes E an element of a homogeneous partition.

Postulate $(P^- 5)$ is then the special case of $(P^- 5w)$ when E is the only element of the partition. If we let $(P^- 5w)$ replace $(P^- 5)$, it is not possible to trivialize (Def Cause) in the same way as before. The drawback of this replacement is that, with this weakening of the postulates for contractions of probability functions, it is no longer possible to prove theorem 5.8, which showed that postulates $(K^- 1)–(K^- 8)$ are satisfied by the belief set associated with P.

9.4   Analysis of Some Examples

It is now time to demonstrate the power of the test for causality introduced in (Def Cause) by applying it to some of the examples that have appeared in the literature on probabilistic causation. In these examples the contractions of epistemic states to be used are presented in an informal, "intuitive" way, and I do not intend to define explicit contraction functions. However, even if this nontechnical strategy is used, the postulates for contractions presented in chapter 5 and in section 9.3 serve as regulative ideals.

The first thing that must be shown is that (Def Cause) in itself can be used to distinguish genuine from spurious causes. Let us consider the classical barometer example. Here three events are involved: the falling barometer reading (F), stormy weather (W), and low air pressure (L). In order to test whether F causes W, we must apply (Def Cause) to an epistemic state, represented by P, where F, W, and L are known to have occurred. The crucial step is the evaluation of the contraction P_F^-. If we give up the belief that F has occurred, the requirement that we should change P as little as possible would, in the most natural interpretation of the example, then make us say something like, "If the barometer had not been falling, it must have been malfunctioning or disturbed in some way, because pressure was low." In other words, this means that the epistemic entrenchment of L is higher than the entrenchment of F. Thus we would keep the belief in L in P_F^- and hence also the belief in W. In other terms, $P_F^-(L) = P_F^-(W) = 1$; so $P_F^-(W/F)$ cannot be greater than $P_F^-(W)$. As desired, (Def Cause) thus yields the result that F is not a cause of W. This line of reasoning can, of course, also be expressed by saying that L *screens off* F from W.[2] However, as will be seen in the following examples, the analysis in terms of contractions can also be applied to cases in which the screening test does not apply.

On the other hand, L is a cause of W (and of F) according to (Def Cause). If we give up our belief in L, it is difficult to retain the belief in W, so $P_L^-(W)$ will be lower than 1 and most naturally of the same magnitude as $P_L^-(L)$. And, of course, $P_L^-(W/L) > P_L^-(W)$, as desired. The reason why the falling barometer F has been called a spurious cause of W is that F can also raise the probability of W in P_L^- because it is an *indication* of L. But the fact that $P_L^-(W/F) > P_L^-(W)$ is not sufficient to make F a cause of W according to (Def Cause). I believe that the strategy of this example can be employed to analyze spurious causes in general.

The second example I want to discuss is due to Hesslow (1976). He suggests (p. 291) that it is possible for a cause to lower the probability of the effect. The example starts from the claim that taking contraceptive pills can cause thrombosis. But pregnancy can also cause thrombosis, and taking the pills lowers the probability of pregnancy. It is perfectly possible that pregnancy is a stronger cause of thrombosis than contraceptive pills, so taking contraceptive pills may *lower* the probability of thrombosis. Thus this example seems to show that the basic thesis of probabilistic causation —that the cause should raise the probability of the effect—is violated.

To analyze this example in relation to (Def Cause), we start from a particular situation in which a woman has been taking contraceptive pills (C) and suffers a thrombosis (T) [and in which she is not pregnant ($-B$)]. If we want to determine whether C caused T, we should, according to (Def Cause), ask what would have happened if she had not been taking the pills.

It is a part of the normal context of this example that the woman has been taking the pills because she wants to avoid becoming pregnant (A). So, if she had not been taking pills, she would most probably have avoided becoming pregnant by some other means. Thus A is still likely in P_C^-; that is, $P_C^-(A)$ is close to 1, and so $P_C^-(B)$ is close to 0. Even if $P_C^-(T/B)$ is higher than $P_C^-(T/C)$, which is what Hesslow claims, it still holds that $P_C^-(T/C) > P_C^-(T)$, at least if we assume that nothing else but B and C are relevant to T. This is all we need according to (Def Cause) in order to say that C caused T.

I next turn to an example, due to Bromberger, that, apart from its relevance to the analysis of causality, also shows in the case of *deductive explanations* that it is necessary to keep different epistemic states separated.[3] The connection between causation and explanation is discussed in section 9.6. An example with a similar structure is also presented in Gärdenfors (1976). This kind of example presents a problem for both regularity analyses of causation and probabilistic theories (as well as for Hempel's theory of explanations), but I want to show that it can be given an appropriate epistemic analysis along the lines of (Def Cause).

Bromberger's example concerns a flagpole of height h that at noon on a sunny day casts a shadow of length l. According to most people's intuitions, the position of the sun and the height of the flagpole cause (and explain) the length of the shadow. But, given the length of the shadow and the elevation of the sun, we can also deductively *infer* the height of the flagpole. However, we protest the idea that the length of the shadow causes (or explains) the height of the flagpole.

This example presents a problem for regularity analyses (and Hempel's theory) because the argument deriving the length of the shadow from the height of the flagpole has the same logical structure as the argument deriving the height of the flagpole from the length of the shadow. Thus there can be no laws or logical conditions that can distinguish the height of the flagpole causing the length of the shadow from the converse relation. Similarly it is a problem for Suppes's analysis, of the kind discussed by Otte, because all probabilities are symmetrical.

My solution to the flagpole example is to investigate the appropriate *contractions* of the outlined epistemic state in the example. Let K be this epistemic state, and let H be the fact that the height of the flagpole is h, L the fact that the length of the shadow is l, and S the fact that the sun is shining (from its particular position). If we now want to show that H causes

L, we should, according to (Def Cause), consider K_H^-. If we give up our belief in H, this would not affect our belief in S, and consequently we would give up the belief in L, that is, $K_H^-(L) < 1$. Because $K_H^-(L/H) = 1$ according to (P$^-$5) (which is valid here because the situation is deterministic), it follows that H causes L in K according to (Def Cause).

In order to determine whether L also causes H, we must consider K_L^-. Now, when giving up L, we must also give up either H or S; that is, we must imagine a situation in which one of these events does not occur. The simplest way to do this is to give up S (that the sun is shining), for example, by assuming that a cloud temporarily covers the sun so that the shadow disappears (this is a smaller change than assuming that the height of the flagpole has been altered). In this situation H would still be accepted, that is, $P_L^-(H) = 1$, which is sufficient to show that L does not cause H.

This analysis can be given a nontechnical description as follows: The smallest variation of the situation to change the height of the flagpole would also change the length of the shadow. On the other hand, the smallest variation to change the shadow would not involve any change in the flagpole. This asymmetry explains the asymmetry in the causal relation. It should be emphasized that the changes involved are of an epistemic nature (and thus need not refer to similarities between possible worlds or their ilk). A related analysis of Bromberger's example is given by Salmon (1971).

Another type of example that is troublesome for Suppes's theory involves so-called *interactive forks*. Salmon (1980) has presented the following instructive example:

Pool balls lie on a table in such a way that the player can put the 8-ball into one corner pocket at the far end of the table if and almost only if his cue-ball goes into the other far corner pocket. Being a relative novice, the player does not realize that fact; moreover, his skill is such that he has only a 50–50 chance of sinking the 8-ball even if he tries. Let us make the further plausible assumption that, if the two balls drop into the respective pockets, the 8-ball will fall before the cue-ball does. Let the event A be the player attempting the shot, B the dropping of the 8-ball into the corner pocket, and C the dropping of the cue-ball into the other corner pocket. Among all of the various shots the player may attempt, a small proportion will result in the cue-ball landing in that pocket. Thus $P(C/B) > P(C)$; consequently, the 8-ball falling into one pocket is a prima facie cause of the cue-ball falling into the other pocket. This is as it should be, but we must also be able to classify B as a spurious cause of C. It is not quite clear how this is to be accomplished. The event A, which must surely qualify as a direct cause of both B and C does not screen B off from C, for $P(C/A) = \frac{1}{2}$ while $P(C/A \cdot B) = 1$. (pp. 65–66)

The task before us is to show that B is not a cause of C according to (Def Cause). The crucial step is to describe P_B^- in sufficient detail. Here it is important to keep in mind that the contraction is a minimal change so that as few beliefs as possible are given up in P_B^-. There is one event, not considered by Salmon, that I think should be made an explicit part of the story, namely, the collision between the cue ball and the eight ball that leads to the sinking of the eight ball. Let us call the occurrence of this event D. Now, if B had not occurred and we should keep as many beliefs as possible in P_B^-, then the belief in D and consequently also the belief in C should be retained. We can, for example, imagine that we do not know whether the course of the eight ball has been interrupted after the collision, which means that the probability of B $[P_B^-(B)]$ is less than 1, as it should be according to ($\mathrm{P}^- 2$), but we still want to have $P_B^-(D) = 1$. By the conditions of the example, we then know that $P_B^-(C/B) = P_B^-(C/D) = P_B^-(C)$, so B is not a cause of C according to (Def Cause).

The reason why Salmon can claim that $P(C/B) > P(C)$ is that he is describing an epistemic state other than the one represented by P_B^-. The epistemic situation he has in mind is the one in which we know that the player has attempted the shot but we do not yet know whether it will result in the collision D. Recall that D describes a collision of the kind that sinks the eight ball. This is the epistemic state that would be described by P_D^- in the present framework. And in this situation the occurrence of B is indeed a strong indication of the occurrence of C, that is, $P_D^-(C/B) > P_D^-(C)$. But, as I hope has been shown by the analysis, P_D^- is not the correct epistemic state to rely on when testing whether B causes C. The upshot of this and the previous examples is that we must be careful to specify which epistemic situation we presuppose when we make probability comparisons.

In pictorial terms the contraction method applied in the analysis consists in going backward along a sequence of (more or less hypothetical) epistemic states that lead up to the event that is seen as the effect of the causal chain. If this sequence of epistemic states, represented by probability functions, is reversed so that we go forward by conditionalization, the result is essentially the method of *successive reconditionalization* presented as "a modest suggestion" by Salmon (1980, pp. 66–70). The main difference between Salmon's method and the one presented here is that Salmon presumes as additional information an initial epistemic state as a starting point for the reconditionalizations; my method starts from the final epistemic state and traces back to an appropriate initial contracted state.

It may be objected that in my analyses of the pool example and Hesslow's thrombosis example I must resort to artificial events, such as the collision *D* and the desire *A* to avoid pregnancy. Thus it may seem that my analysis is open to the same criticism as was leveled against the strategy demanding full information about the causal chain of events—the strategy that Salmon called the "method of more detailed specification." However, I do not believe that these additional events require any extra information that is not already included in the examples. On the contrary, the events are part of the *background knowledge* that goes along with the stories.

9.5   A Comparison with Granger Causality

Currently the most discussed and presumably the most favored explication of probabilistic causality among statisticians and social scientists is that developed by Granger (1969, 1987). I believe that his analysis can be seen as essentially a special case of the analysis suggested in this chapter. In order to substantiate this claim, let me first give a brief summary of Granger's analysis (1987).

Granger prepares his definition of the causal relation by formulating two basic axioms for causation:

(G1)   A causal event occurs before the effect. (Temporal priority)

(G2)   A causal event contains information that is not contained in any other event occurring no later than the cause. (Special relationship)

The intended application area of Granger's analysis is economic variables. He represents such a variable by a random variable sequence $x(t)$ observed at discrete time intervals $j = 0, 1, 2, \ldots, t$. An event that occurs at time t is identified with the value of such a variable at t. The set of all values of the relevant variables up to time t is denoted $O(t)$. He also lets $O(t) - y(t)$ denote the information contained in $O(t)$ minus the sequence $y(t - j), j \geq 0$, where y is one of the relevant variables. His definition can now be formulated as follows:

(Def Granger)   The event described by $y(t)$ causes the event $x(t + 1)$ iff $P(x(t + 1) \in S/O(t)) \neq P(x(t + 1) \in S/O(t) - y(t))$ for some set S.

Or, in words: If the information about the earlier values of y had not been available, the probability of the event that $x(t + 1)$ has the property encompassed by S would have been different. This definition is essentially the same as (Def Cause) restricted to the special case when all the relevant beliefs can be described by the values of the variables included in $O(t)$ and in which the cause occurs immediately before the effect. Granger interprets the probability function P in the definition as an objective probability. The states of belief are thus represented by the different sets of the form $O(t)$. $O(t)$ itself corresponds to the present epistemic state, that is, P in (Def Cause), and $O(t) - y(t)$ corresponds to the contraction P_C^-. Note that $O(t) - y(t)$ could not contain the values $y(t - 1), y(t - 2), \ldots$ because these may be strongly correlated with $y(t)$ and may thus screen off the causal influence of $y(t)$ on $x(t + 1)$.

Granger then makes this definition operational by replacing $O(t)$ with a smaller, more practical information set $I(t)$, which is assumed to contain at least $x(t - j), y(t - j), j \geq 0$, but which may also contain some other measurable variables $z(t - j), j \geq 0$. Now if $P(x(t + 1) \in S/I(t)) \neq P(x(t + 1) \in S/I(t) - y(t))$ for some set S, then $y(t)$ is said to be a prima facie cause of $x(t + 1)$ with respect to the information set $I(t)$. The reason for this name is that $y(t)$ may fail to be a cause of $x(t + 1)$ in $O(t)$ because some variable that is an actual cause of $x(t + 1)$ may have been eliminated from $I(t)$, and if this variable is added to $I(t)$, it would screen off $y(t)$ from $x(t + 1)$. This is basically the same problem as the one Suppes (1970) tries to solve by his definition of spurious causes. For a comparison between Suppes's and Granger's theories, see Spohn (1983b).

9.6   Causation and Explanation

It is often claimed that there is a close relationship between causation and explanation. In particular, it has been argued that causal relations provide the ground for explanations. In this section I want to show how this relation can be explicated using the analyses of explanation and causation. Recall that both analyses deal primarily with *singular* events.

The models of belief used in this chapter are simpler than those in chapter 8, which involved second-order probabilities. This difference is not essential for the comparison, and I make the simplifying assumption that the epistemic states that are used for both explanations and causations are modeled by single probability functions. For explanations this probability function is the belief function B introduced in section 8.3, which for uniformity is here denoted by P. If we, for the sake of the comparison, disregard the role of the law sentences (the T sentences) in (EXP), we can reformulate this definition as follows:

(Exp') C is an *explanation* of E relative to the epistemic state described by P, iff (i) $P(E) = 1$, $P(C) < 1$ and (ii) $P_E^- (E/C) > P_E^- (E)$.

In order to make the comparison easier, I repeat the definition of causation:

(Def Cause) C is a *cause* of E relative to the epistemic state described by P iff (i) $P(C) = P(E) = 1$ and (ii) $P_C^- (E/C) > P_C^- (E)$.

In both these definitions C and E are taken to be descriptions of single events.

There are two differences between (Exp') and (Def Cause). The first is that the explanans C is assumed to be unknown in P but is assumed to be known when the causal relation is evaluated. The second is that the test for the inequality is applied to P_E^- in (Exp'), whereas it is applied to P_C^- in (Def Cause). This difference may seem to be of crucial importance, but I want to argue that it is mainly superficial.

Let us take a typical example of a causal relation between two events C and E, for instance, that Oscar's drinking of champagne caused his hiccups. We assume that in the present epistemic state P it is known that both C and E have occurred, that is, $P(E) = P(C) = 1$. Why can we claim that the causal relation between C and E is a reason for saying that C is an *explanation* of E? First of all, C cannot be an explanation of E in the epistemic state described by P because C is known in P. But if we in P *imagine* a situation P' in which someone knows that Oscar has hiccups (E) but does not know that he has been drinking champagne (C), then this information would indeed provide an explanation of E *in relation to P'*.

This intuition can now be translated into the terminology of the present work. The key question is, How does the imagined epistemic state P' relate to P? C must be contracted from P, but E must be known. The most natural solution is to take P' to be $(P_C^-)_E^+$. Even if this is not the only possible alternative, I think we can safely assume that $P_E'^-$ is identical with P_C^-. In any case the assumption that $P_E'^- = P_C^-$ is all that is needed, because it then follows immediately that $P_E'^- (E/C) > P_E'^- (E)$ iff $P_C^- (E/C) > P_C^- (E)$. But this establishes what we wanted to show: All conditions of (Exp') are fulfilled with respect to P'.

The upshot is that, *if* C *is a cause of* E *in* P, *then* C *is an explanation of*

E *in* P'. Thus the difference between the inequality tests in (Exp') and (Def Cause) disappears if it is acknowledged that they must apply to different epistemic states. I believe that this strategy works for all cases of causation between single events. This is then a strong argument for the claim that causal relations between events can be used for explanations.

Let us then look at the converse situation, when an explanation of an event described by E has been given. Do all explanations contain information about causal relations? To answer this question, let us assume that E is known to have occurred in the epistemic state described by P, that is, $P(E) = 1$, and that C explains E relative to P, that is, $P(C) < 1$ and $P_E^-(E/C) > P_E^-(E)$. If C is accepted as having occurred (so that it is not just a potential explanation), then the new epistemic state is P_C^+. It is in relation to this situation that the question of whether C is a cause of E is most naturally evaluated.

The key problem is now how $(P_C^+)_C^-$ relates to P and P_E^-. Let us assume, for the sake of the argument, that our intuitions already make it possible for us to say whether or not C is a cause of E. When C is not judged to be causally related to E but merely correlated with E, such as the correlation between a low barometer reading and stormy weather, $(P_C^+)_C^-$ is most likely P itself, that is, the state in which the explanation was given. In this state C does not raise the probability of E, and thus it fails the test in (Def Cause).

If, on the other hand, C is indeed an intuitive cause of E, then $(P_C^+)_C^-$ does not contain E as known, and it is natural to identify $(P_C^+)_C^-$ with P_E^-. Because we have assumed that $P_E^-(E/C) > P_E^-(E)$, we can then conclude that the inequality in (Def Cause) is satisfied, assuming that P_C^+ is the state in relation to which the test for causality is performed.

This argument shows that not all arguments that are explanations according to (Exp') are based on causal relations. For instance, events can be explained by causal epiphenomena, according to (Exp'): Low barometer readings can explain stormy weather. However, the argument suggests a way of strengthening (Exp'):

(C-Exp') C is a *causal explanation* of E relative to the epistemic state described by P iff (i) $P(E) = 1$, $P(C) < 1$; (ii) $P_E^-(E/C) > P_E^-(E)$; and (iii) $(P_C^+)_C^- = P_E^-$.

The addition of clause (iii) guarantees that, if C is an explanation of E *in relation to P*, C is a cause of E *in relation to P_C^+* according to (Def Cause). (C-Exp') can also of course be generalized to cover the epistemic models used in chapter 8. In conclusion, it has been shown that, if the analysis of explanations is based on (C-Exp′), there is a natural symmetry between causation and explanation.

9.7   Some Further Aspects of the Causal Analysis

The causal relation introduced in (Def Cause) should be regarded as a relation of direct causation. It turns out that, given postulates $(P^- 1)$–$(P^- 6)$, the relation is not transitive in general. In my opinion this is as it should be: If C causes D and D causes E, then C may, but need not, cause E. The latter case can occur when C causes a part of D but another part of D causes E [see Granger (1987)]. For example, consider a chemical reaction in which a solution of silver chloride is poured into nitric acid, causing silver nitrate to precipitate and turning the acid into chloric acid. Then one can say that adding the silver chloride is a cause of the formation of chloric acid, because it contributes the chloride ions. The presence of chloric acid is also a cause of the low pH value of the solution, because it contributes the hydrogen ions. But the addition of silver chloride is not a cause of the low pH value of the solution.[4]

Another question that should be considered is what the consequences of (Def Cause) are for cases of *causal overdetermination*. For example, Oscar married Victoria because he loved her and because she was pregnant. Either of these two facts is a sufficient motive for the marriage. Let us denote the fact that Oscar loved Victoria by A, the fact that she was pregnant by B, and the event that they married by C. Furthermore, Oscar's present epistemic state is represented by P. If we apply (Def Cause) to this case, we see that it has the consequence that A does not cause C because B is still accepted in P_A^-, and thus $P_A^-(C/A) = P_A^-(C/B) = P_A^-(C)$. For similar reasons, B does not cause C according to (Def Cause). This may appear counterintuitive. However, I do not consider this a serious problem, for (Def Cause) has the consequence that A *or* B is a cause of C: If P is contracted with respect to $A \vee B$, both A and B must be retracted, and then it follows that $P_{A \vee B}^-(C/A \vee B) = 1 > P_{A \vee B}^-(C)$.

It should be emphasized once again that the analysis of the causal relation given in (Def Cause) applies to *actual causal chains*, not to causal laws in general. The events C and E that are involved in the test for a causal relation are thus known to have occurred [as is required by clause (i) in the definition]. This means that the present probabilities of the events are of no use (because they are both 1); it is other probabilities that must be relied on. Because earlier analyses of probabilistic causation have not been explicit about which epistemic situations these probabilities should be related to, it has been easy to slip between probabilities of single events and probabilities of event types as involved in causal laws. Suppes (1970) makes this quite clear: "A deliberate equivocation in reference between events and kinds of events runs through the earlier systematic sections of this monograph. It is intended that the formalism can be used under either interpretation" (p. 79).

I believe that such an equivocation is dangerous, because which general probability laws are relevant to the evaluation of single events is heavily dependent on the epistemic state that is presupposed for the evaluation. As I tried to show in section 9.4, many of the problems presented for Suppes's theory and related theories are due to such equivocations. In my opinion, it is extremely important to use the correct epistemic background situation in the causal analysis.

According to the analysis presented here, the causal relation between *single events* is the fundamental relation. All general causal claims are derived from causal relations between single events. When we say that stress causes heart attacks, we mean that some events of stress cause some heart attacks. If the relevant background knowledge can be kept relatively fixed, we may even be able to give numerical estimates of how frequently an event of a certain type causes an event of another type. However, such statements are methodologically difficult to evaluate.

On the other hand, when determining the probability of a single event in a particular epistemic state, actual or hypothetical, *probabilistic* laws are crucial. Such fixations of the probabilities of single events are the central part of the specification of the relevant contraction function. And, as we have seen in the earlier examples, it is the contraction function that does the heavy duty in the analysis based on (Def Cause).

It is a fundamental philosophical problem to describe the "direct inference" from laws to individual events [this notion is borrowed from Levi (1977a)]. It is inferences of this kind that are used when the exact content of the contractions of probability functions is determined. Of course, in order to avoid circularity, such inferences must be made without relying on the notion of causality. I have nothing to contribute to the solution of this problem, except for the discussion in section 8.4. I want to emphasize that the real substance of the problem of probabilistic causation lies in the probability relations between single events and probabilistic laws. The test for causality formulated in (Def Cause) presupposes that the probabilities of the single events are already determined.

Thus a full analysis of causation among single events consists in two major steps. The first is an account of the relation between probabilistic laws (accepted in a given epistemic state) and probabilities of single events. Understanding this relation not only is important for a theory of causation but also has applications within many other problem areas. The second step is a test of the probability relations between the single events that are the alleged cause and effect. In this chapter (Def Cause) has been suggested as an appropriate account of the second step.

This two-step picture of causation can be compared with Hume's two definitions of causation. He wrote: "We may define a cause to be an object followed by another, and where all the objects, similar to the first, are followed by objects similar to the second" (Hume 1748, sec. VII). As interpreted in modern probabilistic terminology, this definition contains a sketch of a solution to the problem of the connection between the epistemic values of types of events and single events, that is, the first step in my description. For me the epistemic values are probabilities; for Hume they are connections between impressions. Hume spends most of his analysis describing the "genesis" of these connections in our minds.

Hume's second definition follows the first immediately: "Or, in other words, where, if the first object had not been, the second never had existed." This definition is not supported by any earlier analysis in his text. So the phrase "or, in other words" seems rather misplaced. When presenting (Def Cause), I said that I regard it as a probabilistic version of Hume's second definition. The second definition can thus be seen as a solution to the second step in my description of a causal analysis. If my picture is not misleading, Hume's two definitions are solutions to two different problems: The first is a genetic analysis of causal connections, and the second is a test in terms of contractions for when we find a causal relation between two single events.

9.8 Limitations of the Analysis

The analysis of causation presented in section 9.2 is heavily dependent on using probability functions as models of epistemic states. There are, however, several aspects of beliefs that are not captured by such a representation and that affect the outcome of the causal analysis.

One dimension that has been neglected at large in this book is the *temporal* aspect of the beliefs. The description of a single event naturally involves the time it occurred. Some analyses of causation postulate that the cause must not occur later than the effect. If we want this kind of causality, it is easy to add the appropriate clause to (Def Cause). An alternative is not to rule out backward causation or causal loops a priori but to expect that (Def Cause), by means of the properties of the contraction P_C^-, results in the desired temporal relation between C and E. One way of ensuring this is to postulate that, when the probability function P is contracted to P_C^-, the probabilities of all events that occurred before C remain the same in P_C^- as in P. This means that all beliefs about the history of events up to C are left unaltered in the construction of the hypothetical state of belief P_C^-.

Another aspect that has been treated rather lightheartedly is the notion of *acceptance*. As several philosophers have shown, there are many subtleties to acceptance that cannot be captured by simply using probability functions as models of epistemic states. Especially relevant in this context are Adams's works on probabilities of conditionals (for example, his 1975 book; also see the discussion in section 2.2).

Finally, the probabilistic models of belief are not handy for describing *functional* dependencies of the kind studied, for example, by Simon and Rescher (1966). As they show, causal relations are often determined by functional correlations between different variables. And such correlations are difficult to describe using only probability functions defined over single events.

In conclusion, I hope to have shown that, despite the limitations mentioned here, (Def Cause) provides a viable analysis of causality between single events for the case when epistemic states can be described by probability functions. This analysis reduces the problem of causality, I hope in a noncircular way, to the problem of identifying contractions of states of belief.

In this final section I have indicated some limitations of the analysis that are due to the simplicity of the probabilistic models of epistemic states. Because similar limitations apply to some of the applications presented in earlier chapters, an appropriate topic for future research is to present more comprehensive and realistic models of epistemic states.

Appendix A
Proofs of Main Lemmas and Theorems of Chapter 3

(3.2)   If $B \in K_A^+$, then $K_B^+ \subseteq K_A^+$.

Proof   By (K^+3), $K \subseteq K_A^+$. Applying (K^+5), we derive that $K_B^+ \subseteq (K_A^+)_B^+$. Suppose that $B \in K_A^+$. It then follows from (K^+4) that $(K_A^+)_B^+ = K_A^+$. Hence $K_B^+ \subseteq K_A^+$.

(3.5) $(K_A^+)_B^+ = K_{A \& B}^+$.

Proof   If follows from (K^+1), (K^+2), and (K^+3) that $A \& B \in (K_A^+)_B^+$. Hence (3.2) implies that $K_{A \& B}^+ \subseteq (K_A^+)_B^+$. For the converse, first note that (K^+3) implies that $K \subseteq K_{A \& B}^+$. From (K^+5), applied twice, it then follows that $(K_A^+)_B^+ \subseteq ((K_{A \& B}^+)_A^+)_B^+$. But because A and B are included in $K_{A \& B}^+$, it follows that $((K_{A \& B}^+)_A^+)_B^+ = K_{A \& B}^+$ by two applications of (K^+4).

THEOREM 3.1   The expansion function $+$ satisfies (K^+1)–(K^+6) iff $K_A^+ = Cn(K \cup \{A\})$.

Proof   It is easy to show that, if we define K_A^+ to be $Cn(K \cup \{A\})$, it satisfies (K^+1)–(K^+5). To show that it satisfies (K^+6), that is, that it is the minimal belief set satisfying these conditions, it is sufficient to show that $Cn(K \cup \{A\}) \subseteq K_A^+$ follows from (K^+1)–(K^+5). To establish this, assume that $B \in Cn(K \cup \{A\})$. It then follows from the deduction theorem that $(A \rightarrow B) \in K$. By (K^+1), (K^+2), and (K^+3), we then have $B \in K_A^+$.

The converse implication follows from (3.8).

(3.13) $K_A^* = K_B^*$ if and only if $B \in K_A^*$ and $A \in K_B^*$.

Proof   From left to right is trivial. For the converse, assume that $B \in K_A^*$ and $A \in K_B^*$. Except when $\vdash -A$ and $\vdash -B$, which are trivial anyway, the following series of identities is easily established with the aid of (K^*7) and (K^*8): $K_A^* = (K_A^*)_B^+ = K_{A \& B}^* = (K_B^*)_A^+ = K_B^*$.

(3.14) $K_A^* \cap K_B^* \subseteq K_{A \& B}^*$.

Proof   We show that, given (K^*1)–(K^*6), (K^*7) is equivalent to (3.14). It is first shown that (K^*7) entails (3.14). Assume $C \in K_A^*$. It follows from (K^*6) that $K_A^* = K_{(A \vee B) \& A}^*$. Postulate (K^*7) then entails that $C \in (K_{A \vee B}^*)_A^+$. Hence $(A \rightarrow C) \in K_{A \vee B}^*$. Similarly it follows from the assumption that $C \in K_B^*$ that $(B \rightarrow C) \in K_{A \vee B}^*$. Taken together these two assumptions entail that $(A \vee B \rightarrow C) \in K_{A \vee B}^*$ and thus $C \in K_{A \vee B}^*$.

Conversely suppose that (3.14) is satisfied. Assume that $C \in K_{A \& B}^*$. It follows that $B \rightarrow C \in K_{A \& B}^*$. Because $-B \in K_{A \& -B}^*$, it also follows that

$B \to C \in K^*_{A\,\&\,-B}$. Because $K^*_{A\,\&\,B} \cap K^*_{A\,\&\,-B} \subseteq K^*_A$ by (3.14), it follows that $B \to C \in K^*_A$ and hence $C \in (K^*_A)^+_B$.

(3.15)   If $-B \notin K^*_{A\,\vee\,B}$, then $K^*_{A\,\vee\,B} \subseteq K^*_B$.

Proof   We show that (3.15) is equivalent to (K*8). First, suppose that (K*8) is fulfilled. To show (3.15), assume that $-B \notin K^*_{A\,\vee\,B}$. Postulates (K*8) and (K*6) then immediately validate the sequence $K^*_{A\,\vee\,B} \subseteq (K^*_{A\,\vee\,B})^+_B \subseteq K^*_{(A\,\vee\,B)\,\&\,B} = K^*_B$.

Conversely, assume that (3.15) is satisfied. Assume that $-B \notin K^*_A$. It follows that $-(A\,\&\,B) \notin K^*_A$. Postulate (K*6) entails $-(A\,\&\,B) \notin K^*_{A\,\&\,B\,\vee\,A\,\&\,-B}$. Thus, by (3.15), $K^*_A \subseteq K^*_{A\,\&\,B}$ and then, finally, by (K$^+$5), $(K^*_A)^+_B \subseteq (K^*_{A\,\&\,B})^+_B = K^*_{A\,\&\,B}$.

(3.16) $K^*_{A\,\vee\,B} = K^*_A$ or $K^*_{A\,\vee\,B} = K^*_B$ or $K^*_{A\,\vee\,B} = K^*_A \cap K^*_B$.

Proof   We show that, in the presence of the other axioms, (3.16) is equivalent to the conjunction of (K*7) and (K*8). We first show that (K*7) and (K*8) entail (3.16). When $-B \in K^*_{A\,\vee\,B}$, it follows that $A \in K^*_{A\,\vee\,B}$ and hence from (3.13) that $K^*_{A\,\vee\,B} = K^*_A$. A parallel argument shows that if $-A \in K^*_{A\,\vee\,B}$, then $K^*_{A\,\vee\,B} = K^*_B$. This leaves us with the case when $-A \notin K^*_{A\,\vee\,B}$ and $-B \notin K^*_{A\,\vee\,B}$. Using (3.15), we then know that $K^*_{A\,\vee\,B} \subseteq K^*_A$ and $K^*_{A\,\vee\,B} \subseteq K^*_B$, which means that $K^*_{A\,\vee\,B} \subseteq K^*_A \cap K^*_B$. The inverse inclusion is provided by (3.14), so in this case we have the identity $K^*_{A\,\vee\,B} = K^*_A \cap K^*_B$.

To show that (3.16) entails (K*7), it is sufficient to note that it entails (3.14), which has been shown to be equivalent to (K*7).

Finally, to show that (3.16) entails (K*8), we start from the observation that (3.16) together with (K*6) entail that K^*_A is identical with one of $K^*_{A\,\&\,B}$, $K^*_{A\,\&\,-B}$, or $K^*_{A\,\&\,B} \cap K^*_{A\,\&\,-B}$. In the first case $(K^*_A)^+_B = (K^*_{A\,\&\,B})^+_B = K^*_{A\,\&\,B}$. In the second case, $(K^*_A)^+_B = (K^*_{A\,\&\,-B})^+_B = K_\perp$. In the third case, $(K^*_A)^+_B = (K^*_{A\,\&\,B} \cap K^*_{A\,\&\,-B})^+_B = (K^*_{A\,\&\,B})^+_B \cap (K^*_{A\,\&\,-B})^+_B = K^*_{A\,\&\,B} \cap K_\perp = K^*_{A\,\&\,B}$. In either case it is easy to show that, if $-B \notin K^*_A$, then $(K^*_A)^+_B \subseteq K^*_{A\,\&\,B}$.

(3.19) K^*_A is maximal for any sentence A such that $-A \in K$.

Proof   We show that (3.17) together with (K*1)–(K*6) entail (3.19). Assume that $-A \in K$. Suppose that $-B \notin K^*_A$. It follows that $-A \vee -B \notin K^*_A$. But we have $-A \vee -B \in K$. Expression (3.17) then entails that $-(-A \vee -B) \in K^*_A$ and thus by (K*6) $A\,\&\,B \in K^*_A$. This gives us immediately $B \in K^*_A$.

(3.21) If $A \in K$, then $(K_A^-)_A^+ \subseteq K$.

Proof Postulates (K^-2) and (K^+5) imply that $(K_A^-)_A^+ \subseteq K_A^+$. But if $A \in K$, then $K_A^+ = K$ by (K^+4).

(3.22) $K_A^- = K \cap (K_A^-)_{-A}^+$.

Proof First suppose that $A \in K$. Then, by (K^-5) and (3.21), $K = (K_A^-)_A^+$. By theorem 3.1, $K \cap (K_A^-)_{-A}^+ = (K_A^-)_A^+ \cap (K_A^-)_{-A}^+ = Cn(K_A^- \cup \{A\}) \cap Cn(K_A^- \cup \{-A\}) = Cn(K_A^-) = K_A^-$. Next suppose that $A \notin K$. Then $K_A^- = K$ by (K^-3), and it follows from (K^+3) and (K^-4) that $K \cap (K_A^-)_{-A}^+ = K \cap K_{-A}^+ = K = K_A^-$.

(3.25) $K_A^- \cap Cn(\{A\}) \subseteq K_{A \& B}^-$.

Proof We want to show that, given (K^-1)–(K^-6), (3.25) is equivalent to (K^-7). First, suppose that (K^-7) is satisfied. Suppose that $C \in K_A^-$ and $C \in Cn(\{A\})$; we want to show that $C \in K_{A \& B}^-$. If $A \notin K$ or $B \notin K$, then trivially $K_{A \& B}^- = K$; so $C \in K_{A \& B}^-$. Now suppose that $A \in K$ and $B \in K$. Then we have $K_{A \& B}^- = K_{(-A \vee B) \& A}^-$; so by (K^-7) it suffices to show that $C \in K_{-A \vee B}^-$ and $C \in K_A^-$. We have the latter by supposition. As for the former, (K^-5) gives us $K_{-A \vee B}^- \cup \{-A \vee B\} \vdash A$; so $K_{-A \vee B}^- \cup \{-A\} \vdash A$, and thus $K_{-A \vee B}^- \vdash A$. But $C \in Cn(\{A\})$; so $C \in K_{-A \vee B}^-$.

For the converse, suppose that (3.25) is satisfied and that $C \in K_A^-$ and $C \in K_B^-$; we want to show that $C \in K_{A \& B}^-$. Because $C \in K_A^-$, we have $A \vee C \in K_A^-$, and thus, because $A \vdash A \vee C$, (3.25) gives us $A \vee C \in K_{A \& B}^-$. Similarly, $B \vee C \in K_{A \& B}^-$. Because $C \vee A \& B$ is equivalent to $(A \vee C) \& (B \vee C)$, we have $C \vee A \& B \in K_{A \& B}^-$. But by (K^-5), $K_{A \& B}^- \cup \{A \& B\} \vdash C$; so $C \vee -(A \& B) \in K_{A \& B}^-$. Putting these together gives us $C \in K_{A \& B}^-$.

(3.27) Either $K_{A \& B}^- = K_A^-$ or $K_{A \& B}^- = K_B^-$ or $K_{A \& B}^- = K_A^- \cap K_B^-$.

Proof We show that a contraction function satisfies (3.27) iff it satisfies both (K^-7) and (K^-8). First, suppose that (3.27) is satisfied. Then (K^-7) holds immediately. For (K^-8), let A and B be such that $A \notin K_{A \& B}^-$; we need to show that $K_{A \& B}^- \subseteq K_A^-$. When $A \notin K$, this holds trivially; so we suppose that $A \in K$. Now $Cn(A \& B) = Cn(A \& (-A \vee B))$; so by (3.27) $K_{A \& B}^-$ is identical with one of K_A^-, $K_{-A \vee B}^-$, or $K_A^- \cap K_{-A \vee B}^-$. In the first and last cases we have the desired inclusion; we need only show that the middle case is impossible. By recovery, $K_{-A \vee B}^- \cup \{-A \vee B\} \vdash A$; thus $K_{-A \vee B}^- \cup \{-A\} \vdash A$, and so $A \in K_{-A \vee B}^-$. But by hypothesis, $A \notin K_{A \& B}^-$; so $K_{A \& B}^- \neq K_{-A \vee B}^-$, as desired.

For the converse, suppose that $(K^- 7)$ and $(K^- 8)$ are satisfied, and suppose that $K_{A \& B}^- \neq K_A^-$ and $K_{A \& B}^- \neq K_B^-$; we want to show that $K_{A \& B}^- = K_A^- \cap K_B^-$. By $(K^- 7)$ it suffices to show that $K_{A \& B}^- \subseteq K_A^-$ and $K_{A \& B}^- \subseteq K_B^-$. By (3.26), which is an immediate consequence of $(K^- 8)$, we have at least one of these inclusions. So it remains to show that under our hypothesis either inclusion implies the other. We prove one; the other is similar. Suppose for contradiction that $K_{A \& B}^- \subseteq K_A^-$ but $K_{A \& B}^- \nsubseteq K_B^-$. Because by hypothesis $K_{A \& B}^- \neq K_A^-$, we have $K_A^- \nsubseteq K_{A \& B}^-$; so there is a $C \in K_A^-$ with $C \notin K_{A \& B}^-$. Because $K_{A \& B}^- \nsubseteq K_B^-$, we have by $(K^- 8)$ that $B \in K_{A \& B}^-$. Hence, because $C \notin K_{A \& B}^-$, we have $-B \vee C \notin K_{A \& B}^-$. Hence by $(K^- 7)$ $-B \vee C \notin K_A^-$ or $-B \vee C \notin K_B^-$. But because $C \in K_A^-$, the former alternative is impossible, and the second alternative is also impossible, because by $(K^- 5)$ $K_B^- \cup \{B\} \vdash C$, so that $-B \vee C \in K_B^-$. This contradiction concludes the proof.

(3.29) If $B, C \in K$ and $B \vee C \in K_A^-$, then either $B \in K_A^-$ or $C \in K_A^-$.

Proof We show that $(K^- F)$ is equivalent to (3.29). Suppose that $(K^- F)$ is satisfied. Assume that $B \in K$, $C \in K$, and $B \vee C \in K_A^-$; we want to show that either $B \in K_A^-$ or $C \in K_A^-$. If $\vdash A$, then $K_A^- = K$, and the desired conclusion follows trivially. So assume that not $\vdash A$. Suppose for contradiction that $B \notin K_A^-$ and $C \notin K_A^-$. By $(K^- F)$ we then have $B \to A \in K_A^-$ and $C \to A \in K_A^-$ and so $B \vee C \to A \in K_A^-$ and hence $A \in K_A^-$, which contradicts $(K^- 4)$.

For the converse, suppose that (3.29) is satisfied, and suppose that $B \in K$ and $B \notin K_A^-$. We need to show that $B \to A \in K_A^-$. Now $\vdash B \vee (B \to A)$, and so $B \vee (B \to A) \in K_A^-$. Also by hypothesis $B \in K$, and because $B \notin K_A^-$, it follows from $(K^- 3)$ that $A \in K$ and hence $B \to A \in K$. We can now apply (3.29) to get $B \to A \in K_A^-$, which is the desired conclusion.

(3.30) Either $K_{A \& B}^- = K_A^-$ or $K_{A \& B}^- = K_B^-$.

Proof We show that (3.30) entails $(K^- F)$. Suppose for contradiction that $B \in K$, $B \notin K_A^-$, and $B \to A \notin K_A^-$. Note that this implies by $(K^- 3)$ that $A \in K$. Now $\vdash A \leftrightarrow (A \vee B) \& (A \vee -B)$ so by (3.30) we have either $K_A^- = K_{A \vee B}^-$ or $K_A^- = K_{A \vee -B}^-$. In the former case $B \to A \notin K_{A \vee B}^-$. But by $(K^- 5)$ $K_{A \vee B}^- \cup \{A \vee B\} \vdash A$; so $K_{A \vee B}^- \cup \{B\} \vdash A$, and thus $B \to A \in K_{A \vee B}^-$, giving a contradiction. And in the latter case $B \notin K_{A \vee -B}^-$, whereas by $(K^- 5)$ $K_{A \vee -B}^- \cup \{A \vee -B\} \vdash B$; so $K_{A \vee -B}^- \cup \{-B\} \vdash B$; so $K_{A \vee -B}^- \vdash B$, again giving a contradiction.

THEOREM 3.2   If the contraction function $-$ satisfies $(K^-1)-(K^-4)$ and (K^-6) and the expansions satisfy $(K^+1)-(K^+6)$ (that is, expansions can be defined as in theorem 3.1), then the revision function $*$ obtained from (Def $*$) satisfies $(K*1)-(K*6)$.

Proof   Postulates $(K*1)$ and $(K*2)$ are trivial. Postulate $(K*3)$ follows from the fact that $K_A^- \subseteq K$. To show $(K*4)$, assume that $-A \notin K$. Then $K = K_{-A}^-$; so $K_A^+ = (K_{-A}^-)_A^+ = K_A^*$. Postulate $(K*5)$ follows essentially from (K^-4), and $(K*6)$ follows directly from (K^-6).

THEOREM 3.3   Suppose that the assumptions of theorem 3.2 are fulfilled. Then (a) if (K^-7) is satisfied, $(K*7)$ is satisfied for the defined revision function, and (b) if (K^-8) is satisfied, $(K*8)$ is satisfied for the defined revision function.

Proof   Suppose that (K^-7) is satisfied, and suppose that $C \in K_{A\&B}^*$. We want to show that $C \in (K_A^*)_B^+ = ((K_{-A}^-)_A^+)_B^+ = (K_{-A}^-)_{A\&B}^+$. Because $-A$ is logically equivalent to $-(A\&B)\&(A \to B)$, it suffices by (K^-7) to show that $C \in (K_{-(A\&B)}^-)_{A\&B}^+$ and $C \in (K_{A\to B}^-)_{A\&B}^+$. But because $(K_{-(A\&B)}^-)_{A\&B}^+ = K_{A\&B}^*$, the former is given by hypothesis; so we need verify only the latter. Because $C \in K_{A\&B}^*$, we know that $A \& B \to C \in K$, and hence by (K^-5) $(A \to B) \to (A \& B \to C) \in K_{A\to B}^-$. But this entails by propositional logic that $A \& B \to C \in K_{A\to B}^-$, and hence $C \in (K_{A\to B}^-)_{A\&B}^+$, as desired.

Next assume that (K^-8) is satisfied. We want to show that $(K*8)$ holds for all A and B. Because $-A$ is logically equivalent to $(-A \lor -B)\& -A$, it follows that $K_{-A}^- = K_{(-A \lor -B)\& -A}^-$. If we now suppose that $-B \notin K_A^* = (K_{-A}^-)_A^+$, it follows that $-A \lor -B \notin K_{-A}^-$. We may thus apply (K^-8) to get $K_{-A}^- = K_{(-A \lor -B)\& -A}^- \subseteq K_{-A \lor -B}^- = K_{-(A\&B)}^-$. This inclusion justifies the inclusion in the following chain, whose other steps are trivial: $(K_A^*)_B^+ = ((K_{-A}^-)_A^+)_B^+ = (K_{-A}^-)_{A\&B}^+ \subseteq (K_{-(A\&B)}^-)_{A\&B}^+ = K_{A\&B}^*$.

THEOREM 3.4   If the revision function $*$ satisfies $(K*1)-(K*6)$, then the contraction function $-$ generated by (Def $-$) satisfies $(K^-1)-(K^-6)$.

Proof   The only axiom that is not trivial is (K^-5). To prove this, assume that $A \in K$. $(K_A^-)_A^+$ is by (Def $-$) the same as $(K \cap K_{-A}^*)_A^+$, which by (3.9) is identical with $K_A^+ \cap (K_{-A}^*)_A^+$. Now $K \subseteq K_A^+$ and also $K \subseteq K_\perp = (K_{-A}^*)_A^+$, so $K \subseteq K_A^+ \cap (K_{-A}^*)_A^+ = (K_A^-)_A^+$, as desired.

THEOREM 3.5   Suppose that the revision function $*$ satisfies $(K*1)-(K*6)$ so that theorem 3.4 is applicable. Then (a) if $(K*7)$ is satisfied, (K^-7) is satisfied for the defined contraction function, and (b) if (K*8) is satisfied, (K⁻8) is satisfied for the defined contraction function.

Proof Suppose that (K*7) holds for all A and B, and suppose that $C \in K_A^- \cap K_B^-$. We need to show that $C \in K_{A \& B}^-$. Because A is logically equivalent to $-((-A \vee -B) \& -A)$, it follows that $C \in K_{-((-A \vee -B) \& -A)}^- \subseteq K_{(-A \vee -B) \& -A}^* \subseteq (K_{-A \vee -B}^*)_{-A}^+$. A similar reasoning gives us also $C \in (K_{-A \vee -B}^*)_{-B}^+$. It follows that $C \in K_{-A \vee -B}^* = (K_{A \& B}^-)_{-(A \& B)}^+$. But it follows from (K⁻5) that $C \in (K_{A \& B}^-)_{A \& B}^+$, and by combination of these facts we have $C \in K_{A \& B}^-$.

Next assume that (K*8) is satisfied. Suppose that $A \notin K_{A \& B}^-$. Then clearly $A \notin (K_{A \& B}^-)_{-(A \& B)}^+ = K_{-(A \& B)}^*$; so we may apply (K*8) to get $(K_{-(A \& B)}^*)_{-A}^+ \subseteq K_{-(A \& B) \& -A}^* = K_{-A}^* = (K_A^-)_{-A}^+$. It follows that $K_{A \& B}^- \subseteq (K_A^-)_{-A}^+$. But using (K⁻5), we also have $K_{A \& B}^- \subseteq K \subseteq (K_A^-)_A^+$; so by disjunction of premises we conclude that $K_{A \& B}^- \subseteq K_A^-$, as desired.

(3.28)   If $B \to A \in K_A^-$ and $A \to B \in K_B^-$, then $K_A^- = K_B^-$.

Proof Assume the left-hand side. It follows that $-A \to -B \in K_A^-$ and $-B \to -A \in K_B^-$. By means of the Levi identity, we know that $-B \in K_A^*$ and $-A \in K_B^*$. Thus by (3.13), $K_A^* = K_B^*$, and so, finally, by means of the Harper identity, $K_A^- = K_B^-$.

Appendix B
Proofs of Main Lemmas and Theorems of Chapter 4

LEMMA 4.5 If $A \in K$ and K_A^- is defined by means of a maxichoice contraction function, then for any proposition B either $A \vee B \in K_A^-$ or $A \vee -B \in K_A^-$.

Proof Because $A \in K$, we have both $A \vee B \in K$ and $A \vee -B \in K$. In the limiting case when $\vdash A$, we have $K_A^- = K$, and we are done. Suppose that not $\vdash A$, and suppose for contradiction that $A \vee B \notin K_A^-$ and $A \vee -B \notin K_A^-$. Because $K_A^- \in K \perp A$, it follows that $K_A^- \cup \{A \vee B\} \vdash A$ and likewise $K_A^- \cup \{A \vee -B\} \vdash A$. Hence $K_A^- \cup \{B\} \vdash A$ and $K_A^- \cup \{-B\} \vdash A$, and thus $K_A^- \vdash A$. But this contradicts the fact that $K_A^- \in K \perp A$.

LEMMA 4.9 If K_A^- is defined by means of a full meet contraction and $A \in K$, then $B \in K_A^-$ iff $B \in K$ and $-A \vdash B$.

Proof In the limiting case when $\vdash A$, then trivially $-A \vdash B$, and by the definition of $K \perp A$, we have $K_A^- = K$, and hence $B \in K_A^-$ iff $B \in K$. Suppose for the principal case that not $\vdash A$. Suppose first that $B \in K$ and $-A \vdash B$, and suppose for contradiction that $B \notin K_A^-$. This means that there is some $K' \in K \perp A$ such that $B \notin K'$. But because $B \in K$, we have then by the maximality of K' that $K' \cup \{B\} \vdash A$. And because $-A \vdash B$ we have by contraposition that $-B \vdash A$; so $K' \cup \{-B\} \vdash A$. Putting these together gives us $K' \vdash A$, contradicting $K' \in K \perp A$.

For the converse, we assume that either $B \notin K$ or not $-A \vdash B$. In the former case we have immediately $B \notin K_A^-$, and we are done. In the latter case we have by contraposition that not $-B \vdash A$, so not $A \vee -B \vdash A$. There is then a set $K' \in K \perp A$ with $A \vee -B \in K'$. Now clearly $B \notin K'$, for $\{A \vee -B\} \cup \{B\} \vdash A$, whereas $A \notin K'$. Hence $B \notin \bigcap(K \perp A) = K_A^-$.

LEMMA 4.11 For any contraction function $-$ that satisfies (K^-1), (K^-3), and (K^-5), the set K_A^- includes the full meet contraction $\bigcap(K \perp A)$ for any K and A.

Proof Suppose that (K^-1), (K^-3), and (K^-5) are satisfied. Let A be any proposition. We need to show that $\bigcap(K \perp A) \subseteq K_A^-$. When $A \notin K$, we have trivially $\bigcap(K \perp A) = K_A^- = K$ by (K^-3). When $A \in K$, we have $K = (K_A^-)_A^+$ by (K^-5). Suppose that $B \in \bigcap(K \perp A)$. By lemma 4.9 we have $-A \vdash B$, so $K_A^- \cup \{-A\} \vdash B$. But also, because $B \in \bigcap(K \perp A) \subseteq K = (K_A^-)_A^+$, we have $K_A^- \cup \{A\} \vdash B$. Putting these together, we conclude that $K_A^- \vdash B$, and hence by (K^-1) $B \in K_A^-$.

LEMMA 4.12   Every partial meet contraction function satisfies postulates $(K^{-}1)$–$(K^{-}6)$.

Proof $(K^{-}1)$ holds because, when K is a belief set, each $K' \in K \perp A$ is also, and the intersection of belief sets is a belief set. Postulates $(K^{-}2)$, $(K^{-}3)$, $(K^{-}4)$, and $(K^{-}6)$ are trivial. It remains to prove $(K^{-}5)$. In the limiting case when $A \notin K$, we have $K_A^- = K$, and we are done. We may thus suppose that $A \in K$. Suppose that $B \in K$. We want to show that $B \in (K_A^-)_A^+$, where $K_A^- = \bigcap S(K \perp A)$ for some selection function S. $B \in K$ entails $A \to B \in K$. Now suppose that $A \to B \notin K'$ for some $K' \in K \perp A$. Because K' is maximal, it follows that $(A \to B) \to A \in K'$. And because $((A \to B) \to A) \to A$ is a tautology, it follows that $A \in K'$, which contradicts the fact that $K' \in K \perp A$. Hence $A \to B \in K'$ for all $K' \in K \perp A$. In particular, $A \to B \in K'$ for all $K' \in S(K \perp A)$, and hence $A \to B \in K_A^- = \bigcap S(K \perp A)$. Thus $B \in (K_A^-)_A^+$.

TECHNICAL LEMMA 1   Let K be a belief set and A any proposition. If $K' \in K \perp A$, then $K' \in K \perp B$ for any $B \in K$ such that $B \notin K'$.

Proof   Suppose that $K' \in K \perp A$ and $B \notin K'$, where $B \in K$. To show that $K' \in K \perp B$, it suffices to show that, whenever $K' \subset K'' \subseteq K$, $B \in K''$. Let K'' be such that $K' \subset K'' \subseteq K$. Because $K' \in K \perp A$, we have $A \in K''$. But also, because $K' \in K \perp A$, $K \perp A$ is nonempty, so $\bigcap (K \perp A) \subseteq K'$; so using the proof of lemma 4.12, $K \subseteq Cn(\bigcap (K \perp A) \cup \{A\}) \subseteq Cn(K' \cup \{A\}) \subseteq Cn(K'' \cup \{A\}) = K''$; thus because $B \in K$, we have $B \in K''$.

THEOREM 4.13   Let $-$ be a contraction function. For every belief set K, $-$ is a partial meet contraction function *iff* $-$ satisfies postulates $(K^{-}1)$–$(K^{-}6)$ for contraction over K.

Proof   We have the implication from left to right by lemma 4.12. For the converse, suppose that the contraction function $-$ satisfies $(K^{-}1)$–$(K^{-}6)$. To show that $-$ is a partial meet contraction function, it suffices to find a selection function S such that (i) $S(K \perp A) = K$ in the limiting case that $K \perp A$ is empty; (ii) $S(K \perp A)$ is a nonempty subset of $K \perp A$ when this is nonempty; (iii) $K_A^- = \bigcap S(K \perp A)$. Put $S(K \perp A)$ equal to $\{K\}$ when $K \perp A$ is empty and equal to the set of all $K' \in K \perp A$ such that $K_A^- \subseteq K'$ otherwise. Then (i) holds immediately. When $K \perp A$ is nonempty, then not $\vdash A$; so by $(K^{-}4)$ $A \notin K_A^-$, and hence $S(K \perp A)$ is nonempty. Clearly $S(K \perp A) \subseteq K \perp A$, so (ii) also holds. For (iii) we have the inclusion $K_A^- \subseteq \bigcap S(K \perp A)$

immediately from the definition of S. So it remains only to show that $\bigcap S(K \perp A) \subseteq K_A^-$.

When $A \notin K$, we have by $(K^- 3)$ that $K_A^- = K$; so the desired conclusion holds trivially. Suppose then that $A \in K$, and suppose that $B \notin K_A^-$; we want to show that $B \notin \bigcap S(K \perp A)$. When $B \notin K$, this holds trivially, so we assume that $B \in K$. We need to find a $K' \in K \perp A$ with $K_A^- \subseteq K'$ and $B \notin K'$. Because $-$ satisfies $(K^- 5)$ and $B \in K$, we have $K_A^- \cup \{A\} \vdash B$. Because $B \notin K_A^-$, it follows that $B \notin Cn(K_A^- \cup \{-A\})$, and hence $A \vee B \notin K_A^-$. There is then a $K' \in K \perp A \vee B$ with $K_A^- \subseteq K'$. Because $K' \in K \perp A \vee B$, we have $A \vee B \notin K'$, so $B \notin K'$; so, by the hypothesis that $A \in K$ and technical lemma 1, we have $K' \in K \perp A$.

THEOREM 4.2   Any contraction function $-$ that satisfies $(K^- 1)$–$(K^- 6)$ and $(K^- F)$ can be generated by a maxichoice contraction function.

Proof   Suppose that $-$ satisfies $(K^- 1)$–$(K^- 6)$ and $(K^- F)$. By theorem 4.13 we know that $-$ is a partial meet contraction function generated by some selection function S. Suppose for contradiction that $-$ is not a maxichoice contraction function, that is, that for some A there are $K', K'' \in S(K \perp A)$, where $K' \neq K''$. There is then some $B \in K''$ such that $B \notin K'$. Hence $B \notin K_A^-$, and because $B \in K$, it follows from $(K^- F)$ that $B \rightarrow A \in K_A^-$. Hence $B \rightarrow A \in K''$; but because $B \in K''$, it follows that $A \in K''$, which contradicts the assumption that $K'' \in K \perp A$. We conclude that $K' = K''$ and hence that $-$ is a maxichoice contraction function.

THEOREM 4.8   Any contraction function that satisfies $(K^- 1)$–$(K^- 6)$ and $(K^- I)$ can be generated by a full meet contraction function.

Proof   Suppose that $-$ satisfies $(K^- 1)$–$(K^- 6)$ and $(K^- I)$. By theorem 4.13 we know that $-$ is a partial meet contraction function generated by some selection function S. We need to show that, for any A and any K, $S(K \perp A) = K \perp A$, for which it suffices to show that $K_A^- \subseteq \bigcap(K \perp A)$ in the light of lemma 4.11. In the case $A \notin K$, this holds trivially. In the case $A \in K$, we have by lemma 4.9 that $\bigcap(K \perp A) = K \cap Cn(-A)$, so we need only show that $K_A^- \subseteq Cn(-A)$. Suppose that $B \in K_A^-$. Then by $(K^- I)$ and $(K^- 6)$, $K_A^- = K_{A \vee B}^- \cap K_{A \vee -B}^-$; so $B \in K_{A \vee B}^-$ and hence $A \vee B \in K_{A \vee B}^-$; so by the postulate $(K^- 4)$ $\vdash A \vee B$, and $B \in Cn(-A)$, as desired.

TECHNICAL LEMMA 2   Let K be any belief set and $A, B \in K$. Then $K \perp A \,\&\, B = K \perp A \cup K \perp B$.

Proof We apply technical lemma 1. When $K' \in K \perp A \& B$, then $A \& B \notin K'$; so $A \notin K'$ or $B \notin K'$; so by the lemma either $K' \in K \perp A$ or $K' \in K \perp B$. Conversely, if $K' \in K \perp A$ or $K' \in K \perp B$, then $A \& B \notin K'$; so by the same lemma again, $K' \in K \perp A \& B$.

LEMMA 4.14 Any relational partial meet contraction function satisfies postulate $(K^- 7)$.

Proof Suppose that $-$ is a relational partial meet contraction function that is generated by a selection function S, which in turn is generated from a relation $\leqslant$ by means of (Def S). In the cases $\vdash A$, $\vdash B$, $A \notin K$, and $B \notin K$, $(K^- 7)$ holds trivially, so we may suppose that not $\vdash A$, not $\vdash B$, $A \in K$, and $B \in K$. Because $K^-_{A \& B} = \bigcap S(K \perp A \& B)$ and $K^-_A \cap K^-_B = \bigcap S(K \perp A) \cap \bigcap S(K \perp B)$, which by general set theory is the same as $\bigcap (S(K \perp A) \cup S(K \perp B))$, we need to show that $\bigcap (S(K \perp A) \cup S(K \perp B)) \subseteq \bigcap S(K \perp A \& B)$. This can be done by showing the following condition:

(S7) $S(K \perp A \& B) \subseteq S(K \perp A) \cup S(K \perp B)$.

To do this, assume that $K' \in S(K \perp A \& B)$. Because $S(K \perp A \& B) \subseteq K \perp A \& B = K \perp A \cup K \perp B$, by technical lemma 2 it follows that $K' \in K \perp A$ or $K' \in K \perp B$. Consider the former case, as the latter is similar. Let $K'' \in K \perp A$. Then $K'' \in K \perp A \cup K \perp B = K \perp A \& B$, and so $K'' \leqslant K'$ because $K' \in S(K \perp A \& B)$ and S is relational over A. Thus, by relationality again, $K' \in S(K \perp A) \subseteq S(K \perp A) \cup S(K \perp B)$, as desired.

LEMMA 4.15 Any transitively relational partial meet contraction function satisfies $(K^- 8)$.

Proof Suppose that $-$ is a transitively relational partial meet contraction function that is generated by a selection function S, which in turn is generated from a relation $\leqslant$ by means of (Def S). In the cases $\vdash A$, $\vdash B$, $A \notin K$, and $B \notin K$, $(K^- 8)$ holds trivially, so we may suppose that not $\vdash A$, not $\vdash B$, $A \in K$, and $B \in K$. We prove the lemma by first showing that any transitively relational partial meet contraction function satisfies the following condition:

(S8)   Whenever $K \perp A \cap S(K \perp A \& B) \neq \emptyset$, $S(K \perp A) \subseteq S(K \perp A \& B)$.

To do this, suppose that $K \perp A \cap S(K \perp A \& B) \neq \emptyset$. Suppose for contraction that there is some $K' \in S(K \perp A)$ with $K' \notin S(K \perp A \& B)$. Because $K' \in S(K \perp A) \subseteq K \perp A \subseteq K \perp A \& B$, by technical lemma 2, although

$K' \notin S(K \perp A \& B)$, we have by relationality that there is a $K'' \in K \perp A \& B$ with $K'' \not\leqslant K'$. Now by the hypothesis $K \perp A \cap S(K \perp A \& B) \neq \varnothing$, there is a $K^* \in K \perp A$ with $K^* \in S(K \perp A \& B)$. Hence by relationality $K'' \leqslant K^*$ and also $K^* \leqslant K'$. Transitivity gives us $K'' \leqslant K'$ and thus a contradiction.

We then show that (S8) entails (K$^-$8). Suppose that $A \notin K_{A \& B}^-$, that is, $A \notin \bigcap S(K \perp A \& B)$. We need to show that $K_{A \& B}^- \subseteq K_A^-$. Because $A \in K$ and $A \notin \bigcap S(K \perp A \& B)$, there is a $K' \in S(K \perp A \& B)$ with $A \notin K'$. So, by technical lemma 1, $K' \in K \perp A$ and thus $K' \in K \perp A \cap S(K \perp A \& B)$. By applying (S8), we have $S(K \perp A) \subseteq S(K \perp A \& B)$; so $K_{A \& B}^- = \bigcap S(K \perp A \& B) \subseteq \bigcap S(K \perp A) = K_A^-$, as desired.

THEOREM 4.16   Let K be any belief set, and let $-$ be a contraction function defined over K. Then $-$ is a transitive relational partial meet contraction function *if and only if* $-$ satisfies (K$^-$1)–(K$^-$8).

Proof   We have left to right by theorem 4.13, lemma 4.14, and lemma 4.15. To prove the converse, define the relation $\leqslant$ over the set of all subsets of K as follows: For all K' and K'', $K'' \leqslant K'$ iff either $K'' = K' = K$ or the following three all hold: (i) $K'' \in K \perp A$ for some $A \in K$; (ii) $K' \in K \perp A$ and $K_A^- \subseteq K'$ for some $A \in K$; (iii) for all A, if K', $K'' \in K \perp A$ and $K_A^- \subseteq K''$, then $K_A^- \subseteq K'$.

For the proof the following notion will be useful: The *completion* S^* of a selection function S is defined by $S^*(K \perp A) = \{K' \in K \perp A: \bigcap S(K \perp A) \subseteq K'\}$ for all A such that not $\vdash A$ and $S^*(K \perp A) = \{K\}$ in the limiting case that $\vdash A$. It is easily verified that S^* is also a selection function for K and determines the same partial meet contraction function as S does.

To prove the theorem, we need to show that the relation is transitive and that it satisfies the marking-off identity (Def S) with respect to S^* for all A such that not $\vdash A$.

For the identity, suppose first that $K' \in S^*(K \perp A)$. Because not $\vdash A$, we know that $S^*(K \perp A) \subseteq K \perp A$. Let $K'' \in K \perp A$; we need to show that $K'' \leqslant K'$. If $A \notin K$, then $K'' = K' = K$, so $K'' \leqslant K'$. Suppose that $A \in K$. Then clearly conditions (i) and (ii) are satisfied. Let B be any proposition, and suppose that K', $K'' \in K \perp B$ and $K_B^- \subseteq K''$; we need to show that $K_B^- \subseteq K'$. Now by (3.26), which followed from (K$^-$8), either $K_{A \& B}^- \subseteq K_A^-$ or $K_{A \& B}^- \subseteq K_B^-$. And in the latter case $K_{A \& B}^- \subseteq K_B^- \subseteq K'' \in K \perp A$; so $A \notin K_{A \& B}^-$; so by (K$^-$8) $K_{A \& B}^- \subseteq K_A^-$. Thus in either case $K_{A \& B}^- \subseteq K_A^-$. Now suppose for contradiction that there is a $C \in K_B^-$ with $C \notin K'$. Then $B \lor C \in$

K_B^-, and so because $B \vdash B \vee C$, we have by (3.25), which was a consequence of (K$^-$7), that $B \vee C \in K_{A\&B}^- \subseteq K_A^- = \bigcap S^*(K \perp A) \subseteq K'$; so $B \vee C \in K'$. But also, because $K' \in K \perp B$ and $C \notin K'$ and $C \in K$, we have $K' \cup \{C\} \vdash B$, so $C \to B \in K'$. Putting these together, we get $B \in K'$, contradicting $K' \in K \perp B$.

For the converse, suppose that $K' \notin S^*(K \perp A)$ and $K' \in K \perp A$; we need to find a $K'' \in K \perp A$ with $K'' \not\leqslant K'$. Clearly the supposition implies that $A \in K$, so $K' \neq K$. Because $K' \in K \perp A$, the latter is nonempty, so $S^*(K \perp A)$ is nonempty; let K'' be one of its elements. Noting that K', $K'' \in K \perp A$, $K'' \in S^*(K \perp A)$, but $K' \notin S^*(K \perp A)$, we see that condition (iii) fails, so that $K'' \not\leqslant K'$, as desired.

Finally, we check out transitivity. Suppose that $K^\# \leqslant K''$ and $K'' \leqslant K'$; we want to show that $K^\# \leqslant K'$. In the case that $K' = K$, then clearly, because $K'' \leqslant K'$, we have $K'' = K' = K$, and thus, because $K^\# \leqslant K''$, we have $K^\# = K'' = K$, $K^\# = K' = K$ and thus $K^\# \leqslant K'$. Suppose for the principal case that $K' \neq K$. Then because $K'' \leqslant K'$, clearly $K'' \neq K$. Because $K'' \leqslant K'$, we have $K' \in K \perp C$ and $K_C^- \subseteq K'$ for some $C \in K$, so (ii) is satisfied. Because $K^\# \leqslant K''$, we have $K^\# \in K \perp C$ for some $C \in K$, so (i) is satisfied. It remains to verify (iii). Suppose that $K^\#$, $K' \in K \perp B$ and $K_B^- \subseteq K^\#$; we need to show that $K_B^- \subseteq K'$. First, note that, because $K' \neq K$ by the condition of the case, we have $B \in K$. Also, because $K^\# \leqslant K''$ and $K'' \neq K$, there is an $A \in K$ with $K'' \in K \perp A$ and $K_A^- \subseteq K''$. Because A, $B \in K$, we have by technical lemma 2 that $K \perp A \& B = K \perp A \cup K \perp B$, so $K^\#$, K'', $K' \in K \perp A \& B$. Now by (3.26), which was a consequence of (K$^-$8), either $K_{A\&B}^- \subseteq K_B^-$ or $K_{A\&B}^- \subseteq K_A^-$. The former case gives us $K_{A\&B}^- \subseteq K^\#$; so because $K^\# \leqslant K''$ and $K'' \neq K$, we have $K_{A\&B}^- \subseteq K''$; so again because $K'' \leqslant K'$ and $K' \neq K$, we have $K_{A\&B}^- \subseteq K'$. Likewise the latter case gives us $K_{A\&B}^- \subseteq K''$ and thus, as before, $K_{A\&B}^- \subseteq K'$. Thus in either case $K_{A\&B}^- \subseteq K'$. Now let $C \in K_B^-$; we need to show that $C \in K'$. Because $C \in K_B^-$, we have $B \vee C \in K_B^-$; so by (3.25), which was a consequence of (K$^-$7), we have $B \vee C \in K_{A\&B}^- \subseteq K'$. Hence $K' \cup \{-B\} \vdash C$. But because $K' \in K \perp B$ and $C \in K$, we also have $K' \cup \{B\} \vdash C$; so $K' \vdash C$ and thus $C \in K'$, as desired.

THEOREM 4.4 Any contraction function that satisfies (K$^-$1)–(K$^-$6) and (3.30) can be generated by an orderly maxichoice contraction function.

Proof Because (3.30) entails (K$^-$7), (K$^-$8), and (K$^-$F), the theorem follows from the combination of theorems 4.2 and 4.16.

THEOREM 4.17   Let K be any belief set, and let $-$ be a partial meet contraction function over K. Then $-$ is transitively relational iff it is transitively and connectively relational.

Proof Suppose that $-$ is determined by the transitively relational selection function S. Then by lemma 4.14 and lemma 4.15, $-$ satisfies (K^-7) and (K^-8); so the conditions of theorem 4.16 hold, and the relation $\leqslant$ defined in its proof is transitive and satisfies the marking-off identity for S^*. To show that $-$ is transitively and connectively relational, we need to show that $\leqslant$ is connected over the set $U_K = \bigcup_{A \in K}(K \perp A: A \in K, \nvdash A)$. Let K'', $K' \in U_K$, and suppose that $K'' \nleqslant K'$. Because K'', $K' \in U_K$, conditions (i) and (ii) in the proof of theorem 4.16 are satisfied for both K'' and K'. Hence, because $K'' \nleqslant K'$, we have by (iii) that there is an A with K'', $K' \in K \perp A$, $K_A^- \subseteq K''$ and $K_A^- \nsubseteq K'$. But because $K_A^- \subseteq K'' \in K \perp A$, we have by the definition of S^* that $K'' \in S^*(K \perp A)$; so, by (Def S) applied to S^*, because $K' \in K \perp A$, we have $K' \leqslant K''$, as desired.

LEMMA 4.20   Suppose that the ordering $\leqslant$ satisfies (EE1)–(EE3). Then it also has the property that for any A and B either $A \leqslant B$ or $B \leqslant A$. (Connectivity)

Proof By (EE2), we have $A \& B \leqslant A$ and $A \& B \leqslant B$. From (EE3) it follows that either $A \leqslant A \& B$ or $B \leqslant A \& B$. Hence (EE1) gives us either $A \leqslant B$ or $B \leqslant A$.

LEMMA 4.21   Suppose that the ordering $\leqslant$ satisfies (EE1) and connectivity. Then it satisfies (EE3) iff, for any A, B, and C in K, if $C \leqslant A$ and $C \leqslant B$, then $C \leqslant A \& B$.

Proof From left to right is trivial. For the converse, suppose that the right-hand side holds. By connectivity we know that either $A \leqslant B$ or $B \leqslant A$. Suppose that $A \leqslant B$ (the latter is similar). By connectivity again, $A \leqslant A$. So we have both $A \leqslant A$ and $A \leqslant B$ and thus, replacing C by A, $A \leqslant A \& B$, as desired.

LEMMA 4.22   Suppose that the ordering $\leqslant$ satisfies (EE1)–(EE3). Then, for all A, B, and C in K, if $B \& C \leqslant A$, then $B \leqslant A$ or $C \leqslant A$.

Proof Assume that $B \& C \leqslant A$. By (EE3) we know that $B \leqslant B \& C$ or $C \leqslant B \& C$. Hence by (EE1), $B \leqslant A$ or $C \leqslant A$.

LEMMA 4.23 Suppose that the ordering $\leqslant$ satisfies (EE1)–(EE3). Then $A < B$ iff $A \& B < B$.

Proof If $A < B$, then by (EE2) $A \& B \leqslant A$, and hence, by (EE1) applied both positively and negatively, $A \& B < B$.

Conversely, if $A \& B < B$, then it follows from (EE3) that $A \leqslant A \& B$ and hence by (EE1) again $A < B$.

LEMMA 4.26 If $\leqslant_G$ satisfies ($\leqslant_G 1$)–($\leqslant_G 5$), then $\leqslant$ introduced by (Def $\leqslant$) satisfies (EE1)–(EE5).

Proof (EE1): Assume that $A \leqslant B$ and $B \leqslant C$, that is, $-A \leqslant_G -B$ and $-B \leqslant_G -C$. By ($\leqslant_G 2$), $-A \leqslant_G -C$, that is, $A \leqslant C$.

(EE2): Assume $A \vdash B$. It follows, by the deduction theorem, that $\vdash -B \to -A \vee -A$ and hence by ($\leqslant_G 3$) that $-A \leqslant_G -B$, that is, $A \leqslant B$.

(EE3): Because $\vdash -(A \& B) \to -A \vee -B$, it follows from ($\leqslant_G 3$) that $-A \leqslant_G -(A \& B)$ or $-B \leqslant_G -(A \& B)$, that is, $A \leqslant A \& B$ or $B \leqslant A \& B$.

(EE4): $A \notin K$ iff $-A \leqslant_G B$ for all B by ($\leqslant_G 4$) iff $A \leqslant B$ for all B by (Def $\leqslant$).

(EE5): If $B \leqslant A$ for all B, then $B \leqslant_G -A$ for all B by (Def $\leqslant$), and then $\vdash A$ by ($\leqslant_G 5$).

LEMMA 4.27 If $\leqslant$ satisfies (EE1)–(EE5), then $\leqslant_G$ introduced by means of (Def $\leqslant$) satisfies ($\leqslant_G 1$)–($\leqslant_G 5$).

Proof ($\leqslant_G 1$) and ($\leqslant_G 2$): As in lemma 4.26.

($\leqslant_G 3$): Assume that $\vdash A \to B \vee C$. It follows that $\vdash -B \& -C \to -A$. By (EE2) $-B \& -C \leqslant -A$. (EE3) says that $-B \leqslant -B \& -C$ or $-C \leqslant -B \& -C$ and hence by (EE1) $-B \leqslant -A$ or $-C \leqslant -A$, that is, $B \leqslant_G A$ or $C \leqslant_G A$, as desired.

($\leqslant_G 4$): $-A \notin K$ iff $-A \leqslant B$ for all B [by (EE4)] iff $A \leqslant_G B$ for all B [by (Def $\leqslant$)].

($\leqslant_G 5$): From left to right follows from ($\leqslant_G 3$) because, if $\vdash -A$, then $\vdash A \to B \vee B$ for all B and hence $B \leqslant_G A$ for all B. For the converse implication, assume that $B \leqslant_G A$ for all B. It follows by (Def $\leqslant$) that $B \leqslant -A$ for all B and hence by (EE5) that $\vdash -A$.

LEMMA 4.28 Assume that $\leqslant_G$ and $*$ satisfy ($C \leqslant_G$). Then $\leqslant$ introduced by (Def $\leqslant$) and $-$ introduced by (Def $-$) satisfy ($C \leqslant$).

Proof Assume that $B \in K_A^*$ iff $A \& B <_G A \& -B$. Because $\vdash A \& B \to A$, it follows from ($\leqslant_G 3$) that $A \leqslant_G A \& B$ and hence $A <_G A \& -B$. Conversely, assume that $A <_G A \& -B$. It follows from ($\leqslant_G 3$) that $A \& B \leqslant_G A$ or $A \& -B \leqslant_G A$. The second is impossible by assumption, so $A \& B \leqslant_G A$ and hence $A \& B <_G A \& -B$ by ($\leqslant_G 2$). So ($C \leqslant_G$) is equivalent to

(1) $B \in K_A^*$ iff $A \leqslant_G A \& -B$ for all A and B.

Now using (Def $\leqslant$), this is equivalent to

(2) $B \in K_A^*$ iff $-A < -A \vee B$ for all A and B.

If we replace A by $-(A \& B)$ in (2), we obtain

(3) $B \in K_{-(A \& B)}^*$ iff $A \& B < B$.

Next, look at $K_{A \& B}^-$. When $B \in K$, $B \in K_{A \& B}^-$ iff $B \in K_{-(A \& B)}^*$ because $K_{A \& B}^- = K \cap K_{-(A \& B)}^*$ by the Harper identity. And when $B \notin K$, $B \notin K_{A \& B}^-$, and it also follows from (EE4) that $B \leqslant A \& B$, so not $A \& B < B$. So in both cases $B \in K_{A \& B}^-$ iff $B \in K_{-(A \& B)}^*$. Putting this into (3) we obtain

(4) $B \in K_{A \& B}^-$ iff $A \& B < B$.

Now lemma 4.23 shows us that $A \& B < B$ iff $A < B$. Thus

(5) $B \in K_{A \& B}^-$ iff $A < B$.

Finally, by negating both sides,

(6) $B \leqslant A$ iff $B \notin K_{A \& B}^-$,

which is ($C \leqslant$).

LEMMA 4.29   Assume that $\leqslant$ and $-$ satisfy ($C \leqslant$). Then $\leqslant_G$ introduced by (Def $\leqslant$) and $*$ introduced by (Def $*$) satisfy ($C \leqslant_G$).

Proof   Assume ($C \leqslant$). From the previous lemma we know that this is equivalent to

(4) $B \in K_{A \& B}^-$ iff $A \& B < B$.

Replacing A by $-A$ and B by $-A \vee B$, it follows that

(3$'$) $-A \vee B \in K_{-A}^-$ iff $-A < -A \vee B$.

Now look at K_A^*. We want to show that $-A \vee B \in K_{-A}^-$ iff $B \in K_A^*$. From left to right follows from the Levi identity. To prove the converse, we first note that, when $-A \in K$, $-A \vee B \in K$; and because it also follows from

$B \in K_A^*$ that $-A \vee B \in K_A^*$, we conclude by the Harper identity that $-A \vee B \in K_{-A}^-$. And when $-A \notin K$, $K_A^* = K_A^+$. Because $B \in K_A^*$, it follows that $A \to B \in K$ and thus $-A \vee B \in K = K_{-A}^-$. Thus (3') is equivalent to

(2) $B \in K_A^*$ iff $-A < -A \vee B$ for all A and B,

which was shown to be equivalent to $(C \leqslant_G)$ in lemma 4.28.

Appendix C
Proofs of Main Lemmas and Theorems of Chapter 5

LEMMA 5.1   Conditionalization is the only function from $\mathbf{P} \times \mathbf{L}$ to $\mathbf{P}$ satisfying $(\mathrm{P}^+ 1)$–$(\mathrm{P}^+ 4)$.

Proof   From $(\mathrm{P}^+ 1)$ it follows that, for all C, $P_{A \vee -A}^+(C \,\&\, A) = P(A) \cdot P_A^+(C \,\&\, A) + P(-A) \cdot P_{-A}^+(C \,\&\, A)$. Then note that it follows from $(\mathrm{P}^+ 3)$ that $P_{A \vee -A}^+(C \,\&\, A) = P(C \,\&\, A)$ for all C. In the principal case when $0 < P(A) < 1$, $(\mathrm{P}^+ 2)$ entails that $P_{-A}^+(C \,\&\, A) = 0$, and so $P(C \,\&\, A) = P(A) \cdot P_A^+(C \,\&\, A)$. But because $P_A^+(C \,\&\, A) = P_A^+(C)$, by $(\mathrm{P}^+ 2)$ it immediately follows that, for all C, $P_A^+(C) = P(C \,\&\, A)/P(A) = P(C/A)$, which is what we wanted to show. In the limiting case when $P(A) = 1$, it follows from $(\mathrm{P}^+ 4)$ that $P_{-A}^+ = P_\perp$, so by the definition of an a-mixture $P(C/A) = P(C \,\&\, A) = P_A^+(C \,\&\, A) = P_A^+(C)$ for all C. Finally, in the limiting case when $P(A) = 0$, by $(\mathrm{P}^+ 4)$ again $P_A^+ = P_\perp$, which is how conditionalization has been defined in this case.

THEOREM 5.2   A finite probabilistic revision function $*$ is homomorphic iff $P_A^* = P_A^\#$, that is, P_A^* comes from P by general imaging on A for all probability functions P in the model and for all possible propositions A.

Proof   Suppose first that the revision function $*$ is homomorphic. To show that P_A^* comes from P by general imaging on A for any P and possible A, it is sufficient to show that $P_A^*(S^j) = \sum_i P(S^i) \cdot P_A^{i*}(S^j)$ for all determiners S^j, because the values $P_A^*(S^j)$ uniquely determine P_A^*. But because $P(S^j) = \sum_i P(S^i) \cdot P^i(S^j)$, the required identity follows by iterated applications of the linearity condition.

Next suppose that P_A^* comes from P by general imaging on A for all P and all possible A. We want to show that the revision function is homomorphic. Let P be any probability function such that there are P' and P'', all in $\mathbf{P}$, for which $P(B) = a \cdot P'(B) + (1 - a) \cdot P''(B)$ for all sentences B. Now the following series of identities establishes the desired conclusion:

$$a \cdot P_A'^*(B) + (1 - a) \cdot P_A''^*(B)$$
$$= a \cdot \sum_j P_A'^*(S^j) \cdot P^j(B) + (1 - a) \cdot \sum_j P_A''^*(S^j) P^j(B) \quad \text{(since there is a}$$

finite set of determiners S^j in a finite revision function)

$$= a \cdot \sum_j P^j(B) \cdot \sum_i P'(S^i) \cdot P_A^{i*}(S^j) + (1 - a) \cdot \sum_j P^j(B) \cdot \sum_i P''(S^i) \cdot P_A^{i*}(S^j)$$

(by the definition of general imaging)

$$= \sum_j P^j(B) \cdot \sum_i (a \cdot P'(S^i) + (1 - a) \cdot P''(S^i)) \cdot P_A^{i*}(S^j) \quad \text{(by algebra)}$$

$$= \sum_j P^j(B) \cdot \sum_i P(S^i) \cdot P_A^{i*}(S^j) \qquad \text{(by the assumption about } P' \text{ and } P'')$$

$$= \sum_j P^j(B) \cdot P_A^*(S^j) \qquad \text{(by the definition of general imaging)}$$

$$= P_A^*(B) \qquad \text{(by the definition of imaging)}.$$

THEOREM 5.3   There is no nontrivial and rich probabilistic revision function that is both homomorphic and preservative.

Proof   Assume that the revision function $*$ is nontrivial, rich, and homomorphic. Let P be a probability function in $\mathbf{P}$ such that, for three pairwise disjoint sentences A, B, and C, $P(A) > 0$, $P(B) > 0$, and $P(C) > 0$. According to the earlier assumption [postulate (P*2)], we have $P_A^*(A) = 1$. For the same reason we also have $(P_A^*)_{B \vee C}^*(B \vee C) = 1$. It follows that either $(P_A^*)_{B \vee C}^*(B) > 0$ or $(P_A^*)_{B \vee C}^*(C) > 0$. Without loss of generality, it may be assumed that $(P_A^*)_{B \vee C}^*(C) > 0$. Because $*$ is rich, there is a probability function $P' = P_A^* \, a \, P_B^*$ for some a, $0 < a < 1$, also in the domain of $*$. It follows that $P'(A \vee B) = 1$. Because it is assumed that $*$ is homomorphic, we conclude the $P_{B \vee C}'^* = (P_A^*)_{B \vee C}^* \, a \, (P_B^*)_{B \vee C}^*$. Because B and C are disjoint, $P_{B \vee C}'^*(B) + P_{B \vee C}'^*(C) = 1$. But, from $a > 0$ and $(P_A^*)_{B \vee C}^*(C) > 0$, it follows that $P_{B \vee C}'^*(C) > 0$ and hence $P_{B \vee C}'^*(B) < 1$. However, from the assumption that A and C are disjoint, it follows that $P_{B \vee C}'^*(A \vee B) = P_{B \vee C}'^*(B)$, which entails that $*$ is not preservative, because $P'(A \vee B) = 1$ and $P'(B \vee C) > 0$ (recall that $a < 1$), but $P_{B \vee C}'^*(A \vee B) < 1$.

LEMMA 5.5   For all B, if $P_A^-(B) = 1$, then $P(B) = 1$.

Proof   In the limiting case when $P(A) < 1$, the lemma follows immediately from (P$^-$4). For the principal case when $P(A) = 1$, it follows from (P$^-$5) that $P(B) = P_A^-(B/A)$ for all B. So, if $P_A^-(B) = 1$, then $P_A^-(B/A) = 1$ and hence $P(B) = 1$, as desired.

LEMMA 5.6   If $P \neq P_\perp$, then $P_A^- = P \, a \, (P_A^-)_{-A}^+$ [where $a = P_A^-(A)$ when $P(A) = 1$ and $a = 1$ otherwise].

Proof   In the limiting case, when $P(A) < 1$, then by (P$^-$4) $P_A^- = P$; so by selecting $a = 1$, we get the desired result. In the principal case when $P(A) = 1$, then, for all B, $P_A^-(B) = P_A^-(A) \cdot P_A^-(B/A) + P_A^-(-A) \cdot P_A^-(B/-A)$, because $0 < P_A^-(A) < 1$ by (P$^-$2) and lemma 5.5. So by (P$^-$5) $P_A^-(B) = P_A^-(A) \cdot P(B) + (1 - P_A^-(A)) \cdot (P_A^-)_{-A}^+(B)$ for all B, which is the desired conclusion.

LEMMA 5.7   Given the basic postulates, $(P^- 6)$, $(P^- D)$, and $(P^- M)$ are mutually equivalent.

Proof   Note that the value of a in $(P^- M)$ is uniquely determined by putting $C = A \lor B$. For the lemma itself, we first show that $(P^- 6)$ entails $(P^- D)$. Suppose that $P_A^-(-A \& -B) > 0$. Using logical equivalences and applying $(P^- 3)$, we can rewrite this as $P_{(A \lor B) \& A}^-(-(A \lor B)) > 0$. By $(P^- 6)$ we then have $P_{A \lor B}^-(C/-(A \lor B)) = P_{(A \lor B) \& A}^-(C/-(A \lor B))$. Applying $(P^- 3)$ again, this is equivalent to $P_{A \lor B}^-(C/-A \& -B) = P_A^-(C/-A \& -B)$, as desired.

Second, $(P^- D)$ entails $(P^- M)$. Suppose that $P_A^-(-A \& -B) > 0$. Then $P_{A \lor B}^-(C) = P_{A \lor B}^-(A \lor B) \cdot P_{A \lor B}^-(C/A \lor B) + P_{A \lor B}^-(-(A \lor B)) \cdot P_{A \lor B}^-(C/-(A \lor B))$. It follows from $(P^- 5)$ that $P_{A \lor B}^-(C/A \lor B) = P(C)$ because $P(A \lor B) \geqslant P(A) = 1$ and from $(P^- D)$ that $P_{A \lor B}^-(C/-(A \lor B)) = P_A^-(C/-(A \lor B))$, which gives us the desired mixture.

Finally, we show that $(P^- M)$ entails $(P^- 6)$. In the limiting case when $P(A) < 1, P_A^- = P_{A \& B}^- = P$, so $(P^- 6)$ holds trivially. Suppose that $P(A) = 1$, and suppose that $P_{A \& B}^-(-A) > 0$. It follows that $P_{A \& B}^-(-(A \& B) \& -A) > 0$. Applying $(P^- M)$, we get $P_A^-(C/-A) = P_{A \& B \lor A}^-(C/-A) = P_{A \& B \lor A}^-(C \& -A)/P_{A \& B \lor A}^-(-A) = (P(C \& -A) a P_{A \& B}^-(C \& -A))/(P(-A) a P_{A \& B}^-(-A))$. Now because $P(A) = 1$, we have $P(-A) = P(C \& -A) = 0$, and the quotient simplifies to $P_{A \& B}^-(C \& -A)/P_{A \& B}^-(-A) = P_{A \& B}^-(C/-A)$, as desired.

THEOREM 5.8   If a contraction function from $\mathbf{P} \times \mathbf{L}$ to $\mathbf{P}$ satisfies $(P^- 1)$–$(P^- 5)$, then the contraction function from $\mathbf{K} \times \mathbf{L}$ to $\mathbf{K}$, defined by the associated belief sets, satisfies $(K^- 1)$–$(K^- 6)$, and if $(P^- 6)$ is satisfied, the corresponding contraction function satisfies $(K^- 7)$ and $(K^- 8)$.

Proof $(K^- 1)$ follows from the fact that P_A^- is a probability function. Postulate $(K^- 2)$ follows from lemma 5.5. Postulate $(K^- 3)$ is immediate from $(P^- 4)$, $(K^- 4)$ follows from $(P^- 2)$, and $(K^- 6)$ from $(P^- 3)$. Postulate $(K^- 5)$ follows from $(P^- 5)$ and from the association of expansions of belief sets with conditionalizations (Gärdenfors 1978a, p. 387). Only $(K^- 7)$ and $(K^- 8)$ need some details. In section 3.4 it was shown that $(K^- 7)$ is equivalent to the following condition, there called (3.25): If $C \in K_A^-$ and $A \vdash C$, then $C \in K_{A \& B}^-$. To show this condition, assume that $P_A^-(C) = 1$ and $A \vdash C$. We want to show that $P_{A \& B}^-(C) = 1$. But this follows from the equality $P_{A \& B}^-(C) = P_{A \& B}^-(A) \cdot P_{A \& B}^-(C/A) + P_{A \& B}^-(-A) \cdot P_{A \& B}^-(C/-A)$, because $A \vdash C$ entails that $P_{A \& B}^-(C/A) = 1$ and, by $(P^- 6)$, $P_{A \& B}^-(C/-A) =$

$P_A^-(C/-A) = P_A^-(C/-A) = 1$, because $P_A^-(C) = 1$ [the case when $P_{A\&B}^-(-A) = 0$ is trivial]. This shows that $(\text{K}^- 7)$ is satisfied.

To show $(\text{K}^- 8)$, assume that $A \notin K_{A\&B}^-$, that is, $P_{A\&B}^-(A) < 1$. Suppose that $P_{A\&B}^-(C) = 1$. We want to show that $P_A^-(C) = 1$. To obtain this, consider the following equality: $P_A^-(C) = P_A^-(A) \cdot P_A^-(C/A) + P_A^-(-A) \cdot P_A^-(C/-A)$. It follows from $(\text{P}^- 5)$ that $P_A^-(C/A) = 1$ and from $(\text{P}^- 6)$ that $P_A^-(C/-A) = P_{A\&B}^-(C/-A) = 1$, because $P_{A\&B}^-(C) = 1$. Hence $P_A^-(C) = 1$, as desired.

LEMMA 5.9   If a revision function satisfies (P^*1)–(P^*6), it also satisfies (P^*I).

Proof   If $P_A^*(B) = 1$, then, by (P^*6), $P_{A\&B}^*(C) = P_A^*(C/B) = P_A^*(C)$ for all C. Similarly, if $P_B^*(A) = 1$, then $P_{A\&B}^* = P_B^*$. Hence $P_A^* = P_{A\&B}^* = P_B^*$.

LEMMA 5.10   Given postulates (P^*1)–(P^*5), (P^*6) is equivalent to (P^*M).

Proof   It is first shown that (P^*6) entails (P^*M). Suppose that $\vdash -(A \& B)$. It follows that $P_{A\vee B}^*(A) + P_{A\vee B}^*(B) = P_{A\vee B}^*(A \vee B) = 1$ by (P^*2) and the disjunction postulate for probability functions. Now assume both that $P_{A\vee B}^*(A) > 0$ and that $P_{A\vee B}^*(B) > 0$. The limiting cases when $P_{A\vee B}^*(A) = 0$ or $P_{A\vee B}^*(B) = 0$ are similar. By (P^*3) and (P^*6) we then have $P_A^*(C) = P_{(A\vee B)\&A}^*(C) = P_{A\vee B}^*(C/A)$ and $P_B^*(C) = P_{(A\vee B)\&B}^*(C) = P_{A\vee B}^*(C/B)$. It follows that, for all C, $P_{A\vee B}^*(C) = P_{A\vee B}^*(C \& A) + P_{A\vee B}^*(C \& B) = P_{A\vee B}^*(A) \cdot P_{A\vee B}^*(C/A) + P_{A\vee B}^*(B) \cdot P_{A\vee B}^*(C/B) = P_{A\vee B}^*(A) \cdot P_A^*(C) + P_{A\vee B}^*(B) \cdot P_B^*(C)$, which gives us the desired mixture.

Conversely we show that (P^*M) entails (P^*6). Suppose that $P_A^*(B) > 0$. Postulate (P^*M) entails that, for all C, $P_A^*(B \& C) = P_A^*(B) \cdot P_{A\vee B}^*(B \& C) + P_A^*(-B) \cdot P_{A\&-B}^*(B \& C)$. However, it follows from (P^*2) that $P_{A\&-B}^*(B \& C) = 0$ and so $P_A^*(C) = P_{A\&B}^*(B \& C) = P_A^*(C \& B)/P_A^*(B) = P_A^*(C/B)$ for all C, as desired.

LEMMA 5.11 $P_A^* = (P a P_A^*)_A^+$ (for any a).

Proof   The proof uses the general fact about mixtures that, if $P = (P' a P'')$ for some a, then $P_A^+ = P_A'^+ b P_A''^+$, where $b = a \cdot P'(A)/P(A)$ (Domotor 1983, p. 59). Using this, we have $(P a P_A^*)_A^+ = P_A^+ b (P_A^*)_A^+$. When $P(A) = 0$, $P_A^+ = P_\perp$ and $(P_A^*)_A^+ = P_A^*$, then the expression reduces to $P_\perp b P_A^*$, which by the definition of the mixture procedure is identical with P_A^*. And when $P(A) > 0$, $P_A^+ = P_A^*$ by (P^*5), and then the expression reduces to $P_A^* b P_A^*$, which again is P_A^*. [Note that (P^*6) is not used in the proof.]

THEOREM 5.12   If a revision function from $\mathbf{P} \times \mathbf{L}$ to $\mathbf{P}$ satisfies (P*1)–(P*5), then the revision function from $\mathbf{K} \times \mathbf{L}$ to $\mathbf{K}$ defined from the associated belief sets satisfies (K*1)–(K*6), and if (P*6) is satisfied, the corresponding revision function also satisfies (K*7) and (K*8).

Proof   Postulate (K*1) follows from the fact that P_A^* is a probability function. Postulate (K*2) is immediate from (P*2); (K*3) and (K*4) follow essentially from (P*5); (K*5) is a direct consequence of (P*4); and (K*6) follows from (P*3). I give the details only for (K*7) and (K*8). In order to show (K*7), suppose that $C \in K_{A\,\&\,B}^*$, that is, $P_{A\,\&\,B}^*(C) = 1$. We want to show that $(P_A^*)_B^+(C) = 1$, that is, $P_A^*(C/B) = 1$. If $P_A^*(B) > 0$, this follows immediately from (P*6). And in the limiting case when $P_A^*(B) = 0, (P_A^*)_B^+(C) = P_\perp(C) = 1$. Finally, to show that (K*8) is satisfied, assume that $-B \notin K_A^*$, that is, $P_A^*(B) > 0$. Postulate (P*6) then gives directly $(P_A^*)_B^+ = P_{A\,\&\,B}^*$ and hence $(K_A^*)_B^+ \subseteq K_{A\,\&\,B}^*$, as desired.

THEOREM 5.13   If a contraction function satisfies (P⁻1)–(P⁻5), then the revision function generated by (Def P*) satisfies (P*1)–(P*5), and, if the contraction function also satisfies (P⁻6), then the revision function satisfies (P*6).

Proof   Postulate (P*2) follows from the definition of expansions. For (P*3), suppose that $\vdash A \leftrightarrow B$. Then $\vdash -A \leftrightarrow -B$ and hence, by (P⁻3), $P_{-A}^- = P_{-B}^-$ and thus $(P_{-A}^-)_A^+ = (P_{-B}^-)_B^+$, that is $P_A^* = P_B^*$. For (P*4), first suppose that not $\vdash -A$. It then follows from (P⁻2) that $P_{-A}^-(A) > 0$ and hence $(P_{-A}^-)_A^+ \neq P_\perp$. For the converse, suppose that $\vdash -A$. Then, by (P⁻2) again, $P_A^-(A) = 0$ and hence $(P_{-A}^-)_A^+ = P_\perp$. To prove (P*5), assume that $P(A) > 0$. It then follows from (P⁻4) that $P_{-A}^- = P$ and hence $P_A^* = (P_{-A}^-)_A^+ = P_A^+$, as desired. Finally, to show (P*6) assume that $P_A^*(B) > 0$, that is, $P_{-A}^-(B/A) > 0$. It follows that $P_{-A}^-(B\,\&\,A) > 0$. With the aid of (P⁻6), we derive the following series of identities, which gives the desired conclusion:
$$P_{A\,\&\,B}^*(C) = P_{-A\,\vee\,-B}^-(C/A\,\&\,B) = P_{-A}^-(C/A\,\&\,B) = (P_{-A}^-)_A^+(C/B) = P_A^*(C/B).$$

THEOREM 5.14   If a revision function satisfies (P*1)–(P*5), then the contraction function generated by (Def P⁻) satisfies (P⁻1)–(P⁻5), and, if the revision function also satisfies (P*6), the contraction function satisfies (P⁻6).

Proof   Postulate (P⁻1) is immediate from (Def P⁻). To show that (P⁻2) is fulfilled, assume first that not $\vdash A$. By (P*4) it follows that $P_{-A}^* \neq P_\perp$ and hence $P^*_{-A}(A) = 0$. Thus $P^-_A(A) = P(A) \, a \, P^*_{-A}(A) = a \cdot P(A)$. This value is $P(A)$ iff $P(A) < 1$ and a iff $P(A) = 1$. So in both cases $P^-_A(A) < 1$, as desired. In the limiting case when $\vdash A$, by (P*4) again, $P^*_{-A} = P$ and hence $P^-_A(A) = P(A) \, a \, P(A) = 1$ by the definition of a-mixture.

In order to show (P$^-$3), assume that $\vdash A \leftrightarrow B$. It follows that $\vdash -A \leftrightarrow -B$ and then, by (P*3), that $P^*_{-A} = P^*_{-B}$. Hence $P^-_A = P \, a \, P^*_{-A} = P \, a \, P^*_{-B} = P^-_B$. Postulate (P$^-$4) follows immediately from (Def P$^-$) because, when $P(A) < 1$, $a = 1$ and hence $P^-_A = P$. To show that (P$^-$5) is satisfied, assume that $P(A) = 1$. This means that $P^+_A = P$. We then use the same general fact about mixtures as in lemma 5.11 to establish the following series of identities: $(P^-_A)^+_A = (P \, a \, P^*_{-A})^+_A = P^+_A \, b \, (P^*_{-A})^+_A = P \, b \, P_\perp = P$ by the definition of mixtures (b is the same as in lemma 5.11).

Finally, to show that (P$^-$6) is fulfilled, we exploit lemma 5.7 and show that (P$^-$D) follows [essentially from (P*6)]. In the limiting case when $P(A) < 1$, we can apply (P$^-$4), which we have already shown to be valid, and conclude that $P^-_A = P^-_{A \vee B} = P$; so (P$^-$D) holds trivially. Suppose that $P(A) = 1$. Now if we suppose that $P^-_A(-A \, \& -B) > 0$, then by (Def P$^-$), $P(-A \, \& -B) \, a \, P^*_{-A}(-A \, \& -B) > 0$. Because $P(-A \, \& -B) = 0$, it follows that $P^*_{-A}(-A \, \& -B) = P^*_{-A}(-(A \vee B)) > 0$. Using (Def P$^-$) again, we have $P^-_A(C/-A \, \& -B) = P^-_A(C \, \& -A \, \& -B)/P^-_A(-A \, \& -B) = (P(C \, \& -A \, \& -B) \, a \, P^*_{-A}(C \, \& -A \, \& -B))/(P(-A \, \& -B) \, a \, P^*_{-A}(-A \, \& -B))$. However, because both $P(C \, \& -A \, \& -B) = 0$ and $P(-A \, \& -B) = 0$, this quotient reduces to $P^*_{-A}(C \, \& -A \, \& -B)/P^*_{-A}(-A \, \& -B) = P^*_{-A}(C/-A \, \& -B) = P^*_{-A}(C/-B)$. In a similar way it can be shown that $P^-_{A \vee B}(C/-A \, \& -B) = P^*_{-A \, \& -B}(C)$. Now applying (P*6), we conclude that $P^*_{-A \, \& -B}(C) = P^*_{-A}(C/-B)$ and hence $P^-_{A \vee B}(C/-A \, \& -B) = P^-_A(C/-A \, \& -B)$, as desired.

THEOREM 5.15   If a revision function $*$ is generated from a selection function by means of (Def S*), then it satisfies (P*1)–(P*6).

Proof   The only condition that is not immediately obvious is (P*6). Suppose that $P^*_A(B) > 0$, that is, $P^S_A(B/A) > 0$. It follows that $P^S_A(A \, \& \, B/A) > 0$ and hence, by (iii) of (Def S), that $P^S_A = P^S_{A \, \& \, B}$. Then, for any C, $(P^*_A)^+_B(C) = P^S_A(C \, \& \, A/B)/P^S_A(A/B) = (P^S_A(C \, \& \, A \, \& \, B) \cdot P^S_A(B))/(P^S_A(B) \cdot P^S_A(A \, \& \, B)) = P^S_A(C/A \, \& \, B) = P^S_{A \, \& \, B}(C/A \, \& \, B) = P^*_{A \, \& \, B}(C)$, as desired.

LEMMA 5.16   Any revision function obtained from (Def O*) can be generated from some revision selection function by means of (Def S*).

Proof Suppose that an ordinal family $O(P)$ is given for each probability function P. Define the selection function S as follows: $P_A^S = P^a$, where P^a is defined by (Def O*). Then the only thing that needs to be verified is (iii) in (Def S). Suppose that $P_A^S(B/A) = P^a(B/A) > 0$ and $P_B^S(A/B) = P^b(A/B) > 0$. It follows that $P^a(B) > 0$, and then we know that P^b does not come after P^a in the well-ordering, and similarly, because $P^b(A) > 0$, P^a does not come after P^b. Hence $P_A^S = P^a = P^b = P_B^S$, as desired.

LEMMA 5.18   If the revision function $*$ satisfies (P*1)–(P*6), then $\geq *$ is connected and transitive for any P.

Proof Because either $P_{A \vee B}^*(A) > 0$ or $P_{A \vee B}^*(B) > 0$ for any A and B, it follows immediately that $\geq *$ is connected. To prove transitivity, assume that $A \geq * B$ and $B \geq * C$, that is, $P_{A \vee B}^*(A) > 0$ and $P_{B \vee C}^*(B) > 0$. We want to show that $P_{A \vee C}^*(A) > 0$. Suppose for contradiction that $P_{A \vee B \vee C}^*(A \vee B) = 0$. Then $P_{A \vee B \vee C}^*(B \vee C) > 0$. Applying (P*6), we derive that $0 = P_{A \vee B \vee C}^*(A \vee B/B \vee C) = P_{(A \vee B \vee C) \& (B \vee C)}^*(A \vee B) = P_{B \vee C}^*(A \vee B)$. But this contradicts that $P_{B \vee C}^*(B) > 0$. Hence $P_{A \vee B \vee C}^*(A \vee B) > 0$. Applying (P*6) again, we have $P_{A \vee B \vee C}^*(A/A \vee B) = P_{(A \vee B \vee C) \& (A \vee B)}^*(A) = P_{A \vee B}^*(A) > 0$ and hence $P_{A \vee B \vee C}^*(A) > 0$. Thus $P_{A \vee B \vee C}^*(A \vee C) > 0$ and, applying (P*6) a third time, $P_{A \vee B \vee C}^*(A/A \vee C) = P_{(A \vee B \vee C) \& (A \vee C)}^*(A) = P_{A \vee C}^*(A)$. But if $P_{A \vee B \vee C}^*(A) > 0$, then also $P_{A \vee B \vee C}^*(A/A \vee C) > 0$. Hence $P_{A \vee C}^*(A) > 0$, as desired.

THEOREM 5.20   Suppose that the revision function $*$ satisfies (P*1)–(P*6) and that the equivalence classes on **L** generated by $\geq *$ are complete for all P. Then $*$ is generated by an orthogonal selection function.

Proof Suppose that a revision function $*$ with the properties of the theorem is given. Define a function S from **P** $\times$ **L** to **P** as follows: $S(P, A) = P_{A'}^*$, where A' is the determiner for $[A]$ (and where $[A]$ is defined relative to P). We first show that S is indeed a revision selection function. Because A' is in $[A]$, it follows that $A =* A'$ and hence $P_A^S(A) = P_A^*(A) > 0$, which shows that (i) of (Def S) is satisfied. To show (ii) of (Def S), assume that not $\vdash - A$. Then by (P*4), $P_A^* \neq P_\perp$, and it follows that $P_{A'}^* \neq P_\perp$. The converse is trivial. To establish (iii) of (Def S), assume that $P_A^S(B/A) > 0$ and $P_B^S(A/B) > 0$ for some A and B. Let A' be the determiner for $[A]$ and B' the determiner for $[B]$. Then $P_{A'}^*(A \& B) > 0$. Because $P_{A' \vee A \& B}^* = P_{A'}^*$, it follows that $A \& B \geq * A'$. And, of course, $P_{A' \vee A \& B}^*(A') > 0$, so $A' \geq * A \& B$, and hence $A' =^* A \& B$. In a parallel way it can be shown that $B' =^* A \& B$ and hence $A' =^* B'$. Because both A' and B' are determiners, it follows that $P(A'/B') = 1$ and $P(B'/A') = 1$, and hence it follows from lemma 5.9 that $P_A^S = P_B^S$, as desired.

Finally, we need to show that for each P the set of selected probability functions is orthogonal. Assume that $[A]$ and $[B]$ are two disjoint equivalence classes with determiners A' and B', respectively. We want to show that $P_{A'}^*$ and $P_{B'}^*$ are orthogonal. Because A' and B' do not belong to the same equivalence class, we have either $P_{A' \vee B'}^*(A') = 0$ or $P_{A' \vee B'}^*(B') = 0$. Suppose the former (the latter is similar). If $P_{A' \vee B'}^*(A') = 0$, then $P_{A' \vee B'}^*(B') = 1$, and it follows easily from lemma 5.9 that $P_{A' \vee B'}^* = P_{B'}^*$. But then we know that $P_{A'}^* \,!\, P_{B'}^*$, as desired, because $P_{A'}^*(A') = 1$, but $P_{B'}^*(A') = 0$.

LEMMA 5.21   If the revision function $*$ satisfies (P*1)–(P*6) and if all probability functions are σ-additive, then, for any P, $>^*$ is a well-ordering.

Proof   Assume for contradiction that there is a class $\{A_i\}_{i<w}$ of propositions such that $\ldots >^* A_i >^* \ldots >^* A_2 >^* A_1$. It follows from the definition that, for all $j > i$, $P_{A_j \vee A_i}^*(A_i) = 0$. Let $A = A_\vee$, that is, the disjunction of the class $(A_i)_{i<w}$. Because, for all i, $\vdash A \leftrightarrow A \vee A_i$, we know that $P_{A \vee A_i}^* = P_A^*$. From the fact that $P_A^*(A) = 1$, it then follows that $A \geqslant^* A_i$ for all i. Now if, for some j, $P_A^*(A_j) > 0$, then $P_{A \vee A_j}^*(A_j) > 0$ and thus $A_j =^* A$. But, by means of lemma 5.18, this contradicts that $A_{j+1} >^* A_j$ and $A >^* A_{j+1}$. Hence, for all i, $P_A^*(A_i) = 0$. Because P_A^* is σ-additive, it then follows that $P_A^*(A) = 0$, which contradicts (P*2). This contradiction proves the lemma.

THEOREM 5.22   If the revision function $*$ satisfies (P*1)–(P*6) and if all probability functions are σ-additive, then $*$ is generated by a dimensional ordinal function.

Proof   Let $[A]$ be an equivalence class generated by $\geqslant^*$. Let $A_\vee$ be the disjunction of all elements in $[A]$. Then let $\{P^a\}_{a<y}$ consist of all the probability functions of the form $P_{A_\vee}^*$, one for each equivalence class. Because the class of $A_\vee$'s is well ordered by $>^*$, according to lemma 5.21, we can transfer this ordering to $\{P^a\}_{a<y}$. We want to show that the class $\{P^a\}_{a<y}$ defined in this way is a dimensional ordinal family for P. To verify (i) of (Def DO) we note that the sentence functioning as $A_\vee$ for the equivalence class $[I]$ is $\top$ itself. Because $P_{A \vee \top}^*(\top) = 1$, we know that $\top \geqslant^* A$ for all A, and hence $P_\top^* = P$ is the first element in the well-ordering. In a similar way

it can be shown that $P_\perp$ is the last element. To verify (ii) of (Def DO), we can for each b choose A_b to be the $A_\vee$ that corresponds to P^b. We then know that $P^b(A_b) = P^*_{A_\vee}(A_\vee) = 1$ and from the construction of the $A_\vee$'s it follows that $P^a(A_\vee) = 0$ for all $a < b$. This also verifies (ii) of (Def O). Thus $\{P^a\}_{a<y}$ is a dimensional ordinal family. It follows from (P*6) essentially that $\{P^a\}_{a<y}$ generates the revision function $*$.

Appendix D
Proofs of Main Lemmas and Theorems of Chapter 6

LEMMA 6.1   For any belief model $\langle \mathbf{K}, \mathbf{Prop} \rangle$ and any propositions A, B, and C in $\langle \mathbf{K}, \mathbf{Prop} \rangle$, $B \& A = C \& A$ iff $(B \leftrightarrow C) \& A = A$.

Proof   Suppose first that $B \& A = C \& A$ in some belief model $\langle \mathbf{K}, \mathbf{Prop} \rangle$. Because $B \leftrightarrow C$ is the weakest proposition D that satisfies the equation $B \& D = C \& D$, it follows that $B \leftrightarrow C$ is a consequence of A, that is, $(B \leftrightarrow C) \& A = A$.
  For the converse, suppose that $(B \leftrightarrow C) \& A = A$. Because $B \& (B \leftrightarrow C) = C \& (B \leftrightarrow C)$, it follows that $B \& A = B \& (B \leftrightarrow C) \& A = C \& (B \leftrightarrow C) \& A = C \& A$.

LEMMA 6.3 $\langle \mathbf{K}, \mathbf{Prop} \rangle$ is a belief model that satisfies (P1)–(P7) and, for any a in $\mathbf{K}$, $a = 1$ iff $P^a = \top$.

Proof   In most cases it is easy to show that $\langle \mathbf{K}, \mathbf{Prop} \rangle$ satisfies (P1)–(P7) with $P_a \& P_b = P_{a \cap b}$, $P_a \vee P_b = P_{a \cup b}$, $P_a \leftrightarrow P_b = P_{(a \Rightarrow b) \cap (b \Rightarrow a)}$, and $\perp = P_0$. Only the details for (P5) are given here. Suppose that for all x in $\mathbf{B}$, $P_a(P_d(x)) = P_b(P_d(x))$ for some elements a, b, and d in $\mathbf{B}$. By choosing $x = 1$, it follows that $a \cap d = b \cap d$. From the definition of the pseudocomplement $a \Rightarrow b$, it follows that $d \leqslant a \Rightarrow b$ iff $a \cap d \leqslant b$. Hence $d \leqslant a \Rightarrow b$. Similarly, $d \leqslant b \Rightarrow a$. It follows that $d = d \cap (a \Rightarrow b) \cap (b \Rightarrow a)$. This shows that $P_{(a \Rightarrow b) \cap (b \Rightarrow a)}$ is a consequence of P_d and thus $P_a \leftrightarrow P_b = P_{(a \Rightarrow b) \cap (b \Rightarrow a)}$ is the weakest element as desired. Finally, if $a = 1$, then $P_a(x) = x$ for all x in $\mathbf{B}$, and hence $P_a = \top$. And if $P_a = \top$, then $P_a(x) = x \cap 1 = P_1(x)$ for all x in $\mathbf{B}$. It follows that $a = 1$.

LEMMA 6.4 $\langle \mathbf{B}, \leqslant \rangle$ is a PBA such that $A = \top$ iff $C_A = 1$.

Proof   Properties (ii) and (iv) in the definition of a PBA are easily established by putting $C_A \cap C_B = C_{A \& B}$, and $0 = C_\perp = K_\perp$. In order to establish property (i), it is shown that $C_{A \vee B}$ is the least upper bound of C_A and C_B. It is trivial to show that $C_A \leqslant C_{A \vee B}$ and $C_B \leqslant C_{A \vee B}$. Suppose that $C_A \leqslant C_D$ and $C_B \leqslant C_D$ for some D in **Prop**. This means that for any K in $\mathbf{K}$, $A(D(K)) = A(K)$ and $B(D(K)) = B(K)$. Hence, by (P7), $(A \vee B)(D(K)) = (A \vee B)(K)$ for all $K \in \mathbf{K}$. Suppose that $K \in C_{A \vee B}$. From (P3) it follows that $(A \vee B)(K) = K$. Hence $K = (A \vee B)(K) = D \& (A \vee B)(K) = D(K)$. It follows that $K \in C_D$ and hence $C_{A \vee B} \leqslant C_D$, which shows that $C_{A \vee B}$ is the lower upper bound of C_A and C_B. (Note that it is not true in general that $C_{A \vee B} = C_A \cup C_B$.)

In order to show that property (iii) is satisfied, it is shown that $C_{A \to B}$ is the pseudocomplement of C_A relative to C_B. This is equivalent to showing that, for all objects C_D in $\mathbf{B}$, $C_D \leqslant C_{A \to B}$ iff $C_A \cap C_D \leqslant C_B$. This is equivalent to showing that, for all C_D, $C_D = C_D \cap C_{A \to B}$ iff $C_A \cap C_B \cap C_D = C_A \cap C_D$, which is easily shown with the aid of lemma 6.1. This establishes property (iii).

Finally, it is trivial to verify, with the aid of (P2), that $A = \top$ iff $C_A = 1 = C_\top = \mathbf{K}$.

THEOREM 6.5   The class of all belief models satisfying (P1)–(P7) determines the propositional intuitionistic logic $\mathbf{I}$.

Proof   Let $\langle \mathbf{B}, \leqslant \rangle$ be a PBA, and let h be a homomorphism from formulas in $\mathbf{L}$ to $\langle \mathbf{B}, \leqslant \rangle$. A formula is said to be algebraically valid in $\langle \mathbf{B}, \leqslant \rangle$ iff $h(A) = 1$ for all homomorphisms. It is well known (Rasiowa and Sikorski 1968, ch. 9) that the set of formulas that are algebraically valid in all PBAs is exactly the logic $\mathbf{I}$. So, if A is not a theorem in $\mathbf{I}$, there is some PBA $\langle \mathbf{B}, \leqslant \rangle$ and some h such that $h(A) \neq 1$. By lemma 6.3 it follows that $P_{h(A)} \neq \top$. Because the mapping from A to $P_{h(A)}$ is a homomorphism, there is some substitution instance of A that is not a tautology in some belief model.

For the converse, suppose that A is not a tautology in some belief model $\langle \mathbf{K}, \mathbf{Prop} \rangle$. By lemma 6.4 there is some PBA $\langle \mathbf{B}, \leqslant \rangle$ where $C_A \neq 1$. The mapping from A (interpreted as a formula in $\mathbf{L}$) to C_A is a homomorphism, and hence A is not a theorem in $\mathbf{I}$.

THEOREM 6.6   The class of all belief models that satisfy (P1)–(P8) determines the classical propositional logic $\mathbf{C}$.

Proof   It is easy to show that the logic determined by (P1)–(P8) includes $\mathbf{C}$. For the converse it is sufficient to note that a belief model containing only two elements K and $K_\perp$ with $\top$ and $\perp$ as the only functions in $\mathbf{Prop}$ satisfies (P1)–(P8) and has as tautologies exactly the classical tautologies.

Appendix E
Proofs of Main Lemmas and Theorems of Chapter 7

LEMMA 7.3 All instances of (A5) are valid in a belief revision system $\langle \mathbf{K}, * \rangle$ iff the system satisfies (K*3).

Proof Assume first that all instances of (A5) are valid in the belief revision system. Suppose that $B \in K_A^*$. We want to show that $B \in K_A^+$. Because $B \in K_A^*$, it follows by (RT) that $A > B \in K$. Hence, by the validity of (A5), $A \to B \in K$ and thus $B \in K_A^+$.

Suppose next that the belief revision system satisfies (K*3). Suppose for contradiction that there is some K in $\mathbf{K}$ and some sentences A and B such that $(A > B) \to (A \to B) \notin K$. Consider the expansion $K' = K_{(A>B)\ \&\ A\ \&\ -B}^+$. Because $\mathbf{K}$ is closed under expansions, it follows that $K' \in \mathbf{K}$ and $K' \neq K_\perp$. But because (K*3) implies that $K_A'^* \subseteq K_A'^+ = K'$ and (RT) requires that $B \in K_A'^*$, it follows that $B \in K'$, which contradicts that $K' \neq K_\perp$. This contradiction establishes the lemma.

LEMMA 7.4 All instances of (A6) are valid in a belief revision system $\langle \mathbf{K}, * \rangle$ iff the system satisfies (K*4w).

Proof Assume first that all instance of (A6) are valid in the belief revision system. Suppose that $A \in K$ and $K \neq K_\perp$. We want to show that $K_A^* = K$. Suppose that $B \in K$. Then $A\ \&\ B \in K$, and by (A6) we have $A > B \in K$. Thus by (RT) $B \in K_A^*$.

Assume next that the belief revision system satisfies (K*4w). Suppose for contradiction that there is some K in $\mathbf{K}$ and some sentences A and B such that $A\ \&\ B \to (A > B) \notin K$. Consider the expansion $K' = K_{A\ \&\ B\ \&\ -(A>B)}^+$. Because $\mathbf{K}$ is closed under expansions, it follows that $K' \in \mathbf{K}$ and $K' \neq K_\perp$. But then (K*4w) implies that $K' \subseteq K_A'^*$ and thus $B \in K_A'^*$; it follows by (RT) that $A > B \in K'$, which contradicts that $K' \neq K_\perp$. This contradiction establishes the lemma.

LEMMA 7.5 If a belief system $\langle \mathbf{K}, * \rangle$ satisfies (K*5), then (A7) is valid in $\langle \mathbf{K}, * \rangle$.

Proof Assume for contradiction that the belief system $\langle \mathbf{K}, * \rangle$ satisfies (K*5) but that (A7) is not valid, that is, that there is some consistent K such that $(A > -A) \to (B > -A) \notin K$. Consider the expansion K' of K by $(A > -A)\ \&\ -(B > -A)$. We know that K' is consistent. Because $(A > -A) \in K'$, it follows that $-A \in K_A'^*$ and thus by (K*5) that $\vdash -A$. Hence $-A \in K_B'^*$, which contradicts the facts that $-(B > -A) \in K'$ and that K' is consistent.

LEMMA 7.7   Assume that (A4)–(A8) are valid in the belief revision system $\langle \mathbf{K}, * \rangle$. Then all instances of (A9) are valid in $\langle \mathbf{K}, * \rangle$ iff the system satisfies (K*7).

Proof   To show the validity of (A9), it suffices to show that, for all K in $\langle \mathbf{K}, * \rangle$, if $A > C \in K$ and $B > C \in K$, then $(A \vee B > C) \in K$. So assume the antecedent. It follows that $C \in K_A^*$ and $C \in K_B^*$. Because (K*7) is equivalent to (3.14), it follows that $C \in K_{A \vee B}^*$ and hence $(A \vee B > C) \in K$.

For the converse we show (K*7) by proving that (3.14) is valid. Assume that $C \in K_A^*$ and $C \in K_B^*$. It follows that $A > C \in K$ and $B > C \in K$, and by (A9) we then have $(A \vee B > C) \in K$ and thus $C \in K_{A \vee B}^*$, as desired.

LEMMA 7.8   Assume that (A4)–(A8) are valid in the belief revision system $\langle \mathbf{K}, * \rangle$. Then all instances of (A10) are valid in $\langle \mathbf{K}, * \rangle$ iff the system satisfies (K*L).

Proof   To show the validity of (A10), it suffices to show that, for all K in $\langle \mathbf{K}, * \rangle$, if $A > B \in K$ and $-(A > -C) \in K$, then $(A \& C > B) \in K$. So assume the antecedent. It follows from (K*L) that $(K_A^*)_C^+ \subseteq K_{A \& C}^*$. Because $B \in K_A^*$, it follows that $B \in K_{A \& C}^*$, as desired.

For the converse, assume that $-(A > -B) \in K$ and that $C \in (K_A^*)_B^+$. We want to show that $C \in K_{A \& B}^*$. It follows that $(B \to C) \in K_A^*$ and hence that $(A > (B \to C)) \in K$. From (A10) it then follows that $(A \& B > (B \to C)) \in K$ and hence that $(B \to C) \in K_{A \& B}^*$. But because $B \in K_{A \& B}^*$, we conclude that $C \in K_{A \& B}^*$, as desired.

THEOREM 7.9   A formula A is a theorem in **VC** iff it is derivable from **CM** together with the axiom schemata (A4)–(A10).

Outline of Proof   [We follow the presentation in Lewis (1973b, p. 132).] Lewis proves that **VC** is decidable. Using this decision procedure or some more heuristic device, one can check that all instances of the axiom schemata (A1)–(A10) are theorems in **VC**. The derivation rules in **CM** are special cases of those in **VC**.

To prove the converse, one may check the derivation rules and axiom schemata of **VC** one by one. The validity of the derivation rules is easy to check. Axiom schemata (A1)–(A3), (A6), and (A7) are immediately given. Scheme (A4) is only a notational variant of (A7), and scheme (A5), finally, follows essentially from (A9) and (A10).

LEMMA 7.12   (a) Expression (7.6) entails (WRT); (b) (7.7) and (K*3) entail (WRT); (c) (7.8) and (K^-3) entail (WRT).

Proof   Assume that $A \vee C \notin K$. (a) It follows trivially that $C \notin K$ and hence from (7.6) that $A > C \in K$ iff $C \in K_A^*$. (b) If $A \vee C \notin K$, then $-A \to C \notin K$ and hence $C \notin K_A^+$. Then, by (K*3), $C \notin K_{-A}^*$. It then follows from (7.7) that $A > C \in K$ iff $C \in K_A^*$. (c) Trivially $C \notin K$, and hence by (K^-3) $K_C^- = K$. Thus, by (7.8), $A > C \in K$ iff $C \in K_A^*$.

LEMMA 7.13   (WRT) entails (K*WM).

Proof   Assume that $K \subseteq K'$, $A \vee C \notin K'$, and $C \in K_A^*$. It follows that $A \vee C \notin K$ and thus immediately from (WRT) that $A > C \in K$. Then $A > C \in K'$, and it follows from the other half of (WRT) that $C \in K_A'^*$.

THEOREM 7.14   There is no nontrivial belief revision system that satisfies (K*4), (K*5w), and (K*WM).

Proof   Assume for contradiction that some nontrivial belief revision method satisfies all the conditions. Suppose that the sentences A, B, and C are pairwise disjoint and that, for some belief set K, K is consistent with all three of them, that is, $-A \notin K$, $-B \notin K$, and $-C \notin K$. This means that K_A^+, K_B^+, K_C^+, $K_{A \vee B}^+$, and $K_{A \vee C}^+$ are all nonabsurd belief sets.

Consider the double revision $(K_{A \vee B}^+)_{B \vee C}^*$. Now because $-(B \vee C) \notin K_{A \vee B}^+$, it follows from (K*4) that $(K_{A \vee B}^+)_{B \vee C}^+ \subseteq (K_{A \vee B}^+)_{B \vee C}^*$. But (7.4) entails that $(K_{A \vee B}^+)_{B \vee C}^+ = K_{(A \vee B) \& (B \vee C)}^+ = K_B^+$. Thus $B \in (K_{A \vee B}^+)_{B \vee C}^+$. Then (7.3) shows that $K_{A \vee B}^+ \subseteq K_A^+$. Because we know that $B \vee C \notin K_A^+$, truth-functional logic gives us $(B \vee C) \vee B \notin K_A^+$. It was shown that $B \in (K_{A \vee B}^+)_{B \vee C}^+$, and it now follows from (K*WM) that $B \in (K_A^+)_{B \vee C}^*$.

By considering the revision $(K_{A \vee C}^+)_{B \vee C}^*$ it can be shown in an exactly parallel fashion that we also have $C \in (K_A^+)_{B \vee C}^*$. However, this means that $B \& C \in (K_A^+)_{B \vee C}^*$. But it was assumed that $\vdash -(B \& C)$ and thus $(K_A^+)_{B \vee C}^* = K_\perp$, which contradicts (K*5w). This contradiction proves the theorem.

Notes

Chapter 1

1. Compare Ellis (1979), ch. 1.1, and Levi (1980), ch. 1.5.
2. See Forrest (1986), ch. 3.
3. See Ellis (1979), pp. 2–3.
4. For some ideas, see Ellis (1979), ch. 4.
5. Also see Levi (1980), pp. 17–19.
6. See van Fraassen (1980b) for a discussion of other examples.
7. See, for example, Jeffrey (1965), Stalnaker (1970), Harper (1976), van Fraassen (1980b), Williams (1980), Field (1978), and Domotor (1980, 1983).
8. See, for example, Harper (1977).
9. For example, Renyi (1955), Popper (1959), Stalnaker (1970), Harper (1976), van Fraassen (1976b), and Spohn (1986).
10. For example, see van Fraassen (1980b) for some of the results.
11. See Levi (1983) and Levi (1980, section 1.6).

Chapter 2

1. See the discussion in Stalnaker (1984), ch. 5.
2. See Stalnaker (1984), pp. 79–80.
3. See, for example, Harman (1986, pp. 11–15), Stalnaker (1984, ch. 5), and Levi (1980, pp. 10–11).
4. Compare this with the discussion in section 1.2.
5. On this point see Levi (1980), in particular ch. 5 and sec. 10.3.
6. On infallibilism, see also Levi (1980, section 1.6).
7. See Rasiowa and Sikorski (1968). The Lindenbaum algebra of a complete logic is a complete Boolean algebra.
8. Ellis (1979, p. 5). His notion of belief system should not be confused with the more complex structure introduced in section 1.6.
9. Possible worlds models of belief have been investigated by, among others, Hintikka (1962), Harper (1977, 1978), Stalnaker (1976, 1984), and Lenzen (1980).
10. See, for example, Lenzen (1978, 1980) for surveys of the area.
11. See Janlert (1985) for a presentation of the frame problem and an analysis of several attempts to solve the problem.
12. See, for example, Kemeny (1955) and Vickers (1976) for the details of the argument.
13. See Stalnaker (1970, pp. 67–68) and the references therein.
14. Harper (1978), Lewis (1976), Gärdenfors (1980), Lenzen (1980), and Spohn (1986). Also see the analysis of the dynamics of probabilistic models in chapter 5.
15. Dempster (1967), Kyburg (1974), Shafer (1976), Gärdenfors (1979b).

16. For example, Dempster (1967), Good (1962b), Schick (1979), Gärdenfors and Sahlin (1982), Levi (1974, 1980), Smith (1961, 1965), and Wald (1950).

Chapter 3

1. See, for example, McCarthy (1980) and McDermott and Doyle (1980). Despite these efforts, there seems so far to be no satisfactory theory of nonmonotonic logic.

2. This has been shown to my by Hans Rott. The proof that (3.15) is equivalent to (K*8) is found in appendix A.

3. Again, this was pointed out to me by Hans Rott. See appendix A for a proof.

4. I owe this example to David Makinson.

5. This example is due to David Makinson.

6. For further discussion of this point, see Alchourrón and Makinson (1982, sec. 4). Also see Makinson (1985b).

7. Alchourrón et al. (1985), observation 6.4.

8. Alchourrón et al. (1985), observation 3.3.

9. See appendix A for a proof.

10. This was shown to me by Hans Rott. The proof is found after the proof of theorem 3.5 in appendix A because the simplest proof presumes this result. However, it is possible to prove (3.28) directly from (K⁻1)–(K⁻8).

11. Alchourrón et al. (1985), observations 6.1 and 6.2.

12. Also see Stalnaker (1984), pp. 127–129.

13. On this point also see the discussion in sections 7.4 and 7.6.

14. I owe this example to Peter Forrest.

15. Here it is interesting to compare with Teller's (1976) discussion of Jeffrey conditionalization.

Chapter 4

1. This notion was called "epistemic importance" in Gärdenfors (1984b) and (1985a).

2. This lemma is proved in Alchourrón and Makinson (1982). It is a consequence of lemma 4.12, which is proved in appendix B.

3. Compare Alchourrón et al. (1985), observation 6.1.

4. This lemma is a consequence of theorem 4.16, which is proved in appendix B.

5. Compare Alchourrón et al. (1985), observation 6.3.

6. This lemma is a consequence of lemma 4.12, which is proved in appendix B.

7. Compare observation 2.5 in Alchourrón et al. (1985).

8. These are theorems 1 and 2 in Groves (1986). I have changed his notation.

9. Compare Rescher (1964), Gärdenfors (1984b, sec. 4), and Levi (1977b, sec. 2 and 3).

10. See section 5 of Gärdenfors (1984b) for an elaboration of this.

11. The importance of this postulate was pointed out to me by Hans Rott. The present axiomatization replaces a less successful one presented in Gärdenfors (1985a).

12. I owe this result to David Makinson.

13. See theorems 3 and 4 in Grove (1986).

14. This is observation 4.3 in Alchourrón and Makinson (1985).

15. Observation 5.3 in Alchourrón and Makinson (1985).

16. Observation 6.2 in Alchourrón and Makinson (1985).

17. Fagin et al. (1983) call these conditions "integrity constraints."

18. Compare Ginsberg (1986) for some further supporting arguments for this connection.

19. See Fagin et al. (1983), p. 354.

20. See also Fagin et al. (1986).

21. See Alchourrón and Bulygin (1971).

22. See Alchourrón and Makinson (1982) for some technical results.

Chapter 5

1. See Domotor (1983) for a survey.

2. Teller (1976), pp. 210–212.

3. This property was called "linearity" in Gärdenfors (1982a).

4. This property was called "conservative" in Gärdenfors (1982a).

5. This property is introduced merely for the proof of theorem 5.3. In fact, the property is stronger than what is needed for the proof, but it is comparatively easy to formulate.

6. See Levi (1974, 1980).

7. See Teller (1976) and Lewis (1976, p. 311).

8. See Popper (1959), Stalnaker (1970), Harper (1976), and van Fraassen (1976b).

9. See the strategy employed in (Def Prob) in section 2.7.

10. It seems as if van Fraassen's (1976b, p. 428) example can be translated into the present framework; then it would be possible to construct a revision function that cannot be generated by any orthogonal selection function.

Chapter 6

1. See, for example, Stalnaker (1970, 1976, 1984) and Lewis (1973b, 1986).

2. Compare Quine's notion of stimulus synonymy.

3. See Goldblatt (1979), section 3.10.

4. A thorough treatment of pseudo-Boolean algebras can be found in Rasiowa and Sikorski (1968). These algebras are called Heyting algebras in Goldblatt (1979, ch. 8).

5. This is lemma 2 in Gärdenfors (1985b).

6. Compare Segerberg (1968), section 7.

7. I owe this idea to Lloyd Humberstone.

8. Compare Goldblatt (1979), in particular chapters 6 and 8. In the terminology of category theory a pseudo-Boolean algebra is a finitely bicomplete poset with exponentials.

Chapter 7

1. See Ramsey (1931a, p. 248), Stalnaker (1968, p. 102), and Veltman (1985).

2. See, for example, Rescher (1964), Stalnaker (1968, 1970), Harper (1975), Levi (1977b), Gärdenfors (1978a, 1981, 1986a, 1987d), and Veltman (1985).

3. **CM** is equivalent to the system **Ck** mentioned in footnote 14 in Chellas (1975, pp. 149–150). Chellas's basic logic **Ck** is equivalent to **CM** + (A5) (to be introduced).

4. Note the close correspondence between (A9) and (3.14), which was shown to be equivalent to (K*7).

5. Compare Pollock (1976) and Gärdenfors (1979a).

6. For a related analysis of the 'might' conditional, see Stalnaker (1984, pp. 142–146).

7. For other examples, see Stalnaker (1984, pp. 142–146).

8. This theorem is a corollary of theorem 7.14 and is thus not given a separate proof in appendix D.

9. Peter Lavers's proof is in an unpublished manuscript. For an axiomatization of the minimal logic, see chapter 6 or Segerberg (1968).

10. However, Collins (1986) has pointed out that theorem 7.10 presumes belief *revisions* and not merely expansions, whereas Lewis's triviality result utilizes only expansion. So, in this sense theorem 7.10 is not more general than Lewis's theorems.

11. See, for example, Levi (1977b, 1980, 1987b). In fact, this may be the proper way of reading Ramsey's own position. For an analysis, see Sahlin (1986).

12. See Levi (1980, pp. 246–248) and in particular Levi (1987b) for an elaboration of this position.

13. Van Fraassen (1976a) has criticized Lewis's analysis of counterfactuals along similar lines.

Chapter 8

1. This was assumed in Küttner (1984). I believe that for this reason, his main criticism of my theory is not valid.

2. This answers a question of Stegmüller's (1983, p. 1000).

3. Strictly the sentence $p(Qx/-Sx) = 0$ is not necessary for this derivation.

4. See also Stegmüller (1983), pp. 971–973.

5. See Stegmüller (1983), pp. 999–1000.

6. Also see the discussion in Sintonen (1984).

7. This example is due to Carnap (1966), pp. 191–192.

8. For such an attempt in connection with deductive explanations, see Gärdenfors (1976).

Chapter 9

1. An outline of a related theory is presented in Sahlin (1982).
2. See Suppes (1970) and Salmon (1971) for a formal definition of this notion.
3. See Hempel (1965) and Salmon (1971).
4. For further discussion of the transitivity of causation, see Hesslow (1981).

References

Adams, E. 1966. "Probability and the logic of conditionals," in *Aspects of Inductive Logic*, J. Hintikka and P. Suppes, eds. Amsterdam: North-Holland, 265–316.

Adams, E. 1975. *The Logic of Conditionals*. Dordrecht: Reidel.

Alchourrón, C. E., and E. Bulygin. 1971. *Normative Systems*. Wien: Springer.

Alchourrón, C. E., and D. Makinson, 1980. "Hierarchies of regulations and their logic," in *New Studies in Deontic Logic*, R. Hilpinen, ed. Dordrecht: Reidel, 123–148.

Alchourrón, C. E., and D. Makinson. 1982. "The logic of theory change: Contraction functions and their associated revision functions." *Theoria* 48: 14–37.

Alchourrón, C. E., and D. Makinson. 1985. "On the logic of theory change: Safe contraction." *Studia Logica* 44: 405–422.

Alchourrón, C. E., and D. Makinson. 1986. "Maps between some different kinds of contraction function: The finite case." *Studia Logica* 45: 187–198.

Alchourrón, C. E., P. Gärdenfors, and D. Makinson. 1985. "On the logic of theory change: Partial meet functions for contraction and revision." *Journal of Symbolic Logic* 50: 510–530.

Beauchamp, T. L., and A. Rosenberg. 1981. *Hume and the Problem of Causation*. Oxford: Oxford University Press.

Bulygin, E., and C. E. Alchourrón. 1977. "Unvollständigkeit, widersprüchlichkeit und Unbestimmtheit der Normenordnungen," in *Deontic Logic and Semantics*, G. Conte, R. Hilpinen, and G. H. von Wright, eds., Wiesbaden: Athenaion, 20–32.

Carnap, R. 1966. *Philosophical Foundations of Physics*. New York: Basic Books.

Cartwright, N. 1979. "Causal laws and effective strategies." *Nôus* 13: 419–437.

Chellas, B. 1975. "Basic conditional logic." *Journal of Philosophical Logic* 4: 133–153.

Coffa, J. A. 1974. "Hempel's ambiguity." *Synthese* 28: 141–163.

Collins, J. D. 1986. "Belief revision." Paper read at the Australasian Association for Philosophy Conference, Monash, August 1986.

De Finetti, B. 1937. "La prévision: ses lois logiques, ses sources subjectives." *Annales de l'Institut Henri Poincaré* 7: 1–68.

Dempster, A. P. 1967. "Upper and lower probabilities induced by a multivalued mapping." *Annals of Mathematical Statistics* 38: 325–339.

Domotor, Z. 1980. "Probability kinematics and representation of belief change." *Philosophy of Science* 47: 384–403.

Domotor, Z. 1983. "The structure of probabilistic knowledge." Department of Philosophy, University of Pennsylvania.

Doyle, J. 1979. "A truth maintenance system." *Artificial Intelligence* 12: 231–272.

Doyle, J. 1983. *The Ins and Outs of Reason Maintenance*. Report CMU-C5-83-126. Department of Computer Science, Carnegie-Mellon University.

Dray, W. 1957. *Laws and Explanation in History*. Oxford: Oxford University Press.

Dretske, F. 1981. *Knowledge and the Flow of Information*. Oxford: Blackwell.

Ellis, B. 1976. "Epistemic foundations of logic." *Journal of Philosophical Logic* 5: 187–204.

Ellis, B. 1979. *Rational Belief Systems*. Oxford: Blackwell.

Fagin, R., J. D. Ullman, and M. Y. Vardi. 1983. "On the semantics of updates in databases," in *Proceedings of Second ACM SIGACT-SIGMOD*. New York: Association for Computing Machinery, 352–365.

Fagin, R., G. M. Kuper, J. D. Ullman, and M. Y. Vardi. 1986. "Updating logical databases." *Advances in Computing Research* 3: 1–18.

Field, H. H. 1977. "Logic, meaning and conceptual role." *Journal of Philosophy* 74: 379–409.

Field, H. H. 1978. "A note on Jeffrey conditionalization." *Philosophy of Science* 45: 316–367.

Foo, N., and A. Rao. 1986. "DYNABELS." Department of Computer Science, Sydney University.

Forrest, P. 1986. *The Dynamics of Belief: A Normative Logic.* Cambridge: Cambridge University Press.

Gärdenfors, P. 1976. "Relevance and redundancy in deductive explanations." *Philosophy of Science* 43: 420–431.

Gärdenfors, P. 1978a. "Conditionals and changes of belief," in *The Logic and Epistemology of Scientific Change (Acta Philosophica Fennica* 30 (2–4)), I. Niiniluoto and R. Tuomela, eds. Amsterdam: North-Holland, 381–404.

Gärdenfors, P. 1978b. "On the logic of relevance." *Synthese* 37: 351–367.

Gärdenfors, P. 1979a. "Even if," in *Proceedings from 5th Scandinavian Logic Symposium,* F. V. Jensen, B. H. Mayoh, and K. K. Møller, eds. Aalborg: Aalborg University Press, 189–203.

Gärdenfors, P. 1979b. "Forecasts, decisions and uncertain probabilities." *Erkenntnis* 14: 159–181.

Gärdenfors, P. 1980. "A pragmatic approach to explanations." *Philosophy of Science* 47: 404–423.

Gärdenfors, P. 1981. "An epistemic approach to conditionals." *American Philosophical Quarterly* 18: 203–211.

Gärdenfors, P. 1982a. "Imaging and conditionalization." *Journal of Philosophy* 79: 747–760.

Gärdenfors, P. 1982b. "Rules for rational changes of belief." in ⟨320311⟩: *Philosophical Essays Dedicated to Lennart Åqvist on his Fiftieth Birthday* (Philosophical Study 34), T. Pauli, ed. Uppsala: Philosophical Society and the Department of Philosophy, Uppsala University, 88–101.

Gärdenfors, P. 1984a. "The dynamics of belief as a basis for logic." *The British Journal for the Philosophy of Science* 35: 1–10.

Gärdenfors, P. 1984b. "Epistemic importance and minimal changes of belief." *Australasian Journal of Philosophy* 62: 136–157.

Gärdenfors, P. 1985a. "Epistemic importance and the logic of theory change," in *Foundations of Logic and Linguistics,* G. Dorn and P. Weingartner, eds. New York: Plenum Press, 345–367.

Gärdenfors, P. 1985b. "Propositional logic based on the dynamics of belief." *Journal of Symbolic Logic* 50: 390–394.

Gärdenfors, P. 1986a. "Belief revisions and the Ramsey test for conditionals." *Philosophical Review* 95: 81–93.

Gärdenfors, P. 1986b. "The dynamics of belief: Contractions and revisions of probability functions." *Topoi* 5: 29–37.

Gärdenfors, P. 1987a. "Causation and the dynamics of belief," in *Causation in Decision, Belief Change, and Statistics,* W. L. Harper and B. Skyrms, eds. Dordrecht: Reidel, vol. 2, 85–104.

Gärdenfors, P. 1987b. "Sneed's reconstruction of the structure and dynamics of theories," *After Kuhn: Method or Anarchy?* B. Hansson, ed. Lund: Doxa.

Gärdenfors, P. 1987c. "Theoretical concepts and their function," in *After Kuhn: Method or Anarchy?* B. Hansson, ed. Lund: Doxa.

Gärdenfors, P. 1987d. "Variations on the Ramsey test: More triviality results." *Studia Logica* 46: 319–325.

Gärdenfors, P., and N.-E. Sahlin. 1982. "Unreliable probabilities, risk taking, and decision making." *Synthese* 53: 361–386.

Gibbard, A. 1981. "Two recent theories of conditionals," in *Ifs*, W. L. Harper, R. Stalnaker, and G. Pearce, eds. Dordrecht: Reidel, 211–247.

Ginsberg, M. L. 1986. "Counterfactuals." *Artificial Intelligence* 30: 35–79.

Goldblatt, R. 1979. *Topoi: The Categorial Analysis of Logic*. Amsterdam: North-Holland.

Good, I. J. 1961. "A causal calculus I." *British Journal for the Philosophy of Science* 11: 305–318.

Good, I. J. 1962a. "A causal calculus II." *British Journal for the Philosophy of Science* 12: 43–51.

Good, I. J. 1962b. "Subjective probability as a measure of a nonmeasurable set," in *Logic Methodology and Philosophy of Science: Proceedings of the 1960 International Congress*, E. Nagel, P. Suppes, and A. Tarski, eds. Stanford, Calif.: Stanford University Press, 319–329.

Granger, C. W. J. 1969. "Investigating causal relations by econometric models and cross-spectral methods." *Econometrica* 37: 424–438.

Granger, C. W. J. 1987. "Causality testing in a decision science," in *Causation in Decision, Belief Change, and Statistics*, W. L. Harper and B. Skyrms, eds. Dordrecht: Reidel.

Grove, A. 1986. *Two Modellings for Theory Change*, Auckland Philosophy Papers 13.

Halmos, P. 1962. *Algebraic Logic*. New York: Chelsea.

Hansson, B. 1975. "Explanations—Of what?" Department of Philosophy, Stanford University. Mimeo.

Harman, G. 1986. *Change in View: Principles of Reasoning*. Cambridge, Mass.: MIT Press.

Harper, W. L. 1975. "Rational belief change, Popper functions and counterfactuals." *Synthese* 30: 221–262.

Harper, W. L. 1976. "Ramsey test conditionals and iterated belief change," in *Foundations of Probability Theory, Statistical Inference, and Statistical Theories of Science*, W. L. Harper and C. Hooker, eds. Dordrecht: Reidel, vol. 1, 117–135.

Harper, W. L. 1977. "Rational conceptual change," in *PSA 1976*. East Lansing, Mich.: Philosophy of Science Association, vol. 2, 462–494.

Harper, W. L. 1978. "Bayesian learning models with revision of evidence." *Philosophia* 7: 357–367.

Harper, W. L. 1981. "A sketch of some recent developments in the theory of conditionals," in *Ifs*, W. L. Harper, R. Stalnaker, and G. Pearce, eds. Dordrecht: Reidel, 3–38.

Hempel, C. G. 1965. *Aspects of Scientific Explanation*. New York: Free Press.

Hempel, C. G. 1968. "Maximal specificity and lawlikeness in probabilistic explanation." *Philosophy of Science* 35: 116–134.

Hesslow, G. 1976. "Two notes on the probabilistic approach to causality." *Philosophy of Science* 43: 290–292.

Hesslow, G. 1981. "The transitivity of causation." *Analysis* 41: 130–133.

Hilpinen, R. 1981. "On normative change," in *Ethics: Foundations, Problems, and Applications*, E. Morscher and R. Stranzinger, eds. Wien: Hölder-Pichler-Tempsky, 155–164.

Hintikka, J. K. K. 1962. *Knowledge and Belief*. Ithaca, N.Y.: Cornell University Press.

Hume, D. 1748. *An Enquiry Concerning Human Understanding*. London.

Janlert, L.-E. 1985. "Studies in knowledge representation." Ph.D. dissertation, Institute of Information Processing, Umeå University, Umeå.

Jeffrey, R. C. 1965. *The Logic of Decision*. New York: McGraw-Hill.

Johnson-Laird, P. N. 1983. *Mental Models*. Cambridge: Cambridge University Press.

Kemeny, J. 1955. "Fair bets and inductive probabilities." *Journal of Symbolic Logic* 20: 263–273.

Keynes, J. M. 1921. *A Treatise on Probability*. London: Macmillan.

Kratzer, A. 1979. "Conditional necessity and possibility," in *Semantics from Different Points of View*, R. Bauerle, U. Egli, and A. von Stechow, eds. Berlin: Springer-Verlag, 117–147.

Kratzer, A. 1981. "Partition and revision: The semantics of counterfactuals." *Journal of Philosophical Logic* 10: 201–216.

Kuhn, T. S. 1970. *The Structure of Scientific Revolutions*, second edition. Chicago, Ill.: University of Chicago Press.

Küttner, M. 1984. "Glaube, Wissen und die Pragmatik des Erkläens: Zur Kritik des Ansatzes von Gärdenfors und Stegmüller," in *Philosophy of Religion*, W. L. Gombocz, ed. Wien: Hölder-Pichler-Tempsky, 102–107.

Kyburg, H. 1974. *The Logical Foundations of Statistical Inference*. Dordrecht: Reidel.

Lakatos, I. 1970. "Falsification and the methodology of scientific research programmes," in *Criticism and the Growth of Knowledge*, I. Lakatos and A. Musgrave, eds. Cambridge: Cambridge University Press, 91–196.

Leblanc, H. 1983. "Alternatives to standard first-order semantics," in *Handbook of Philosophical Logic*, D. M. Gabbay and F. Guenthner, eds. Dordrecht: Reidel, 189–274.

Lenzen, W. 1978. *Recent Work in Epistemic Logic*. Amsterdam: North-Holland.

Lenzen, W. 1980. *Glauben, Wissen und Wahrscheinlichkeit*. Wien: Springer.

Levi, I. 1974. "On indeterminate probabilities." *Journal of Philosophy* 71: 391–418.

Levi, I. 1977a. "Direct inference." *The Journal of Philosophy* 74: 5–29.

Levi, I. 1977b. "Subjunctives, dispositions and chances." *Synthese* 34: 423–455.

Levi, I. 1980. *The Enterprise of Knowledge*. Cambridge, Mass.: MIT Press.

Levi, I. 1983. "Truth, fallibility and the growth of knowledge," in *Boston Studies in the Philosophy of Science*, R. S. Cohen and M. W. Wartofsky, eds. Dordrecht: Reidel, vol. 31, 153–174.

Levi, I. 1987a. "Four themes in statistical explanation," in *Causation in Decision, Belief Change, and Statistics*, W. L. Harper and B. Skyrms, eds. Dordrecht: Reidel, vol. 2, 195–222.

Levi, I. 1987b. "Iteration of conditionals and the Ramsey test." *Synthese*.

Lewis, D. K. 1973a. "Causation." *Journal of Philosophy* 70: 556–567.

Lewis, D. K. 1973b. *Counterfactuals*. Oxford: Blackwell.

Lewis, D. K. 1976. "Probabilities of conditionals and conditional probabilities." *The Philosophical Review* 85: 297–315.

Lewis, D. K. 1979. "A problem about permission," in *Essays in Honour of Jaakko Hintikka*, E. Saarinen, R. Hilpinen, I. Niiniluoto, and M. Provence-Hintikka, eds. Dordrecht: Reidel, 163–179.

Lewis, D. K. 1986. *On the Plurality of Worlds*. Oxford: Blackwell.

Mackie, J. L. 1974. *The Cement of the Universe*. Oxford: Oxford University Press.

Makinson, D. 1985a. "How to give it up: A survey of some formal aspects of the logic of theory change." *Synthese* 62: 347–363.

Makinson, D. 1985b. "Revisions are themselves contractions." Department of Philosophy, UNESCO, Paris.

Makinson, D. 1987. "On the status of the postulate of recovery in the logic of theory change." *Journal of Philosophical Logic* 16: 383–394.

McCarthy, J. 1980. "Circumscription: A form of non-monotonic reasoning." *Artificial Intelligence* 13: 27–39.

McDermott, D., and J. Doyle. 1980. "Non-monotonic logic I." *Artificial Intelligence* 13: 41–72.

Niiniluoto, I. 1976. "Inductive explanation, propensity and action," in *Essays on Explanation and Understanding*, J. Manninen and R. Tuomela, eds. Dordrecht: Reidel, 335–368.

Otte, R. 1981. "A critique of Suppes' theory of probabilistic causality." *Synthese* 48: 167–189.

Peirce, C. S. 1932. *Collected Papers*, C. Hartshorne and P. Weiss, eds. Cambridge, Mass.: Belknap Press.

Pollock, J. L. 1976. *Subjunctive Reasoning*. Dordrecht: Reidel.

Popper, K. R. 1959. *The Logic of Scientific Discovery*. London: Hutchinson.

Quine, W. V. O. 1952. *Methods of Logic*. London: Routledge & Kegan Paul.

Ramsey, F. P. 1931a. "General propositions and causality," in his *Foundations of Mathematics and Other Logical Essays*. New York: Routledge & Kegan Paul, 237–257.

Ramsey, F. P. 1931b. "Truth and probability," in his *Foundations of Mathematics and Other Logical Essays*. New York: Routledge & Kegan Paul, 156–198.

Rasiowa, H., and R. Sikorski. 1968. *The Mathematics of Metamathematics*. Warszawa: Polish Scientific Publishers.

Reichenbach, H. 1956. *The Direction of Time*. Berkeley, Calif.: University of California Press.

Renyi, A. 1955. "On a new axiomatic theory of probability," *Acta Mathematica Hungarica* 6: 285–333.

Rescher, N. 1964. *Hypothetical Reasoning*. Amsterdam: North-Holland.

Rosen, D. 1978. "In defense of a probabilistic theory of causality." *Philosophy of Science* 45: 604–613.

Ross, L., and C. A. Anderson. 1982. "Shortcomings in the attribution process: On the origins and maintenance of erroneous social assessments," in *Judgement under Uncertainty: Heuristics and Biases*, D. Kahneman, P. Slovic, and A. Tversky, eds. Cambridge: Cambridge University Press, 129–152.

Rott, H. D. 1982. "Gärdenfors' epistemologische Explikation wissenschaftlichen Erklärung." Seminar für Logik und Wissenschaftstheorie, Universität München. Mimeo.

Rott, H. D. 1984. *Epistemische Interpretationen von wenn-dann- und weil-Sätzen nach Kratzer, Gärdenfors und Spohn*. München: Magisterarbeit, Ludwig-Maximilians-Universität.

Rott, H. D. 1986. "Ifs, though and because." *Erkenntnis* 25: 345–370.

Sahlin, N.-E. 1982. "Towards a counterfactual probabilistic theory of causality." *Logique et Analyse* 99: 327–332.

Sahlin, N.-E. 1986. "F. P. Ramsey." Department of Philosophy, Lund University.

Salmon, W. C. 1971. *Statistical Explanation and Statistical Relevance*. Pittsburgh, Penn.: University of Pittsburgh Press.

Salmon, W. C. 1980. "Probabilistic causality." *Pacific Philosophical Quarterly* 61: 50–74.

References

Schick, F. 1979. "Self-knowledge, uncertainty, and choice." *British Journal for the Philosophy of Science* 30: 235–252.

Schurz, G. 1983. "Wissenschaftliche Erklärung." Dissertation, Karl-Franzens-Universität, Graz.

Scriven, M. J. 1959. "Explanation and prediction in evolutionary theory." *Science* 130(3374): 477–482.

Segerberg, K. 1968. "Propositional logics related to Heyting's and Johansson's." *Theoria* 34: 26–61.

Segerberg, K. 1986a. *Conditional Logic and the Logic of Theory Change*. Auckland Philosophy Papers 12.

Segerberg, K. 1986b "On the logic of small changes in theories I." *Acta Philosophica Fennica*.

Segerberg, K. 1986b. "On the logic of small changes in theories II," in *Mathematical Logic and Applications*, D. Skordev, ed.

Shackle, G. L. S. 1961. *Decision, Order and Time in Human Affairs*. Cambridge: Cambridge University Press.

Shafer, G. 1976. *A Mathematical Theory of Evidence*. Princeton, N.J.: Princeton University Press.

Simon, H. A., and N. Rescher. 1966. "Cause and counterfactual." *Philosophy of Science* 33: 323–340.

Sintonen, M. 1984. *The Pragmatics of Explanation*. Amsterdam: North-Holland.

Skyrms, B. 1980. *Causal Necessity*. New Haven, Conn.: Yale University Press.

Smith, C. A. B. 1961. "Consistency in statistical inference and decision." *Journal of the Royal Statistical Society*, ser. B, 23: 1–25.

Smith, C. A. B. 1965. "Personal probabilities and statistical analysis." *Journal of the Royal Statistical Society*, ser. A, 128: 469–499.

Sneed, J. D. 1971. *The Logical Structure of Mathematical Physics*. Dordrecht: Reidel.

Spohn, W. 1983a. "Deterministic and probabilistic reasons and causes." *Erkenntnis* 19: 317–396.

Spohn, W. 1983b. "Probabilistic causality: From Hume via Suppes to Granger," in *Causalità e modelli probabilistici*, M. C. Galavotti and G. Gambetta, eds. Bologna: CLUEB, 69–87.

Spohn, W. 1986. "The representation of Popper measures." *Topoi* 5: 69–74.

Spohn, W. 1987. "Ordinal conditional functions: A dynamic theory of epistemic states," in *Causation in Decision, Belief Change, and Statistics*, W. L. Harper and B. Skyrms, eds. Dordrecht: Reidel, vol. 2, 105–134.

Stalnaker, R. 1968. "A theory of conditionals," in *Studies in Logical Theory* (American Philosophical Quarterly Monograph Series, no. 2, N. Rescher, ed. Oxford: Blackwell, 98–112.

Stalnaker, R. 1970. "Probability and conditionals." *Philosophy of Science* 37: 64–80.

Stalnaker, R. 1972. "Letter to David Lewis," in *Ifs*, W. L. Harper, R. Stalnaker, and G. Pearce, eds. Dordrecht: Reidel, 151–152.

Stalnaker, R. 1976. "Propositions," in *Issues in the Philosophy of Language*, A. F. MacKay and D. D. Merrill, eds. New Haven, Conn.: Yale University Press, 79–91.

Stalnaker, R. 1984. *Inquiry*. Cambridge, Mass.: MIT Press.

Stegmüller, W. 1976. *The Structure and Dynamics of Theories*. New York: Springer-Verlag.

Stegmüller, W. 1980. "Two successor concepts of the notion of statistical explanation," in *Logic and Philosophy*, G. H. von Wright, ed. The Hague: International Institute of Philosophy, 37–52.

Stegmüller, W. 1983. *Erklärung, Begründung, Kausalität*, second edition. Berlin: Springer-Verlag.

Suppes, P. 1970. *A Probabilistic Theory of Causality*. Amsterdam: North-Holland.

Teller, P. 1976. "Conditionalization, observation and change of preference," in *Foundations of Probability Theory, Statistical Inference, and Statistical Theories of Science*, W. L. Harper and C. H. Hooker, eds. Dordrecht: Reidel, vol. 1, 205–259.

Thomason, R. H., and A. Gupta. 1980. "A theory of conditionals in the context of branching time." *Philosophical Review* 89: 65–90.

Tichy, P. 1976. "A counterexample to the Stalnaker-Lewis analysis of counterfactuals." *Philosophical Studies* 29: 271–273.

van Fraassen, B. C. 1976a. "Probabilities of conditionals," in *Foundations of Probability Theory, Statistical Inference, and Statistical Theories of Science*, W. L. Harper and C. Hooker, eds. Dordrecht: Reidel, vol. 1, 261–308.

van Fraassen, B. 1976b. "Representation of conditional probabilities." *Journal of Philosophical Logic* 5: 417–430.

van Fraassen, B. 1977. "The pragmatics of explanation." *American Philosophical Quarterly* 14: 143–150.

van Fraassen, B. 1980a. "Critical notice of Brian Ellis: Rational belief systems." *Canadian Journal of Philosophy* 10: 497–511.

van Fraassen, B. 1980b. "Rational belief and probability kinematics." *Philosophy of Science* 47: 165–87.

van Fraassen, B. 1980c. *The Scientific Image*. Oxford: Clarendon Press.

Veltman, F. 1976. "Prejudices, presuppositions and the theory of counterfactuals," in *Amsterdam Papers in Formal Grammar*, J. Groenendijk and M. Stokhof, eds. Amsterdam: Centrale Interfaculteit, Universiteit van Amsterdam, vol. 1, 248–281.

Veltman, F. 1985. "Logics for conditionals." Dissertation, Universiteit van Amsterdam.

Vickers, J. 1976. *Belief and Probability*. Dordrecht: Reidel.

Wald, A. 1950. *Statistical Decision Functions*. New York: Wiley.

Williams, P. M. 1980. "Bayesian conditionalisation and the principle of minimum information." *British Journal for the Philosophy of Science* 31: 131–144.

Woods, W. A. 1975. "What's in a link," in *Representation and Understanding*, D. G. Bobrow and A. Collins, eds. New York: Academic Press, 35–81.

Index

Absurd epistemic state, 25, 137, 158
Absurd probability function, 105
Acceptance, 11–13, 21–24, 31, 33, 47, 105, 133, 135, 153, 172–173, 179, 209
    context, 28
    criteria of, ix, 19–20, 26–27, 29, 31, 147, 154–156
    degrees of, 72–74
    state, 24
Accidental generalization, 87–88
Adams, Ernest, 165, 209
Alchourrón, Carlos E., x, xi, 59, 65–66, 76–79, 97–98, 101–102
Algebraic semantics, 139
Amendment (of a legal code), 101–103
Anderson, C. A., 36
Artificial intelligence, ix, 32–33
Assertability, 13, 153
Assumption, 33–34
Awareness (of acceptance), 23

Bach, Johann Sebastian, 55
Background beliefs, 169, 202
Balzer, Wolfgang, x
Bayesian model of belief, 105. *See also* Epistemic state, probabilistic model of
Bayesian statistics, 92
Beauchamp, T. L., 191
Belief function, 173–174, 177
Belief model, 134–141
    contraction-extended, 142
    revision-extended, 143
Belief revision system, 148–151, 157, 159, 162
    nontrivial, 158–159, 161
    probabilistic, 163–164
Belief set, 21–27, 29–30, 38, 43, 47, 67, 134, 141, 143–144, 164
    associated with an ordinal conditional function, 73
    associated with a probability function, 121, 163, 197
    base for, 59, 102
    finite, 98
    maximal, 25, 59, 113, 152
    maximal subset of, 58, 75–82, 97
    minimal subset of, 97
Belief system, 18–20, 26–27, 39
    completable, 26
Boolean algebra, 25. *See also* Pseudo-Boolean algebra
Bromberger, S., 199–200
Broome, John, x
Bulygin, E., 101–102

Carnap, Rudolf, 23, 39
Cartwright, Nancy, 193
Category theory, 136, 141, 144–145
Causal belief, xi, 14, 19, 167, 191–209
Causal chain, 193, 201, 206
Causally relevant background factors, 193–194, 196
Causal overdetermination, 206
Causal reasoning, 48, 61
Causation, 3
    axioms for, 202
    direct, 192, 206
    genuine, 192–193, 196–197
    indirect, 192
    prima facie, 196, 200, 203
    probabilistic, 191–192, 197, 202, 206
    spurious, 192–193, 196–198, 200, 203
    transitivity of, 206
Change of belief. *See* Epistemic change
Classical logic. *See* Propositional logic, classical
Coffa, J. A., 168, 187
Cognitive dissonance, 169
Coherence (probabilistic), 9, 11, 36–37, 41–42, 105
Coherence theory of beliefs, 35–36
Collins, John, x
Commitment function. *See* Epistemic commitment, function
Compactness, 24, 76, 105
Comparative possibility, 94
Complete belief set, 26, 30
Complete language, 25, 128
Complete logic, 25–26
Completeness theorem, 138–141, 149, 151
Composition principle, 50
Computer implementation, ix, 2–3, 7, 10, 99–103
Conditional connective, 148, 157–159, 164
Conditionalization, 16–17, 105–110, 114–120, 122, 163
    (A, a)-, 72–73
    extension of, 116–117
Conditional probability, 375
Conditional sentence, x, 3, 16, 19, 23, 57, 143, 147–166. *See also* Counterfactual sentence; 'Even if' conditional; Might conditional; Open conditional
    belief, 165–166
    iterated, 157, 164–165
    logic of, 28, 148–152
    probability of, 108, 164–165, 209
    semantics of, 109, 147, 156, 162, 165–166

Connective. *See* Conditional connective;
    Logical connective
Consequence set, 25
Conservativity principle, 67
Consistency, 8–9, 11, 22, 26, 29
Construction of contractions and revisions,
    ix, 3, 48, 75–86, 88, 125–128
Contraction, xi, 2–3, 16, 47, 52, 60–66, 68–
    73, 87–88, 99, 106, 133, 135, 142–144,
    152–153, 167–168, 175–176, 178–179,
    187, 191–192, 195–197, 199, 201, 204,
    209
  basic set of postulates for, 63, 119
  function for belief sets, 61, 69–71, 75–86,
    91, 96–97, 100, 102–103
  function for probability functions, 106–
    107, 118–121, 124–125, 188, 207
Conversational context, 93
Convexity (of probability functions), 42,
    116
Counterfactual sentence, 48, 59, 83–84, 94,
    147, 151, 162, 166, 179, 191, 195
Cresswell, Max, x

Dalton, John, 88
Database, 12, 99, 102
  management system, 99
  priority, 100
  update of, 3, 76, 99–101, 103
Debate, 23, 60
Decision theory, 37, 41
Deduction theorem, 24, 211, 224
Deductive closure, 16. *See also* Logical
    consequence, closure under
Deductive-nomological explanation. *See*
    Explanation, deductive-nomological
Deductive reasoning, 11
De Finetti, Bruno, 23, 36, 39
Degree of belief, 30, 36–39, 168
Deontic entrenchment, 102
Derogation (of a legal code), 101–103
Determiner, 127
  for belief set, 26, 30
  for probability function, 111–112
Determinism, 168, 191–192, 196
Dimensional ordinal family of probability
    functions, 128
Direct inference, 207
Disjoint sentences. *See* Logically disjoint
    sentences
Domotor, Zoltan, x, 43, 127, 230
Doyle, Jon, x, 32–35
Dray, William, 186

Dutch book theorem, 36–37, 40, 42, 105,
    107
Dynamics of belief. *See* Epistemic change

Ellis, Brian, x, 19, 26–28, 39
Empiricism, 167, 169
Epiphenomenon, 191, 205
Epistemic attitude, 7, 12–14, 18–19, 22, 26,
    30–32, 36, 48
Epistemic change, 15–18, 23, 47, 131–132,
    144, 179. *See also* Contraction; Expan-
    sion; Revision
  typology of, 2, 8, 39
Epistemic commitment, 8, 48
  function, 15–18, 75
Epistemic entrenchment, 17–18, 64–66, 75–
    76, 80–81, 86–97, 166, 192, 198
  ordering of, 88–94, 100, 102, 188
  origins of, 91–94
  postulates for, 89–91
Epistemic input, 7–10, 13–18, 23, 36, 49,
    132, 142
  composition of, 134–135
  as constraint, 15, 106
  as function, 132–134
Epistemic logic, 29
Epistemic operator, 29
Epistemic possibility, 154
Epistemic reliability (of probability
    functions), 42
Epistemic state, 2, 7–15, 21–46, 167–168
  as equilibrium point, 9–10, 13, 15, 22–23,
    25
  hypothetical, 179
  intersection of, 79, 143–144
  possible worlds model of, 11, 28–31, 40,
    75
  probabilistic model of, xi, 3, 9, 11–12, 14–
    17, 36–43, 62, 92, 105–128, 145, 168, 192
  propositional model of, 8–9, 11–12
Epistemological theory, 7–11, 18–20
Equalizer, 136–138, 141, 144
Equilibrium state. *See* Epistemic state, as
    equilibrium point
'Even if' conditional, 152–154
Expansion, 2–3, 16, 43, 46, 47–52, 73, 99,
    105, 131, 133, 135, 141–142, 155, 158,
    164, 174–175
  closure under, 148
  postulates for, 49–51, 57, 63
  of probability function, 108, 118
Expected probability. *See* Probability
    function, expected

Expected utility, 37
Explanandum, 167–171, 176–179, 182–189
Explanans, 167–171, 176–180, 182–189, 204
Explanation, x, 3, 14, 19, 43, 48, 61, 167–189, 191, 203–206
 causal, 205
 as a communicative act, 188–189
 deductive-nomological, 167–168, 171, 179, 185–187, 199
 degrees of, 185
 elliptic, 180, 189
 how-possibly, 186
 inductive-statistical, 167–168, 171, 187
 pragmatics of, 167, 189
 spurious, 186
 why-necessarily, 186
Explanatory power (or value), 93, 185–186, 188
Explicit belief, 23
Extension, 131
External world, 9, 19–20

Factoring condition
 for contraction, 65
 for revision, 57
Fagin, R., 99–100
Falsity proposition, 21, 137
Field, Hartry, 38
First-order language, 170
First-order logic, 43
Foo, Norman, x, 100
Forrest, Peter, x, 39
Foundations theory of belief, 35
Frame problem, 3, 32–35
Fuhrmann, André, x
Full belief, 39
Full meet contraction function, 78–80, 86
Fullness (condition for contraction), 65, 77
Functional dependency, 209

Game theory, 37
General imaging. See Imaging, general
Gibbard, Allan, 160, 165
Ginsberg, M. L., 147
Good, Irving John, 191
Granger, C. W. J., 191, 202–203, 206
Grove, Adam, x, 83–85, 94–96
Gupta, Anil, 148

Halldén, Sören, x
Halmos, Paul, 144
Hansson, Bengt, x, 169–170, 180, 182–183

Harman, Gilbert, 23, 28, 35–36, 67
Harper, William H., 70, 91, 160, 165
Harper identity, 70–71, 75, 83, 85, 95–96, 152, 216, 225–226
Hemeren, Paul, x
Hempel, Carl, 167–169, 171, 175–176, 178, 181–187
Hesslow, Germund, 192, 194, 198–199, 202
Heyting algebra. See Pseudo-Boolean algebra
Hierarchy of regulations, 102
Hilpinen, Risto, 49, 101
Hintikka, Jaakko, 29
Homomorphic probabilistic revision function, 113–117
Hume, David, 195, 208

Imaging, 108–118
 general, 112–115, 117
 preservative, 117–118
Implicit belief, 23
Indetermined proposition, 12, 22–23, 47
Indicative, 152
Inductive reasoning, 10, 171
Inductive-statistical explanation. See Explanation, inductive-statistical
Infallibility, 23
Informational economy, criterion of, 49, 53, 58, 61–62, 75–76, 89, 157
Informational value, 87, 91, 93
Information-theoretic approach, 91–92
Insufficient information, 193
Intension, 131
Interactive fork, 200
Interpretation function, 29–30, 172
Intersection condition (for contraction), 79

Jackson, Frank, x
Jeffrey, Richard, x, 17, 106
Jeffrey conditionalization, 74, 106
Johansson's minimal logic. See Minimal logic
Johnson-Laird, Philip, 43–46
Justification for beliefs, 33–35

Keynes, John Maynard, 42
Knowledge, 20
 of probability, 173
Kratzer, Angelika, 148
Kuhn, Thomas, 88, 92, 94

Lakatos, Imre, 92
Laplace's demon, 58

Lavers, Peter, x, 161
Lavoisier, A. L., 88
Lawlike sentence, 87–88, 189, 191, 204
Learning, 48, 50–51, 107
Leblanc, Hughes, 38
Legal code, 12, 76, 99, 101–103
Levi, Isaac, x, 8, 23, 30, 35, 39, 41–42, 68–
    71, 87, 90, 117, 124, 155, 164–165, 174,
    207
Levi identity, 69, 75, 78–79, 96, 153, 216,
    226
Lewis, David, 83–86, 94, 101, 107–112,
    118, 126, 131, 151, 154, 163–164, 191,
    195, 240
Logical connective, 19, 21, 26, 135–138,
    140–141, 144
Logical consequence, 9, 22, 24, 135
  closure under, 11, 14, 22, 34, 39, 61, 99,
    171
Logical database. See Database
Logically disjoint sentences, 37, 107, 158
Logically omniscience. See Logical
    consequence, closure under
Logical validity, 148–149
Logic determined by class of belief models,
    139–141
Loss of information, 91–92, 119

Mackie, John, 191
Makinson, David, ix, xi, 59, 71, 75–79, 97–
    98, 102
Marking-off identity, 81
Maxichoice contraction function, 76–79,
    86, 102
  orderly, 77–78
Maximal belief set. See Belief set, maximal
Maximal probability, 23, 87
Mental model, 43–46
Menzies, Peter, x
Method of more detailed specification, 194,
    202
Might conditional, 151, 154–156
Minimal change of belief, 8, 16, 35, 53, 55,
    57–58, 64, 66–67, 69, 86, 92, 109–110,
    119, 122, 147, 157–158
Minimal logic, 141, 161
Mixture of probability functions, 106, 123–
    124
Modal logic, 28, 156
Modus ponens, 24, 137
Monotonicity, 135
  postulate of, 50, 59, 65, 157
  weak, 161

Necessary implication, 156
Nietzsche, Friedrich, 181–182
Nonmonotonicity
  of belief changes, 52–53, 143
  in reasoning, 33–34, 53, 147
Nontrivial belief revision system. See Belief
    revision system, nontrivial
Nontrivial probabilistic revision function,
    116–117
Normal science, 94
Norm system, 101

Object language, ix, 18–19, 144
O'Connell, Conall, x
Omniscience, 25
Ontology, 132
Open conditional, 147, 162
Oppenheim, Paul, 187
Ordinal conditional function, 30–32, 72–73
Ordinal family of probability functions,
    126, 128
Otte, Richard, 192, 199

Paradigm approach, 92–94
Paresis, 169, 180–182, 186
Partial meet contraction function, 80–83,
    85–86, 98
  connectively relational, 82
  relational, 81, 98
  transitively relational, 82, 98
Partition of event space, 193
  homogeneous, 197
Pearce, David, x
Peirce, Charles Saunders, 23, 42–43
Permissible probability function. See
    Probability function, epistemologically
    possible
Personalistic probability, 36–39
Pettit, Philip, x
Phlogiston theory, 88
Plausibility grading, 31
Pollock, John, 152–153
Popper, Karl, 37, 123
Possible worlds, ix, 11, 25, 28, 31, 41, 56,
    72, 83–85, 109–112, 122, 131–132, 134,
    144, 156, 170–175, 177, 195. See also
    Epistemic state, possible worlds model of
  probability of, 109
  similarity between, 126, 191, 195, 200
Pragmatic factor, 93, 170
Prediction, 168–169
Premise semantics, 148
Preservation condition, 156–159, 162.

See also Conservativity principle
probabilistic, 163
Preservative imaging. *See* Imaging,
preservative
Preservative probabilistic revision function,
115–118
Probabilistic laws, 207–208
Probabilistic model of belief. *See* Epistemic
state, probabilistic model of
Probability function (or measure), 36, 38–
42, 105–107, 172–174
axiomatization of, 38–39, 58
classes of, 41–42
completion of, 113
contraction of (*see* Contraction, function
for probability functions)
epistemologically possible, 41–42
expected, 174–175, 177
first-order, 174
opinionated, 110–114
orthogonality of, 127–128
revision of (*see* Revision, function for
probability functions)
Probability interval, 41–42
Probability of conditional sentence. *See*
Conditional sentence, probability of
PROLOG, 101
Proposition, 28, 30–31, 43, 131–145
defined as function on epistemic states,
132–134
defined from possible worlds, 131–132
strongest, 135, 138
weakest, 135–136
Propositional logic, 3, 17, 26, 43, 131–133,
144
classical, 24, 27–28, 105, 141
intuitionistic, 139–140, 145
semantics of, 38
Pseudo-Boolean algebra, 139–140
Pseudocomplement, 139

Quantificational sentence, 171
Question opening, 16. *See also* Contraction
Quine, Willard Van Orman, 66

Rabinowicz, Wlodek, x
Ramsey, Frank Plumpton, 36, 147
Ramsey test, 16, 147–148, 151–166
strong, 160
Rao, Anand, x, 101
Rasiowa, Helena, 238
Rationality criteria (or postulates), ix, 2–3,
7–11, 16, 18, 21–26, 36, 41, 53, 61

Reason for beliefs, 35, 67–68
Recovery (postulate for contraction), 62,
65, 71, 119, 196
Reference class, 170, 183
narrowest, 177, 182
Regularity theory, 191, 199
Reichenbach, Hans, 177, 191
Rejection, 12, 22–23, 29, 31, 34, 47
Relevance, 177–178
Representation theorem, 51, 60, 66, 75, 77,
79, 82, 84, 95, 107, 112, 127–128
Requirement of maximal specificity, 171,
176, 183–184
Rescher, Nicholas, 209
Research program, 92
Retraction. *See* Rejection
Revision, xi, 1–3, 7–8, 17, 33, 35, 46, 48, 52–
61, 68–73, 78, 87–88, 99, 106, 133, 135,
142–144, 148–149, 155, 163, 165, 175,
179, 186
basic set of postulates for, 55
function for belief sets, 54, 65, 69–71, 75,
95, 100, 102–103, 123, 157
function for probability functions, 106–
107, 109–110, 113, 115–119, 121–128
iterated, 55
Rich probabilistic revision function, 116–
117
Roeper, Peter, x
Rosen, Deborah, 194
Rosenberg, A., 191
Ross, L., 36
Rott, Hans, x, 148, 160, 180, 186

Safe contraction, 97–99
Sahlin, Nils-Eric, x, 42
Salmon, Wesley, 168–169, 184–185, 192,
194, 200–201
Satisfiability, 148
Savage, Leonard, 107
Schurz, Gerhard, x, 185
Scientific revolution, 88
Screening off, 198, 200, 203
Scriven, M. J., 169, 180–182
Second-order probabilities, 13, 168, 170,
173–175, 203
Segerberg, Krister, x, 84, 139, 141
Selection function, 77, 80–82
completion of, 221
connectively relational, 82
for probabilistic revision functions, 125–
127
relational, 81

Selection function (cont.)
  transitively relational, 82
Semantical theory, 18–20
Semantic network, 32–33
Separation theorem for intuitionistic logic,
  140
Set-theoretical operation, 131, 144
Shackle, G. L. S., 30
σ-additivity, 128
Sikorski, Roman, 238
Similarity between possible worlds. *See*
  Possible worlds, similarity between
Simon, Herbert, 209
Single-case probability, 176–177
Sintonen, Matti, 169, 183, 188
Skyrms, Brian, 193
Smart, Jack, x
Sneed, Joseph, 92
Spatial reasoning, 45–46
Spohn, Wolfgang, x, 30–31, 35, 42, 47, 72–
  74, 90, 100, 125, 127–128, 192, 194, 203
Stalnaker, Robert, 10–11, 20, 24, 37–38,
  52, 108–109, 131, 151, 154, 163, 165–
  166
Stalnaker assumption, 86
State descriptions, 25
State of belief. *See* Epistemic state
Stegmüller, Wolfgang, 92, 167, 183–184,
  186
Structuralist view of scientific theories, 92
Subjective probability. *See* Personalistic
  probability
Subjunctive, 152
Successive reconditionalization, 201
Suppes, Patrick, 191–193, 195–196, 199–
  200, 203, 207
Surprise, 167, 178, 188
  potential, 30
  value, 167–169, 179, 187
Syllogistic reasoning, 43–45
System of spheres, 83–86, 94–95

Tacit consequence, 180
Tarskian satisfaction, 12
Tautology, 136–138
Teller, Paul, 107–108, 110, 116
Tennant, Neil, x
Thomason, Richmond, 148
Thrombosis, 194, 198, 202
Tichy, Pavel, 67–68
Total evidence, 176, 183–184
Total information, 194, 196, 202
Truth condition, 9, 19–20, 27, 164
Truth maintenance system, 32–35

Validity. *See* Logical validity
Van Benthem, Johan, x
Van Fraassen, Bas, x, 8, 14, 27, 125, 145,
  148, 164, 170, 188
Veltman, Frank, 148

Weight of evidence, 42–43
Well-ordering, 126, 128
Why-question, 169–170, 176, 178, 180,
  182–183, 187
Williams, P. M., 92
Withdrawal function, 71
Wittgenstein, Ludwig, 13
Woods, William, 32